eXtreme HEADSHIP

A CASE STUDY IN EDUCATIONAL
LEADERSHIP AND SCHOOL IMPROVEMENT

PHIL MCNULTY

Note for Librarians: A cataloguing record for this book is available from Library and Archives Canada at www.collectionscanada.ca/amicus/index-e.html
ISBN 1-4120-5586-5

Printed in Victoria, BC, Canada. Printed on paper with minimum 30% recycled fibre. Trafford's print shop runs on "green energy" from solar, wind and other environmentally-friendly power sources.

TRAFFORD.
PUBLISHING™

Offices in Canada, USA, Ireland and UK
This book was published *on-demand* in cooperation with Trafford Publishing. On-demand publishing is a unique process and service of making a book available for retail sale to the public taking advantage of on-demand manufacturing and Internet marketing. On-demand publishing includes promotions, retail sales, manufacturing, order fulfilment, accounting and collecting royalties on behalf of the author.

Book sales for North America and international:
Trafford Publishing, 6E–2333 Government St.,
Victoria, BC v8t 4p4 CANADA
phone 250 383 6864 (toll-free 1 888 232 4444)
fax 250 383 6804; email to orders@trafford.com
Book sales in Europe:
Trafford Publishing (uk) Limited, 9 Park End Street, 2nd Floor
Oxford, UK ox1 1hh UNITED KINGDOM
phone 44 (0)1865 722 113 (local rate 0845 230 9601)
facsimile 44 (0)1865 722 868; info.uk@trafford.com
Order online at:
trafford.com/05-0484

10 9 8 7 6 5 4 3

ACKNOWLEDGEMENTS

IT IS WITH THE greatest respect that I acknowledge the work undertaken by the staff of Shorefields Technology College-a genuine inner-city community school. Through their hard work and dedication the College has developed and thrived as a vital community resource for Liverpool 8 and beyond.

The professionalism and commitment of teachers and headteachers in all the Toxteth schools deserves the widest recognition. I am personally grateful for their comradeship and for all that I learned from their example. Similarly, the work of other professionals and community leaders, working tirelessly towards regeneration in the area, requires full acknowledgement.

The Dingle, Granby, Toxteth area of Liverpool is complex and sophisticated.

Stable and well-established communities absorb diverse new groups and there is a tremendous richness of life experience.

There is an abundance of character, depth, loyalty, tradition and self-belief. It was a real privilege to work with the students, parents, governors, councillors, community and religious groups in Liverpool 8 and to make some contribution to the development of the area.

This book describes a difficult journey, perhaps typical of other successful schools. It provides a personal perspective in order to assist other school leaders. The huge contribution of others – teachers, senior staff, curriculum and pastoral leaders, clerical, site and catering staff-should be taken as read.

I will only, specifically, thank Rodger Lafferty and John Charnock for their immense contribution and for their unwavering personal support.

Phil McNulty

FOR

Pauline, John, Joe and Siobhan

SETTING THE SCENE

In 1993 I took over the Headship of Shorefields Community Comprehensive School, the County Secondary School for Toxteth, Liverpool. The school was in the worst of circumstances. We had a falling roll, poor examination results, completely dilapidated buildings, financial problems and the worst case of governor abuse of their new powers in the country.

The catchment area included some of the most deprived areas in Western Europe. There was little support from the LEA, opposition from other schools, problems with staff, daily intrusions, nightly break-ins and racially divided warring gangs on the streets.

This case study is a description of how we moved the school out of this situation. From an intake of 45 students per year to 210. From an exclusion rate of 136 per year to none. From 4% gaining five or more good GCSEs to 25%. From the brink of closure to over subscription and, on the way, attracting sponsorship, national recognition, huge technological investment and the capability to refurbish or rebuild the entire school.

The tragic death of Philip Lawrence, headteacher of St. George's Catholic School, Maida Vale, North London, on 8th December

1995, highlighted the difficulties faced by those headteachers and those schools facing 'challenging circumstances' right across the country. Philip Lawrence was stabbed to death at the gates of his school when he went to the aid of a pupil. The media spotlight showed the starkly brutal situation in which educationalists were trying to raise standards in the context of heightened political expectations. It also gave a glimpse into the complex and difficult world of school leadership. A world in which survival depends upon top quality management training, personal commitment, profound knowledge of the local terrain, good judgement and luck. Tragically, Philip Lawrence, by all accounts a committed and talented man, was grossly unlucky. There but by the grace of God go many of us who work, and have worked, in Britain's inner cities or outer estates.

Ten years on from that tragedy the local authority, Westminster, had not ruled out closing the school. There had, apparently, been an outbreak of violence following the school's designation as 'a failing school' by inspectors.

We know the sort of characteristics 'a failing school' may exhibit. We know the characteristics of a 'successful' school. How does one progress from one to the other?

In a 'failing school', or one with 'significant weaknesses', levels of attainment tend to be below average. There may be a falling roll and lack of parental trust and support. Senior management may be weak. They may be well meaning but ineffective or rendered ineffective by cynicism and resistance. Teaching is likely to be unsatisfactory and there will be an unwillingness to embrace change. Student learning and behaviour are likely to be unsatisfactory. There may be an inadequate use of data to track and measure performance. The head may be constantly distracted by peripheral activities, which draw his attention away from the core business – achievement on the part of the students. As well as dealing with premises issues and matters of finance, the head may be struggling to deal with wide ranging social, economic and demographic problems impacting on a daily basis. The staff may be unsupported, underdeveloped and demotivated. Where such a school is located in an area of social disadvantage, the staff may adopt a 'fortress mentality', which compounds their problems.

In a successful school levels of attainment tend to be at, or above, average. The curriculum will be well managed and there will be highly effective teaching and clear learning taking place on the part of students. The students will receive good guidance and support and this will be reflected in their attitudes and social behaviour. Strategic leadership and governance will be very sound and there will be a clear sense of direction. In relation to internal processes management will have an accurate view of what is happening in the school. There will be a detailed and regular focus on classroom practice and staff will be supported and challenged in their performance. We would expect to see the quality of the school reflected in the range of additional activities open to students, in the level of parental support and in the general sense of drive and purpose understood by all concerned.

So we know what we do *not* want in a school, one judged as failing or weak, and we know what constitutes 'good'. It is a *huge* challenge to move from one state to the other. It cannot be achieved by simply inverting the problems, changing the rhetoric and wishing that things were better. Although this may be a starting point.

The crucial importance of determining what will work in school improvement is underlined by the number of schools causing concern as we moved into 2005. Nationally there were 314 schools in Special Measures, a further 302 identified as having Serious Weaknesses and 71 seen as Underachieving. There are significant issues of support and development implied here.

At the same time there is a decline in the number of applications for headship. There are, undoubtedly, matters at the heart of school leadership and management requiring detailed analysis. This analysis will impact on the school improvement agenda.

There are few longitudinal studies of school improvement. In other words, studies which detail the process by which improvement has been achieved over time. It is a complex and conflicted business and the passing on of summary accounts of success, key learning outcomes or management tips, while useful in their own right, fail to contextualise the experience for colleagues struggling with intractable strategic and operational problems in their own schools.

This case study is the detailed ten-year story of a struggle to create change and improvement from a starting position of, apparently, terminal decline. There are probably many industrial parallels of success in extraordinary circumstances and aspects of our approach to survival will be transferable.

THE STARTING POSITION

SHOREFIELDS HAD AN UNUSUAL history. Formed under compre-
hensivisation in the 1970s from four Secondary Modern Schools
and a Technical School it, initially, operated on all five sites. The
management difficulties this presented must have been almost insurmountable. It was established as a Community Comprehensive
School, which implied extensive responsibilities towards activities
for local people including the maintenance of full time Youth and
Adult Education Centres. In the 1980s, under secondary school reorganisation in Liverpool, the school was effectively reduced to two
sites. The Head had been relatively successful in retaining or gaining staff in the upheavals of reorganisation across the city. There
were, nevertheless, a group of teachers on protected salaries or on
inflated salaries given their level of responsibility.

The school had been under the leadership of a dynamic head for
the best part of 17 years. There was, however, an inevitable period
of decline in the years prior to her retirement in 1988. An acting
head followed her until the appointment of my predecessor in 1989.
He was in post until August 1993. I was, therefore the fourth head
teacher in five years. Each of my three predecessors departed on

acrimonious terms with members of the governing body.

Upon my joining the school in 1990, as a Deputy Head teacher, the Head made it clear that a significant school improvement programme was required and that it was necessary for us to take advantage of current changes sweeping education at the time. The key external driver was The Education Reform Act (ERA), which had ushered in the radical 'national curriculum', local financial management of schools (LFM), open enrolment and greater powers for school governors. Shorefields was, now, well led. The new Head Teacher was enthusiastic and visionary with a clear sense of the challenges facing us and of the opportunities available to the school.

The challenges included – a historically fractious relationship with the governing body; outdated curriculum and pastoral structures in the school; significant numbers of staff, at all levels, still on protected posts since reorganisation; no staff development structure and an absence of development in the new National Curriculum; no adequate curriculum monitoring; wholesale underachievement; widespread opposition to setting homework amongst the staff; outdated policies; high levels of student absence; outdated teaching styles; significant staff performance, capability and conduct issues; no staff handbook; outdated job descriptions; unacceptable custom and practice in both Sport and Community management; a neglect of Primary School liaison on the part of Senior Management; a significant proportion of disruptive and violent students; no structured reward system for students; a tolerance of informal corporal punishment and blatantly low expectations on behalf of many of the teachers.

Given the vision and drive to bring about improvement, to take advantage of educational opportunities and to invest in new initiatives it was disappointing that, by 1993, we had, overall, made little progress. This needs examining.

The opportunities were significant – we introduced a school information management system; created a staff development policy; used effective strategic development planning to identify the school's needs; undertook training in the new Local Financial Management arrangements; modernised the role of the Governors and provided them with facilities; restructured the curriculum to meet current needs; embarked on a dynamic Design Technology initiative (NDTEF) and introduced Cognitive Ability Tests to benchmark students.

The range of initiatives introduced during this period was also impressive – new academic monitoring arrangements, new student diaries, the introduction of a Year system for Pastoral management, significant investment in Vocational and Work Related developments (Liverpool Compact, TVEI, pre voc. qualifications), a review of 16-19 education, student self assessment, a new PSE curriculum, a homework policy, a pilot to consider the use of OMR for registering students, support for staff interested in flexible learning styles, reorganisation of Community management and responsibilities in Adult education, a review of the race equality policy, a rewards and sanctions policy, formal links with the local business community in the Parliament St. area, a pilot for a student council, the introduction of the Elton(behaviour management) Team to work alongside staff, an attempt to link governors to curriculum areas and compensatory programmes with the local Training and Enterprise Council and Higher Education Institutions.

The key reason behind our failure to develop the school at that time lay in the existing relations with the governing body. This was, clearly, a school with embedded problems and the obvious dilemma was where to start. **From a management perspective it is not only impossible to tackle all issues at once, it is also undesirable.** This was not a view necessarily shared by the Governors. The Heads aim was to create a 'critical mass' of staff in order to effect change throughout the school. There was certainly external support for moving the school forward at that time. We had no less than five HMI visits in one year alone. There was, nevertheless, a degree of cynicism and resistance amongst the staff emanating, partly, from past experiences with the Governors.

We had difficulty persuading middle managers of the importance of academic and pastoral monitoring. There was a resistance
to the development of new teaching and learning styles even with
the intervention of Local Authority Advisers. While student self-
assessment was embraced in some areas it was treated disparag-
ingly in others, as was the introduction of diaries. Managers were
resistant to completing review documents either for their areas of
responsibility or in relation to policies such as Race Equality. When
we were able to undertake analysis it indicated complacency rather
than the good practice of which some staff had felt proud. There
was a general reluctance to use extrinsic rewards, certificates in particular, in order to motivate difficult students. Some staff preferred
to use punishment. We experienced a disastrous inability on the part
of some departments to manage coursework, leading to low exam
entry levels.

Due to the relatively autocratic style of leadership, previously
experienced by the school, we had difficulty with the delegation
of new initiatives. Some bright and enthusiastic staff simply failed
to deliver on projects because they were unused to autonomy and
colleagues would not accept their authority. **The consequences of
a change of leadership style must be considered in any agenda
for change.**

In many respects, this description of staff resistance to change,
and partial success, will not be uncommon. Given time, and persist-
ence, I am sure that we would have made and sustained progress. We
had, for example, seen significant developments in the motivation
of more academic students. Our new staff meeting structure was
very sound. The introduction of technical and vocational initiatives
(TVEI) carried great potential. We were focussing staff training on
what mattered, the underachievement of the students, and, in time,
the Staff Development programme should have had a wide impact.

Unfortunately, the challenges facing the management of the
school conspired to undermine progress. It was a difficult school.

An influx of students from the recently closed Paddington School created real tension. There were racial tensions inside and outside of school. Petty gangsterism was depressingly visible. When faced with the exclusion or disciplining of their children many parents reacted with criticism and hostility. As managers we spent a good proportion of our time dealing with disciplinary matters. The most serious problems often emanated from the midday break or from out of school behaviour in the evenings. We faced daily intrusions into the building. This was an unmanageable situation as long as our Community Team operated a policy of, literally, open access. We experienced a number of serious assaults upon staff by outsiders. We had the contradictory situation in which some staff wanted panic alarms while others wanted free use of the building by the public.

Even the employment of a doorman on the main entrance failed to deter troublemakers.

Each morning we assessed the damage to the school from the previous night. There were frequent break-ins and arson attacks. One night our entire stock of computers was hauled out through a hole in the first floor roof. On another occasion thieves dismantled a wall in the Technology block to steal equipment. We invited a group of business people for an early morning seminar in our Assembly Hall only to find that the projector, video and screen had been removed via a hole smashed in the roof overnight. We proceeded without visual aids.

Meanwhile the governors themselves were demonstrating hostility and aggression towards the leadership of the school and their behaviour became increasingly disturbing and inappropriate. They were demanding massive amounts of management time around the presentation of 'proof' that there was effective development in the school. Despite receiving management reports, the Governors demanded to see actual students diaries. They questioned activities in individual teachers lessons. A genuine initiative to link governors with curriculum areas fell down due to their intolerable attitudes.

They criticised the timing of the day, book sales, break facilities, holidays, leave arrangements, use of offices and stock handling. They challenged minor financial decisions, challenged established financial procedures and refused to accept any incremental approach to school improvement. They demanded action in relation to crime rates in the *whole* Liverpool 8 area. The constant presence of the Chair of Governors was intrusive and debilitating. He was using up huge amounts of staff time – managers, teachers, clerical, ancillary – and, on a day-to-day basis, was preventing the caretakers doing their job. There was a strong sense in which a managerial and inspectorial role had been assumed. This led to a stream of observations and criticisms of real and perceived inadequacies in the school.

Clearly, it is not the role of governors in any school to decide upon whether or not policies are working on the basis of casual observation. They profoundly misunderstood the process of change in an institution like a school. Despite repeated explanations they refused to accept that the decisions of Governors and managers are part of the process of change. Those decisions do not constitute change in themselves. Implementation is the real challenge.

We had a specific concern over the inherent dangers in relating to a single member, or only a handful of members, of the governing body. The written complaints to the school, eventually produced on a daily basis, were often demanding action over individual children. The children of Governors themselves!

In 1990/1 the Governors launched a sustained attack upon the integrity of our 'non-public' funds. In other words monies the school raised outside of its LEA allocation. Their criticisms were mainly historical and were aimed, apparently vindictively, at our Community staff. Our senior deputy, the man who had been the acting Head, now responsible for finance, made his position clear. He would operate professionally and expected to be so treated. When it was clear that the Governors would not respect this position he resigned on the spot. A great loss.

During 1991 the relationship between management and the governors became hopeless. Governors meetings were a battlefield. A number of Governors were manifestly intimidating and the meetings were degenerate. Any and sometimes every action of management was challenged – security, tenancies, kitchens, technicians, homework, references, staff hours and discipline. The main thrust of the attack, though, was towards the Head. There appeared to be a concerted attempt to marginalise his influence. An increasing proportion of management time was wasted in responding to vexatious complaints and spurious requests.

The Governors attempted to sidestep management completely by arguing for the appointment of a Bursar accountable directly to them. It is fair to say that we believed there was a real financial risk in such a proposal. The extraordinary amount of money now being managed at a local level had led to issues of propriety across the country. We were facing a very real challenge and dealing with this challenge – to the right of management to manage the school – was detracting from the business of school improvement.

In the Summer of 1991 the Chair of Governors was reported to have taken over the Heads office during the vacation and this was a catalyst for his removal by the LEA.

Despite this development we still experienced disruption at each Governors meeting and Governors loyal to the school were treated very badly indeed. One reported a death threat and members of staff reported abuse from Governors in the street. The Head and I were receiving dozens of nuisance calls at home around this time and calls to our home phones were being monitored by the Police. The school was being disrupted on at least a weekly basis by bomb scares and bogus fire alarms and there was a campaign of misinformation about the school being waged through the local media. In October and November 1991 there were at least eighteen articles in the press critical of the school. No organisation can sustain this.

The complaints from Governors continued and the Police, LEA and the teacher unions were all involved, somewhat powerlessly, in seeking a solution. The Director of Education was refused permission to speak at a Governors meeting, which stopped, fractionally, short of physical violence. The NUT regarded our situation as the worst case of Governor abuse of power in the country. Between November '91 and July '93, a period of only twenty months, there were a further sixty enquiries, complaints or incidents relating to this ongoing campaign to undermine not only school management but the school itself. These included correspondence from ex governors, councillors, the LEA, DFE, charities and exam boards. We were even referred to the Local Government Ombudsman. In February 1993 we found ourselves, again, in the middle of a storm of adverse publicity generated by the ex chair around alleged bullying. There was a battery of communication generated by the issue – letters, phone calls, visits and radio and newspaper reports. The effect on the image of the school, at a time when parents were finalising their choice of secondary schools, was catastrophic.

Unsurprisingly, the Head, who had carried the brunt of all this erroneous vilification, decided to move to another post.

Despite all the effort involved in attempting to move the school forward, and lasting progress in some areas, the staff were demoralised by the confrontation with Governors. Parents had become disenchanted with their local school due to the adverse publicity. By June 1993 they were appealing, successfully, against placements at Shorefields.

The possibilities for my own Headship of Shorefields Community Comprehensive School looked most unpromising. My three predecessors had all left following disputes with the Governors, parents were deserting the school in droves and we still had most of the management issues to contend with from three years earlier. The only way was up!

START OF FIRST YEAR OF
HEADSHIP SEPTEMBER '93

IN THE TERM PRIOR to taking up post in September 1993 I listened
to the expectations of the people around me. I had the advantage
of knowing the staff quite well by now. I also knew the students
and many of the parents. While I had already made a presentation
of development ideas at interview, what these different groups and
individuals said to me, when they realised that I was to be the new
head teacher, proved most instructive.

The key staff, exhibiting motivation and sound expectations, saw
an opportunity in my appointment. They believed that I knew the
main issues facing the school and might, unlike an outside appointment, have the measure of the governing body. They wanted support. **There was, undoubtedly, some good practice at Shorefields
but the school felt like it was less than the sum of its parts.** Some
staff were working hard but were failing to achieve the results they,
and the students, deserved due to the context in which they were
operating.

The students were very amusing. A number approached me to

confirm or deny rumours that the school was to become very strict and that a radically new uniform policy was to be imposed. I had no sense whatsoever that they saw this as a bad thing. I did not regard myself as particularly authoritarian and had, frankly, given little thought to the issues the students had raised. This was, however, a great opportunity. **When students reveal their own expectations they provide an ideal starting point for improvement.** Before the end of the academic year the students had talked themselves into believing there would be a sea change.

Parents also approached me during that Summer term, concerned over the uniform issue, in particular, and the cost implications of any change. By now I had realised the challenge was to enforce the existing uniform rather than to introduce anything new. This was an undertaking itself as, on any day, the 'uniform' might include blazers, leather jackets, trousers, tracksuits, shoes, and trainers. Every parent I spoke to wanted standards. Their problem was that they couldn't afford to purchase items that their children refused to wear. They refused to wear shoes, for example, if others in the class were allowed to wear trainers. The parents wanted nothing half hearted. They said that if we set standards we had to stick to them. **They made it clear that it was not a question of parents supporting the school but of the school supporting the parents.**

These three simple exchanges gave me my agenda. I set out to give people what they wanted. I was determined not to accept any nonsense from any of the parties and I knew it was going to be difficult. There were huge problems to overcome but I had my motivation. There were going to be arguments, there was going to be conflict, not least with the partially reformed governing body, but this was one opportunity to marry the expectations all the 'partners' had over standards. **There was no doubt that, in September, I had to hit the ground running.**

I spent the whole six-week summer break preparing a programme of improvement and effective management for the school. It was titled 'Shorefields 2000 a Successful Schools Programme' and included reference to – a new staff handbook to ensure consistency; a new community management structure; a clear ethos of **Hard Work, Achievement, Respectability and Personal Fulfilment;** new student responsibilities as prefects and Head Boy and Head Girl; an improved environment; the establishment of a 'Friends' Association in lieu of a PTA; a weekly Community Newsletter to counteract bad press; the full uniform policy; the reorganisation of all supervisory arrangements and the introduction of full accreditation in all curriculum areas.

I was very concerned over staff standards and establishing a consistency of approach. The new staff handbook emphasised procedures in minute detail but, in particular, the new standards expected over issues like uniform. It also made absolutely clear what standards were expected of the staff themselves – in their behaviour, punctuality, conduct of lessons, when on duty and in administering discipline. I wrote to all staff prior to the start of term over this.

The new ethos was necessary in order to consolidate the purposes of the school after years of having a diffuse community identity. It became like a mantra – Hard Work, Achievement, Respectability and Personal Fulfilment. **You need to be completely clear over what you want to achieve. If this runs to more than a couple of lines or, worse, strays from the pragmatic, then question yourself.** 'Wanting every child to fulfil their potential' means little.

I wrote to all parents over the summer regarding school standards. I emphasised the uniform, said that, in future, students would be restricted to the site during the day and wrote of the importance of full equipment. I told them that I was very pleased to be the new head teacher and that I was looking forward to working with them in moving the school on. **It's Very important to acknowledge the expectations of parents and indicate how you are going to meet them.** I was always tired of pundits referring to the low expectations of parents in inner city areas. This was not my experience. Schools tend to *fail* in meeting the aspirations of many parents.

Throughout the summer parents and staff received copies of our new newsletter. This was intended to reinforce the messages about standards and to prepare them for the new term.

Our key issues for students were uniform, behaviour, discipline, responsibility and academic progress. I hoped that by introducing a consistency of approach amongst the staff, by promoting the new ethos and by working better with parents the benefits would be felt directly by the students.

Despite feeling reasonably confident over the general direction in which the school needed to move, I was, inwardly, anxious over my own situation. This job was a colossal undertaking and I had no immediate colleague with whom to discuss philosophy, strategy or operational matters. The only deputy was to retire that year and I felt very unsupported. I knew that in years gone by head teachers had been obliged to maintain a log book in which they recorded incidents in the life of the school. Much like a ship's log. A journal in which the captain can record where he is in order to plan where he is going. This sounded like a useful device to me and one which might help me to maintain my sanity.

I bought an impressive leather bound record book and kept it on my office desk. To a greater or lesser extent I maintained this log for the next decade. I used it as a muse, as a diary, as a record of significant events and as a means of adding gravitas to my dealings with students and parents. It forms a valuable historical record during a period of real educational change.

In the pre-term staff meeting, in September '93, the staff were openly sceptical over our ability to even enforce the uniform policy. I had meticulously worked through procedures for dealing with this in the handbook but most staff could not be persuaded that it was worth the effort. This was a significant challenge. My whole approach was based upon us becoming a self-confident organisation, mutually supportive and with the capacity to do anything we wanted. We were, also, under even more pressure to get it right as we had just been informed of a forthcoming OFSTED inspection in March.

On the first day of term it was apparent that many students and parents had chosen to ignore the request over uniform. Watching them arrive was quite disheartening. It was a situation in which action was needed or the whole framework of improvement would be undermined. The staff had already demonstrated a worrying lack of confidence and this needed addressing.

I refused to let any student out of uniform enter the school site. They were turned back in the street. Initially there were so many I felt they might not comply. But I meant it. I had enough faith in the parents to believe there were probably sufficient uniform items at home. The main issue was trainers and the staff sensed that we could not win this sub cultural battle. As the first seventy or eighty turned away from the school others, coming behind, got the message and turned back of their own accord. They all returned within the hour looking radically different. By the end of the first half term, using the procedures laid down in the handbook, we had completely won the battle over uniform even with the hardline stragglers. We were doing what we said we would do, supporting the parents, and they appreciated it. A friend provided me with free shoes from his market stall, which the students hated wearing. We provided free leather dye where students had deliberately purchased the wrong colour shoes and, in extreme situations where parents claimed they could not afford uniforms, we purchased them. Liverpool is a very proud city and there was not a single occasion when this money wasn't repaid.

As anticipated, only a small number of Year 7 children arrived to register at the school in September. An intake of seventy is simply insufficient to sustain a Secondary School. Our despondency was compounded by the fact that there were individuals effectively picketing the school attempting to dissuade parents from allowing their children to enter. We called the Police.

We came to realise very quickly that the change of headship had made no difference to the campaign to close the school. The fact that present and past governors had orchestrated this was a disgrace.

The letter writing, phone calls, threatening visits and bogus reports in the media began in earnest. A discredited councillor was happy to ask staged questions and many well-meaning organisations were drawn into the vindictive web of accusation being created around us. There was no integrity here. Nobody could be unhappy with my headship, as I hadn't even started. There were, nevertheless, nineteen incidents, items of correspondence and articles in the press arising from the activity of the ex chair in my first fortnight. This, unfortunately, was the pattern for the rest of the year. I had hundreds of issues to deal with all emanating from the same source. Day after day. Sometimes three or four times a day. Individual governors, staff and I were all threatened during the year. I continued to receive dozens of nuisance calls at home. The worst element, however, was the publicity, again staged to coincide with parents' choice of Secondary Schools.

All this was grossly unfair not only to the professionals attempting to improve the situation and working in difficult circumstances anyway but also to the local community. The unpleasant demonstration of personal power, vindictiveness and manipulation we were experiencing was simply aimed at closing a significant resource in Liverpool 8. I found that to be totally unacceptable. I determined to work with the decent people new to the Governing Body. I would handle the attacks on the school for a proportion of my time each day. I would demand that the Local Authority play their appropriate role and I would try to carry out my school improvement plan come what may.

Part of this plan involved the introduction of Head Boys and Girls and a Prefect system. Some staff were hostile to the idea on principle. It smacked of elitism, sounded old fashioned, and they frankly found it ridiculous. Others simply did not believe it could work. How was it possible for an older student to exercise any authority over others when there may be repercussions for them in the neighbourhood after school? They wouldn't be capable of it anyway! For my part I had no choice for two reasons. Firstly, I had said we would have prefects and therefore needed to deliver on the undertaking. Secondly, and as important, I had said that we would contain the students on site during the day. This would require a large number of staff prepared to do duties and, while we had some excellent teachers supervising at midday, the numbers now required were simply not available to me. Quite simply, I needed the older students to control parts of the school in the absence of staff duties. In particular I needed control of the entrances and exits.

Never underestimate the level of responsibility students are capable of holding. The new prefects were incredible! Students had, hitherto, been able to leave the site at lunchtime. Suddenly other students were telling them that they couldn't do so! Who would have thought it would work? Our first prefects took their responsibilities very seriously indeed. There was simply no way a student without permission was going to leave the site. Because I had introduced the Prefects without any consultation with staff, and because they didn't fit in to any area of responsibility, I had to manage them myself. This included organising their duties and training them in handling confrontation. This was essential as their natural inclination was to be rather fascistic.

We managed to contain hundreds of youngsters on site for the first time. This was crucial due to problems in the area at lunchtime, threats to students, nuisance to neighbours, poor afternoon attendance and punctuality and the huge management time wasted each afternoon dealing with problems generated during the lunch period outside the gates. **It *is* easier to stop problems occurring than to deal with the consequences.** Having said this large numbers of students need to be kept occupied and their movement needs to be well managed. The bulk of our students were on free school meals, around 80%, and all were using the canteen at some time during the lunch break. They needed entertaining. At one point we hired two juggling, fire eating unicyclists to entertain the canteen queue!

We had particular problems during wet and cold weather and during November-December '93 we restructured a proportion of our Youth work activity from evening to midday work. This brought me into very swift conflict with the Youth Service managers in the city but our arrangement occupied hundreds of students each day. Our other safety valve was the sports hall and gyms and the Head of PE organised 'FA Cup' competitions indoors, with hundreds of spectators, during the worst months. A lifesaver.

The issue of lunchtime supervision is highly significant for schools. Many have moved to a 'continental day' in order to side-step problems. Staff are often prepared to undertake paid duties but less inclined to run voluntary activities. Some staff, conversely, will voluntarily work with a small club or society or provide extra lessons but would hate general supervision. Eventually, at Shorefields, we made it a condition of employment of all non-teaching staff that they would participate in supervision. This provided security against teacher action and significantly increased the number of staff available for rotas. It also emphasised **that everyone in a school has an inescapable responsibility for the welfare of students** and cemented working relationships between teaching and APTC staff. However it is achieved **the well-being of the school depends upon the lunch period being a satisfactory experience for the students.**

Punctuality and attendance in the afternoons immediately improved due to keeping the students on site and this was despite having to manage a rather cumbersome exeat system for several years while we phased out the old arrangements.

In my first assembly, to the whole school and all the staff, I talked about the film 'The Principal' in which an American High School was turned around and taken back from the bad guys for the sake of the decent majority. I conducted the whole assembly with a baseball bat in one hand and the new staff handbook of watertight procedures in the other. They probably thought they were in the presence of a madman. I needed to project an image of change and of determination to see it through. **Assemblies are a huge opportunity for the Head to lay out his expectations to the students**

and, more importantly, the staff. I addressed the whole school at least once a week for many years, until we outgrew the facilities.

I had started the weekly newsletter to counterbalance our poor press. The newsletter was relentlessly positive. We highlighted all significant visitors. We included a list of 'sponsors' to indicate that the school was well supported and in the ascendancy. Initially these were a little fictitious and included the logo of our bankers, our uniform suppliers, Gary, who had given us the shoes and the local garage who *we* had reimbursed when a student broke their window.

We relentlessly highlighted the achievements of the students and the school. We included 'quotes' about the success of the school and how impressed visitors had been. Some of these were genuine but if we had insufficient material we simply made it up. Nothing was going to get in the way of the 'real' story, which was that Shorefields was on a steep incline of improvement. **Unless you tell people how good you are you cannot assume they know.** We never, publicly, criticised students or admonished parents. We made no criticism of groups of students for poor behaviour. We never wrote to parents en masse complaining of poor punctuality, uniform or lack of homework. We simply provided advice and encouragement. I had seen plenty of school newsletters in which the head or staff gave vent to their negativity. It simply doesn't work. Similarly, I never criticised staff, en masse, for the lateness of their reports, for failing to make curriculum returns on time or for not selling raffle tickets. This actually has the exact opposite effect to that intended. **Never broadcast and potentially amplify your problems!**

Each week we named all the students receiving the new school HARP award –for Hard Work, Achievement, Respectability or Personal Fulfilment. A weekly newsletter prize was provided to encourage students to take the newsletter home and I delivered the prize by hand to their home address. This achieved an insight into the students families and was also good PR. **Schools must be positive and I was relentlessly positive.**

The staff needed tools to support them in maintaining disci-

pline. Years previously they had been used to sending badly behaved students to the head for punishment. In lieu of this we had a Pager System. The Pager System provided a senior member of staff on call for every lesson each day. Staff were entitled, even encouraged, to send for the 'Pager' in order to support them in their teaching. Students were frequently removed from lessons, by the 'Pager', for disruptive behaviour. They were placed with another member of staff, often a Head of Department or Head of Year, for the duration of the lesson. They then returned to their normal timetable and it was the responsibility of the Department to follow up the issue. I always resisted the notion of a 'sin bin' as fundamentally unmanageable. Such an idea places intolerable strain on the senior staff and clusters the worst students, temporarily, in one place. **Staff and students do, however, have a right to enjoy lessons without disruption.** Our arrangement involved no questioning of a teacher's decision to remove the student. It defused a lot of confrontation.

We supported the 'Pager System' with a 'Patrol Book'. Any student causing any level of difficulty in lessons or on corridors was entered in the book. Similarly for break and lunchtimes. The taking and writing down of a name for recording purposes is hugely symbolic and powerful. We recorded what had happened and what punishment, if any, was given. Any staff, at any point, could make entries in the Patrol Book. We were able, at a glance, to see which students were causing widespread disruption and, where a student was repeatedly spoiling lessons we would suspend their timetable.

We realised that staff were crying out for a form of immediate admonishment that gave them control. A form of administrative 'caning'. We introduced our own 'assertive' methods. Firstly, teaching and the expectations set had to be of a good order and this became a main plank in raising standards in the school. Secondly, staff were advised over a range of low-level interventions in the classroom. The first significant punishment was an 'assertive 3' writing exercise. This was standard across the school and staff carried copies of the assertive 3 complete with instructions. Staff were also given 'assertive pocket books' in order to note names and details of offenders. This was backed up by the unquestioning pager system on the part of senior staff and the Patrol Book. Obviously, we had a range of sanctions beyond the classroom and, ultimately, this hierarchy of measures culminated in exclusion.

The role of the pastoral staff in overseeing the behaviour of Year groups was very important. The Heads of Year were, generally, respected colleagues and they had been creating files of information on individual students as staff passed information to them. While this was helpful, it was apparent that the absence of a chronological record in an agreed format was hampering the school in dealing with all levels of disruptive behaviour. In fact, most Heads of Year adopted a 'clean sheet' attitude each September, which undermined a properly incremental approach to dealing with problems. Staff were aware that the school was presenting a very 'flat' response to behavioural issues and this was unacceptable. We introduced an 'Intervention Record', which was held and completed by Heads of Year. This was intended to summarise positive as well as negative interventions with students but was predominantly used for the latter. The record was intended to be continuous and to properly inform pastoral staff in deciding upon appropriate action. Even with the Intervention Record it took several years to persuade, and demand, that the pastoral staff, receiving a new year group each September, make themselves fully familiar with the students and keep to the principle of continuity of care and intervention. We used these records, very effectively, during exclusion hearings.

Clearly, though, a healthy community needs to be praising to a greater extent than it is criticising or punishing. This is the only way to highlight the positives and model the behaviour you want to see. We relentlessly highlighted success on the part of both staff and students. We had our HARP Awards, Log Book Certificates and Good Citizen Awards. We used a Community Book, to record any positive minor activity, and attempted to make more entries here than in the Patrol Book.

An initial problem was staff acceptance of praise and reward for the students. There were some vicious objections to rewarding improvement in punctuality, for example, as opposed to the absolute achievement of high standards. The school had an established Graduation Ceremony for Leavers in year 11. This was a well organised and fulfilling event but even here, year on year, the Head of Year struggled to suppress the inclination of staff to acknowledge and validate some students above others.

I started the 'Friends of Shorefields' with some year 7 parents, EWO, Police and staff. Initially this was a device to suggest strong parental support in the face of external problems. 'The Friends' could voice support and this was reported in the newsletter. We also distributed questionnaires at parents' evenings in order to garner parents' views. Any positive comments were again reported in the newsletter and our surveys helped to counteract the undermining propaganda we were still suffering.

Eventually we had separate Chinese, Somali, Arabic, Bangladeshi, Czech, indigenous white and black groups meeting as 'Friends'. We also held a number of 'house meetings'. This involved me approaching an individual parent and asking them to host a meeting, at home with their friends and neighbours, in order to discuss the future of the school. **Secondary Schools need to organise the support of parents.** This is, universally, harder to achieve than at the Primary stage. Nevertheless the health and well being of the organisation depends upon it. If you are not in control of the communication between home and school and don't genuinely engage in the annual struggle over parental involvement then you lose the opportunity to influence the crucially important informal communication between parents themselves. We, at Shorefields, also needed to listen to the perceptions of the school held by black and minority ethnic parents, who often felt marginalised. We needed to act on their concerns.

Traditionally, the students had tended to drift into school in the morning and this lateness shaded into truancy and absence. We were able to make huge progress with punctuality by introducing systematic procedures, which distinguished between 'unpunctual' and 'late'. This enabled us to harass students causing a nuisance by failing to arrive on time and separated them from the hardline cases. We also found, however, that the problem will always resurface if procedures are not followed and the situation deteriorates very quickly if not monitored! **Monitoring of course is a crucial management information tool.** It must be simple and efficient. Furthermore, each **Post holder must want to achieve high standards** otherwise any procedures are a wasteful and annoying exercise all round.

Attendance was shockingly low in '93 but year on year we incrementally improved from 74% to 86%. Part of our initial problem was 'ghost students'. The school even maintained a 'ghost register'. This related to students we were obliged to maintain on roll but who, in some cases, had not been seen for years. At some point this had probably been of financial advantage to schools but published statistics and league tables of performance meant that they represented disaster. In the face of EWO opposition we ruthlessly challenged our school roll and set about deleting the phantoms. This was costly in every respect but was necessary if the school were to be on an incline of improvement. In addition to the 'ghosts' there were dozens of children who had not been seen for many months and their families failed to respond to correspondence. There were also children who formed part of the shifting population experienced by many inner city schools, itinerant families moving in, out and around the area generating instability in all the schools they attended. We knew that the school experienced a movement factor of around a third in any given year. In some year groups, by the end of year 11, only the minority had been in the school for five years. Later, Between January and Sept '96 we removed 112 students from the school roll. This was a desperate time financially for the school but Shorefields was either going to be a sink school burdened with colossal welfare problems, the flotsam from across the Authority and shocking statistics or it was going to rationalise, refocus and drive forward with a real sense of purpose and identity. We needed to redefine ourselves from a half empty six-form entry school to a full three or four form entry in order to protect the morale of staff and provide a meaningful education to the students. Furthermore, improvements in attendance can only come about from an understandable and manageable base line. We needed to establish this. During this period, the record shows students removed from the roll and continuing their education in a wide range of Liverpool schools, as well as London, Leeds, Devon, Kent, Birmingham, Manchester, Wales, Scotland, Bangladesh, Kazakhstan, Yemen, USA, Somalia and Malaysia.

While we needed to rationalise our roll we also needed to generate per capita funding. Thus, in '93 we tried to capitalise on a social education initiative our youth workers had been running for a couple of years. They had been successful in working with identified groups of disaffected youngsters who attended sessions with them part time. We were well aware that there were hundreds of such youngsters outside of the school system in Liverpool and that it was an LEA priority to track these students and arrange provision Apparently the numbers were sufficient to fill a medium sized secondary school. During 1993 I drew up a business plan for a 'Reintegration Unit' to be run by our youth staff and coordinated with the main school and Educational Welfare. In the plan we would receive full funding for large numbers of these students. We would cycle them through a range of activities suitable for their age and aptitude on a part time basis. We would provide distance learning materials and outreach support for the time they were at home. Each family would engage in a contract with Shorefields and the key outcomes would be behaviour modification and reintegration into full time mainstream education in a Liverpool school. Our proposal was rejected but we set up the unit anyway. Its key purposes initially were to break into the cycle of temporary exclusions and expulsion we were experiencing; to provide respite for school refusers and to integrate students transferring from other schools with poor disciplinary records. Clearly, this arrangement was underpinned by a different attitude to parents and students. With parents there was more negotiation rather than confrontation around disciplinary issues. Eventually the Unit made a huge difference to our record of exclusions. This was an essential step for us. In 1991-92 the school exclusion record was 136. This had actually fallen during 1992-93 but was rising again with another determined push over disciplinary standards. In the next two years we were able to cut the rate of exclusions by 85%. Having started with no funding whatsoever we successfully bid for Single Regeneration Budget (SRB), European Social Fund (ESF) and later used Social Inclusion funds.

There was a desperate need to improve the physical environment. There were appalling conditions in the toilets, the canteen ante-room, the canteen itself, on corridors and in many classrooms. The woodblock flooring on some corridors and in the reception area had bulged upwards to a height of about ten inches. The joke for visitors was that a member of staff was asleep under the carpet. It was awful. In places there was no plaster on the walls, with bare brick exposed. Plaster would regularly fall, in chunks, onto students and staff working in classrooms. We had five boilers heating the main school and another heating the Annexe. The different systems and repeated breakdowns prevented any sensible control over temperature with some staff freezing cold and others experiencing sweltering heat. The general state of dilapidation was compounded by our apparently low priority with the Council. There were rumours that the school would close. Hardly an incentive to put scarce funds into our maintenance. Only extreme circumstances such as contacting the Director to issue a closure notice due to ingress of water or lack of heating brought any response. One freezing February, several years later, we lost the use of four of our five boilers. Nevertheless we never sent students home! We couldn't afford the loss of confidence from parents and we didn't believe it right anyway.

After heavy rain, running water could ruin wall displays and this so demoralised the staff that they were very reluctant to spend time and effort replacing the work.

There was also a widespread objection to putting displays on corridors due to the damage caused by students. Nevertheless, the general environment had to be improved. At the start of term in Sept.93, I bought dozens of potted plants and populated all the window ledges on the ground floor. The Caretakers made display boards for classrooms and corridors. Initially these were completely ignored by many staff although some departments, such as, RE were keen and supportive. An interim solution, and one, which shamed some heads of dept, was to introduce 'wallpaper'. This was advertising material we had paid the local media to distribute. Blown to A3 size I could use these advertising flyers to cover a display board in minutes. **Lead by example was the message**. Later forms of 'wallpaper' comprised of the school achievements writ large or copies of news stories from the local press. When we, eventually, provided laminated sheets to cover the display boards the level of staff support rose dramatically.

Most of the inside of the school hadn't been painted for decades. There was paint peeling from corridor ceilings and, in places, hanging in long unsightly strips. Something had to be done. I arranged with the probation service for offenders carrying out Community Service Orders to repaint the building. They worked as a team with a supervisor. They provided the labour and we provided the paint. The quality of work was really variable but always better than we had experienced previously. We used the newsletter to broadcast Phase One of the 'total refurbishment' of the school. In reality three car thieves and a pot of paint. **You can *always* improve on the physical environment**. As one visiting councillor said, **'the important thing is that progress is being made and that you can point to it.'** I appreciated the generosity of that sentiment at the time.

Having introduced the plants, which, to the amazement of many staff, the students broadly respected, I had the problem of who would tend them. Initially I set about doing this myself. I bought a

watering can with a long spout and a bottle of Baby Bio. I made a
point of being on corridors from 8.00am each day watering plants
and cutting dead leaves. I was able to greet the students and staff as
they arrived. Students frequently offered help but the attitude of a
handful of staff was rather different. Why was I wasting my time?
Was I the highest paid domestic in the country? Obviously I didn't
have real work to do like them. But there was a lot of very real
work in this. For staff to be able to speak to me in passing saved
countless meetings and memos. I was able to express support for,
and show interest in, a mass of people I would, otherwise not reach
personally on a daily basis. I also knew quite finely what time staff
were arriving each day. **Maintaining high visibility is important
whether people feel comfortable with it or not.** From the point of
view of the students the head was a familiar face. One they generally accepted was on their side.

In relation to the plants, I had no idea what I was doing. I did,
however, remove a reasonable amount of chewing gum and sweet
wrappers from the pots. In time staff, particularly some RE and
English staff took responsibility for the plants in their areas and
eventually the cleaning staff took charge.

An unforeseen advantage of the plants was that we could quickly alter the appearance of any area of the school. On, for example,
a parents evening only requiring the use of two corridors and a hall,
we could move greenery from all over the school and more easily
disguise the mouldering state of the building. The caretakers made
two square planters, which we would position at corridor intersec-
tions – a great softening of the environment.

A proportion of every day was spent dealing with the ex chair-
man's correspondence and the avalanche of vexatious complaint
he generated through proxies and the media. The Local Education
Authority, which should have been protecting and supporting us,
were disabled by the harassment the school was suffering. The involvement of the City Solicitor and Learned Counsel made not a jot
of difference to the pressure. When correspondence about us was

directed to the LEA in the form of complaint or, perhaps, bogus councillors questions, the LEA itself simply became another agent from whom we were forced to field correspondence. It continued to pile high.

A particularly unpleasant incident occurred when The 'Mail on Sunday' staff appeared at the school wanting a response to allegations of bullying made by the ex chair. I spoke to them and refused to respond to an outrageous story, which they acknowledged was a set up, and a fabrication. The photographer and reporter hid outside the school and waylaid me on my way home. They published the photograph and a scandalous story without our cooperation.

There were some challenging students in the school particularly incomers from other schools in the city. This was a typical problem for a school below capacity. **A difficult situation is compounded by instability and by being forced to accept problem students from other schools.** Understandably the staff wanted unequivocal action over violence and we instigated immediate expulsion over unprovoked attacks. A fight would lead to the exclusion of both parties temporarily. A general rule was that personal space must not be invaded and this was the easiest test of right and wrong. A teacher must never, ever, be touched. **Staff and students must understand the parameters of good order.**

We **broke down any attempts at gangsterism.** At break and lunchtimes clusters of students in suspicious places e.g. around entry and exit doors, near toilets, in hidden corners, on ramps and stairways would be dispersed. Much of the site could be observed from the building and patterns of movement are easily observable if one is vigilant. There is, apparently, a science developing around the use of CCTV to detect aberrant patterns in shopping malls and town centres. In a school it requires vigilance and common sense. If we were likely to face resistance we would simply request that one or two from a group came into the building to 'have a discussion'. Very polite. No confrontation. No explanation. **The staff were in charge of the school.** Tension was diffused. You have to believe this to make it work. **There is no doubt that high levels of supervision inside and outside contribute to good order.** This, though, needs to be quality supervision.

We had tremendous problems at the end of each school day as students exited the school. We attracted delinquent youths from the area, often excluded from Catholic schools farther afield . They were a general nuisance but were also intent on settling scores from some of the petty rivalries in the neighbourhood. They habitually caused problems for our black students, blocking pavements, pushing and shoving. We knew that we had some vicious individuals on our school roll, white and black, male and female and it was to a great extent their behaviour out of school hours that exacerbated the problems. A gang fight, a beating, rivalry over a girl or boy during the weekend would inevitably bring trouble to the school. We were a multi racial school in a white neighbourhood and an easy venue for reprisals. We also provided a big audience at 3.20 each day. Our students were obliged to use public transport and the nearest bus stops to the school, 50 yards away, were the focus for tension. The students were not safe on the buses themselves and there were instances of white skinheads with dogs boarding the buses en route to cause mayhem. We had a number of instances of stone throwing in which bus windows were smashed and had to deal with the backlash when our students, understandably, acted pre-emptively or retaliated. The local Anti Nazi League organised a march from the school to protest over racism in the area – that wasn't helpful and could easily have exacerbated our problems. Meanwhile, we struggled each night to hold the line. We were well aware that we were dealing essentially with petty gangsterism and local rivalries that were easily perceived along racial lines. Disputes were, increasingly, taking on those characteristics and were in danger of polarising the school.

I took the position of being responsible for the students' behaviour and welfare all the way to and from school. While this was a fiction, the reality is that people generally have this expectation of schools without considering the practical implications. We issued instructions that students must not congregate at the end of the road and directed them back into school if they didn't move off home. We travelled on public service buses, intervened in fights with outsiders, faced down youths with dogs, challenged people carrying knives and sticks and generally became a high profile nuisance.

A number of incidents typified this period. At 3.15 one day I was standing on the street corner and a passing neighbour warned me that we were going to have a problem. 'They're getting tooled up by Beloe St.', he said. I drove up the hill away from the school and found 'the tools' neatly lined up against a wall. Pick axe handles, iron bars, hammers, and chains. The Police riot vans arrived very quickly confiscated the equipment and made arrests. An appalling situation had been averted.

After the installation of CCTV, I was idly watching one of the monitors and noticed that we had a handful of young women outside the school. This was quite odd as it was only mid afternoon. Far too early to be meeting friends. I went outside. They had no explanation for why they were there and I asked them to move on. As they did so a group of up to a dozen men appeared from an alley opposite the school. Each was wearing a full ski mask and carried a wooden stave. I pretended to speak into my mobile phone, which was not working at the time, and the men disappeared back into the labyrinth of passages.

We immediately rang the police who promised support for the end of the day. At 3.10 an elderly man and a young woman in blue uniforms arrived. They were park rangers from Newsham Park. The Police, apparently, were all tied up with a royal visit. The park rangers, understandably, refused to leave the reception area and left the end of the day to us.

I have to say that, while the police response was mediated by the priorities senior officers had on the time of the force, it was generally a good well-intentioned response. We were given priority and enjoyed a police presence nightly for years. The Liverpool force took the issue of race related crime very seriously in respect of our school and we formed some excellent relationships with officers on the ground. We were lucky to have a fantastic officer on our governing body.

Unfortunately, the nightly presence of a marked police vehicle is not ideal for public confidence in a school, although the students understood it was there for their protection.

I did learn to prevent police officers breaking up squabbles between students themselves. They have less authority than teachers in those situations and can exacerbate a problem.

I invited all local councillors into the school and gave students representative roles in greeting and meeting them. **It is important to generate support and respect amongst the decision makers.** All students were told they could be called upon at any time to account for themselves and to represent the school to visitors. My office opened directly onto a corridor and, during meetings with visitors, I would take the first half dozen students walking past and invite them in. I was never once let down or disappointed. The students were sometimes shy, sometimes untidy but always decent, ordinary, young people. This was the message I ceaselessly communicated, ordinariness. **It's all most parents really want.** A straightforward school with no fancy claims but doing what it says it will do.

Unfortunately, the media do not want to know 'ordinary' which is why they continually highlight aberrations in areas such as Toxteth and Mosside.

The morale of students and staff is important and the morale of governors is equally crucial to the development of the school. In our case, we were really struggling with attendance at governors meetings and attributed this, in part, to the negativity the governors were exposed to at each meeting. While it was essential to gain their support in demanding action over our schedule of dilapidations, in considering our financial crisis, dealing with disciplinary cases and enlisting their help in combating the harassment faced by the school and the staff the overall effect was dismal.

We invested considerable effort in making the Governors meetings as convivial as possible with tea, coffee, cake, biscuits and even sherry. We also moved all meetings to the daytime in order to emphasise that the real business was about young people. We started each meeting with a presentation by or to students to emphasise the progress the school was making.

We had particular problems recruiting and retaining parent governors and, in particular, black and minority ethnic parents. We could never assume that nomination forms for election represented genuine interest. Sometimes they had been completed in good faith, sometimes by a child on behalf of a parent and sometimes for a laugh. There were occasions when non-literate parents had signed nomination forms believing them to be regular school returns. I spent considerable time and effort contacting potential governors, not merely in respect of standing for election but to explain that attendance at meetings was a requirement of the post. We offered transport to and from meetings where it was a problem and in the case of one family, I made so many home visits, after the lady had secured a landslide victory in the parent governor elections then changed her mind, that I had an evening meal with the extended family.

A common problem was that many parents felt it would embarrass their children if they played a role in the school. As the school grew recruitment became easier and so keen were we to have the maximum parent governor support that we introduced 'associate' governors well in advance of it being a government initiative. Nevertheless, regardless of numbers, a school must have a healthy representation of decent parents on its governing body. **The time spent in nurturing parents and encouraging the most appropriate parents to step forward is a worthwhile investment. These are the people with the greatest stake in the school. It is only by having decent well meaning people on the governing body that a school can move forward.** This does not mean yes men and yes women. I spent ten years with a challenging and abrasive parent governor but was happy to see him co-opted when his children left the school.

We introduced a New Intake Open Evening for the first time in Nov. 93. Obviously, *all* successful schools held such evenings in order for prospective parents to view the facilities and speak to staff. We had all staff in their classrooms with displays of apparatus and work. There were twenty prefects on duty. It was a huge organisational effort but was a total disaster. Four people turned up. One wasn't even a parent. He was just an inquisitive passer by. We had arranged hundreds of chairs in the Assembly Hall in order for me to address the parents and children but on the evening we quickly changed the venue of the 'head's talk' to my office. **A small crowded space creates a better impression than a room full of empty seats.**

The visitors had no clear idea of how many people were in the building, nor did the staff.

Unfortunately, during the course of the evening, and following my meeting with the parents, my office was broken into from the outside and all the prefects' coats were stolen. We had to pay for them.

The following morning we told staff that the event had been a great success although some were critical of having seen no visitors whatsoever. We also broadcast the success of the evening in the newsletter and invited all parents who had missed this 'remarkable opportunity' to a personal tour of the school during the day. We actually received a reasonable response to this invitation.

By the end of the first term it was clear that the prefects had made a real contribution to running the school. I wrote to them all giving very genuine thanks for the manner in which they had carried out their duties.

By Christmas the staff themselves were exhausted and a number of malign and destructive colleagues exploited this and were publicly undermining any attempt to celebrate the end of term. We did have a good Christmas meal in the staff room, organised by the long-suffering staff association and three very loyal and dedicated colleagues. Beyond that, however, the message was clear .The staff wanted to disappear and had no interest in socialising with each other. This was a real problem. Morale was crucial at this time and I believe that the manner in which you end a term influences the start of the next. **It is also true that people who can socialise together can work better together.** I organised a staff evening meal in a Turkish restaurant, complete with belly dancer and, having initially canvassed some basic support, the response was overwhelming. What a fantastic night! On the last afternoon we provided drinks and sandwiches in the staff room and formally said our goodbyes to a number of staff leaving the school. This is always important. There is a mixture of feelings when colleagues move on and it is the responsibility of Senior Management to imbue the occasion with dignity and to capitalise on the potential for galvanising the staff. **Morale is a fickle commodity and requires nurturing. While staff have a responsibility not to be demoralising, senior management have a responsibility to nurture positive attitudes towards work and good social relations between the staff. If this is already happening, fine, but fail to monitor morale at your peril.**

During this first year the vulnerability of the school, which had been an issue for many years, had to be tackled. We suffered intrusion during the day, break-ins at night, arson attacks and delinquent youths on the streets during and at the end of each day. We installed CCTV but, by the end of the first half term, all the cameras had been stolen as they were stolen from all the other Liverpool schools in the scheme. In desperation a locked gate policy was introduced in an attempt to prevent opportunistic crime and make the school safer for all of us. We reduced seventeen exits from the school site down to one. We locked many of the buildings exit doors for the safety of the students and staff. This was far from being politically correct but was absolutely necessary. The impact was dramatic. The parameters of the school were no longer diffuse, with casual intrusion or casual escape a fact of life. Our community had clear, defendable, physical boundaries. There was an increased sense of security, personal safety and common purpose. **You must define your community and create a sense of communal well-being.**

I had, initially, written to Ofsted asking for our inspection to be deferred, as I was new in post. The rather curt response was that it 'could not be deterred'! The staff were apprehensive about the whole process. It was our first experience and the Registered Inspector's preliminary visit was on one of the worst days of the year. Liverpool, unusually, was practically snow bound and a proportion of the staff wanted snowballing banned. I refused to do it. Liverpool rarely experienced snow and this freak weather presented the experience of a lifetime for many of our youngsters. I remember standing with the inspector watching a colossal battle on the school field. The snow was so heavy that rival groups of students had rolled balls of snow up to six feet across and were battering each other. He was very complimentary over their efforts.

The Ofsted inspection itself was a good experience. I took the view that the largest turnout of parents would be for the best and organised a free bar for the end of the Inspector's meeting. The response was tremendous. We had also realised that the inspector's would see no music or performing arts during the Inspection week so took the opportunity to organise musical performance accompanied by a short Shakespearean scene to entertain parents in the foyer while they awaited the start of the Inspector's meeting. Our juggling unicyclist, previously employed at the school to entertain the canteen queue, also performed to the delight of the Inspectors. As I handed over the twenty pounds, we had agreed for the performance, the Registered Inspector came and shook the jugglers hand declaring him to be 'the most talented sixth former he had come across'!

Undoubtedly, the relationship formed with the Registered inspector and the team influences the outcome of inspections. In our first and all subsequent inspections we invested heavily in creating the right climate for the inspection. This involved tremendous hospitality, assistance in carrying bags, files, laptops, total courtesy, good working facilities, a senior member of staff checking on the inspectors welfare, a great deal of good humour and real honesty over discussing the short comings of the school as well as obviously promoting the strengths. We had staff and students on hand to guide inspectors, responded to their every whim (no matter how frustrating), put real effort into arranging interviews and observations to help the inspection but also to present our best face. Inspectors always want to complete inspections early and individual inspectors 'bought in' for minority subjects are very short of time. Inspectors are only human. If they are treated well and their life is made easier it must affect their general opinion of the school.

Following the inspection we invited in the local press for a presentation buffet. We presented them with certificates marking their support for the school, which, hitherto, had been non-existent. They were quite bemused. We also distributed copies of the official Ofsted report, printed on deep red paper, and our own edited version, printed on clear white. We took photographs of their sub editors receiving awards from us and wrote an article on the event for our newsletter, which we sent to them. It was entirely surreal. The governors and senior students enjoyed the buffet, the media realised they were dealing with real people and we received tremendous coverage of our inspection.

Thereafter we changed our practice of sending press releases and developed fully written articles, complete with tabloid headlines ready for publication. Our success rate with the local media was phenomenal. They started contacting the school for quotes about a range of issues and were happy to highlight positives when fed to them. **You must form an appropriate relationship with the media but remember you are playing with fire.** It only takes personnel change at the local paper for a hungry journalist to reverse all the good work done previously. One damagingly inaccurate or misleading article can influence parents enormously and the trite media view that 'there are two sides to every story' to justify print-ing slander about educational institutions is morally reprehensible. They are in the business of selling papers or attracting TV audiences so beware! Less than six months after our media buffet we were hit by a scandalous front-page article based on false exam results fed to a new and naïve reporter by a rogue councillor. The subsequent front page apology really was too late.

We had planned a Summer Fair for July '94. This was, again about communicating messages – the school as a community; a ma-ture organisation with the emotional reserves to undertake charity work; confidence over opening the gates to the public; positive rela-tionships with parents and the Primary Schools; a means of involv-ing students, parents, governors and staff in a 'fun' extra curricular activity. Ostensibly it was about fund raising and we were relatively successful. Most fundraisers of course know that the real money is made on the 'grand prize draw' and that the day itself is something of a loss leader. The Primary Schools and local community groups really appreciated the opportunity to have free stalls for their own fundraising activity. We had great prizes, all delivered by hand on the night of the fair. We hoped that everyone who participated, every small child enjoying themselves, every prizewinner became an advocate for the school. It all helped towards the 'critical mass' we needed. **It is essential to communicate confidence, to put on a show. To be serious minded but ebullient and life affirming.** This attracts support. We also calendared a Public speaking Competition in that first year and this became an annual event.

We were working all the time to improve staff expectations, classroom standards, school security, the falling roll, student behav-iour, the appalling state of the buildings, overstaffing and the rela-tionship with the governing body. Meanwhile, we were supporting the development of new curriculum models department by depart-ment, reviewing academic progress, developing good practice in respect of lesson planning, delivery, marking, record keeping and homework and keeping the bulk of students on site all day.

Our major academic push with Year 11 students included close monitoring of attendance, punctuality and performance, establishing target exam grades for the students and providing mentoring for each individual in small groups with volunteer staff.

Despite our vigorous approach to facing our challenges and improving the school we continued, right through 1993-94 to suffer from external pressure. Dealing with nearly two hundred items of correspondence, complaint, incident or reporting in the media was draining of my time. Worse, the very public vilification of the school was a disaster for our image with both existing parents and prospective parents. We were making little or no progress on this front despite countless meetings with unions, governors, sympathetic councillors, LEA officers, solicitors and barristers. We had taken action over defamation, sought an injunction, involved the police in two separate investigations, and been exonerated by both an Ombudsman's enquiry and a City Council independent enquiry. During the year we had, also, received a very good Ofsted report.

There was nothing else to do but persevere. This was my job and I had to do it despite it being almost completely time consuming and detracting from my personal and family life. If we had not made such strong progress, on the educational front, during the year it would have been easy for total demoralisation to set in.

We can look at the progress made during that first year of Headship through the five areas I habitually used to analyse the business of the school and report to Governors. They were-Staff, Students, Curriculum, Resources, Wider Constituency Matters.

In terms of Staff there had been substantial guidance over their standards and their behaviour particularly regarding students being on task in lessons, the preparation for and conduct of lessons, and the implementation of consistent procedures. The introduction of the Handbook had been an essential device and acted as a point of reference thereafter on everything from staff absence procedures, disciplinary issues, performing effective supervisory duties and communication, to 'directed time' meetings, the performance standard for tutors and heads of year, booking the minibus and school policies.

In any organisation the introduction of revised expectations and changes to existing practices is likely to meet with both support and resistance. We had already had that experience prior to 1993 under the previous Headteacher. During my first year as Head it was necessary to take informal or formal action over certain issues of standards in respect of staff.

Action was taken with nine staff over issues of competency. Seventeen colleagues had presented problems over punctuality to work, to lessons or to duties. Eight had been of concern regarding their behaviour towards students and six had exhibited unacceptable behaviour towards colleagues. Nine staff had received warnings over their general professional conduct and eight for failing to fulfil their responsibilities. Seven colleagues were instructed personally, in addition to the general imperative, to keep students in lessons. In all, this was sixty four specific actions in relation to twenty three of the staff. The action ranged from informal expressions of management concern and informal and formal warnings to suspension. This was not a popularity contest and what had been achieved was an understanding that the Head was unequivocal over standards and over school improvement.

In relation to Students, we had a range of new Prefect responsibilities, the Head Boys and Girls were regularly representing the school, sixth formers had all been given responsibility as 'stewards', the student council was active, new attendance and punctuality procedures had brought improvement, there was an acceptance of uniform and the sixth form had voted to also have a uniform. There was a wider range of midday activities including the full Youth Club. We had continued the highly successful motivational programmes in years 10 and 11, improved the quality of teaching and also encouraged 'supported self study'. We introduced and promoted a wider range of rewards and, finally, had been more stringent over our disciplinary arrangements. This had resulted in the exclusion, either temporarily or permanently, of 117 students. Shocking as this sounds it was similar to many other schools in the Liverpool County sector at the time. We were making some progress towards an image of order and discipline.

Our Curriculum developments were around the National Curriculum, cross curricular skills, themes and dimensions, assessment, recording and reporting, alternative accreditation, issues of planning and delivery and homework. We were heavily supporting change with appropriate staff development and release for staff to attend courses. We had introduced structural change into some departments and were developing a more authoritative role for curriculum leaders. We were also monitoring and periodically reviewing the delivery of the whole curriculum through lesson observations. Finally, there were a number of additional developments impacting on the curriculum. These included the Public Speaking event, which the English Department reluctantly agreed was relevant to their area, as well as a variety of university trips and study residentials for the older students. There had been significant progress across the curriculum.

Our Resources situation, by the end of the year, was looking desperate. We had however, managed the situation well. The collapse in student numbers had been so rapid that planning from 92-93 to 93-94 had been impossible. Nobody had anticipated the number of parents simply baling out of places at the school. We had been saved financially by three factors. Firstly, we were still in a transitional phase of Local Financial Management and our budget was somewhat enhanced by this. Secondly, our funding was historical and based on the preceding year's census return. Thirdly, we had a substantial reserve. Unfortunately, we were forced into the situation of supporting staffing, to which we were already committed, rather than spending reserve funds on school development. Nevertheless, we had achieved the redecoration of parts of the building and had used our caretaking/maintenance team to complete minor works, which staff appreciated. In anticipation of a growing financial problem we had been very protective of the budget, had retrieved nearly £100,000 of funds incorrectly accounted by the LEA, had placed a moratorium on new staff appointments and had managed to remain solvent moving into the new financial year in April '94.

In terms of what we called our Constituency we had achieved a significantly better working relationship with the Governing body. We had succeeded in attracting new governors who were very supportive of the school and who were impatient with our detractors. We had restructured our Community management arrangements in order to create a clearer accountability to the Head teacher. We had a number of very supportive Councillors within and outside the Governing Body who were working politically on our behalf and we were communicating with every councillor and parent directly each week via the newsletter. We had also held our first Open Evening earlier in the year, which had been disappointing, but we were determined to build on this for the future.

LEARNING POINTS YEAR ONE

- Be clear over the challenges you are facing and identify the opportunities immediately available to you. A 'SWOT' analysis of Strengths, Weaknesses, Opportunities, Threats, is helpful as a 'desktop' exercise but beware of making assumptions and thinking only in boxes.

- Listen to the governors, staff, students and parents.

- Form your own simple agenda. Be sure that *you* understand the nature of the overall mission.

- Be clear over the ethos of the school or your interpretation of that ethos.

- Maintain a diary and a log as efficient management tools and to encourage reflection on progress.

- Communicate with all staff and parents.

- Ensure that staff have clear guidance over expectations, procedure and conduct.

- Set out an improvement programme as soon as possible. Clearly the circumstances of an internal and external appointee are different. There are advantages and disadvantages in both situations.

- Start a weekly newsletter as a vehicle for school improvement. Send this to all staff, students, parents, governors, Primary Schools and Councillors and local shops.

- When you give an undertaking always follow it through. This increases support for any future decisions.

- Budget time for dealing with problems. Do not allow problems to derail the main agenda.

- Give students responsibility.

- Introduce procedures to guarantee the security of the site, the staff and the students.

- Be proactive. Put time and effort into preventing problems occurring. Be healthily pessimistic.

- Recognise the importance of the lunchtime period. Look at the experience from a student's perspective. Give everyone a good experience.

- Lead from the front. Use Assemblies to motivate and inspire students…and staff!

- Broadcast successes widely but deal with problems discreetly.

- Create practical, human tools for supporting progress – certificates, discipline books, reward books, and chronological records. They are understandable, symbolic and familiar.

- Organise parental support.

- Be clear over school strategies for improving attendance, punctuality, uniform and academic success and, crucially, employ simple monitoring devices to gauge progress.

- Immediately take a range of measures to improve the school environment. These can cost very little. The important thing is to demonstrate progress.

- Be highly visible and lead by example.
- Publish a clear statement on behaviour and discipline. Be vigilant around the school and act quickly to disempower threatening students.
- Be concerned about the neighbourhood. Form good relations with residents, local shopkeepers and the police. The school is not an island. Extend the limits of your authority, parents will appreciate it.
- Invite councillors, parents and business people into school during the working day. Inform staff of the visitors. Always involve students. Be optimistic. Publish visitors names and any positive quotes.
- Put time and effort into recruiting, managing and nurturing the Governing Body. Hold daytime meetings. Make life interesting. Organise presentations and introduce students and staff.
- Stage manage Open Days and turn any failure into an opportunity. Do not reveal a lack of parental support to staff.
- Organise staff social events and appropriately dignified leaving/retirement parties.
- Stage manage everything about an Ofsted Inspection. Leave nothing to chance. Over prepare. Form a good relationship with the team. Manage the release of the report.
- Be very supportive of curriculum leaders. Develop their responsibility for improving staff and monitoring performance. Give time for planning curriculum change. Personally monitor and review the delivery of the curriculum across the school and involve all senior managers in this.
- Be intolerant of Performance, Capability and Conduct issues amongst the staff. This does not mean being unsympathetic but

the Head's responsibility is to ensure professionalism.

- Maintain a very tight control of the budget.

- Be positive, enthusiastic and optimistic. Communicate a high level of self-belief. Constantly 'talk up' the school, praise the staff and praise the students, the parents and the community. Genuinely enjoy the job and believe that you will succeed. If you don't believe this then nobody else will.

START OF SECOND YEAR OF HEADSHIP SEPTEMBER '94.

W E HAD DISASTROUS NUMBERS on the first day. Only forty five Year 7 students enrolled. This now had huge budgetary implications. We had actually improved on previous exam results with 4% gaining five or more good GCSEs. Despite this, apparently, minimal level of success both staff and governors were pleased that there had been progress. As mentioned previously, we had excluded 117 students during the 93-94 academic year. We entered the new academic year with a number of clear staff disciplinary problems identified from work the previous year and with a growing staff absence problem. **Effort doesn't always bring immediate success, things often get worse!**

We calendared quality assurance points throughout the year... homework monitoring, uniform and equipment, punctuality and attendance and were paying very close attention to preparation and marking. **The calendar is a crucial management tool**. The creation of the calendar should involve the widest consultation and requires careful scrutiny and oversight. It drives the year and the overall performance of the school. In-year, problems, mistakes and modifications should be carefully recorded in order to inform the following year's exercise.

We engaged in a vigorous review of PR and marketing. This included a concentration on uniform and standards of behaviour. **The students are your key ambassadors!** We looked critically at the newsletter and how it was distributed. We developed a 'road show' of staff, students, materials and display stands to take to Primary open evenings and we visited Primaries for recruitment talks. I began a heavy involvement with the Primary 'Cluster' of heads. **Neglect a relationship with Primary Heads at your peril.** We sent dozens of articles to the local press and purchased advertising 'flyers' through the press. These professional adverts for the school were delivered to every home in the area.

While we relentlessly highlighted the positives, it was necessary from time to time, within school, to make a very clear demonstration of how any seriously undisciplined students were being treated. This was as important for staff as for students. **We created an 'At Risk' register.** This referred to being 'at risk' of ultimate permanent exclusion. It served a number of purposes. It highlighted the students for Pastoral heads and SMT and emphasised the importance of record keeping and evidence. In some cases the level of difficulty presented by a student was impressionistic. The explanation was that either staff held prejudicial attitudes or they were failing to report issues for the Head of Year's attention. It had to be acknowledged that low-level disruption was very undermining but difficult to record unless staff were entirely clear over standards. The 'At Risk' register put pressure on staff to record incidents of concern and to record what actions they had taken. It also put clear pressure on SMT to support staff when poor behaviour was compromising the quality of life in the school. Finally, we used it publicly to affirm standards.

Every whole school assembly focussed on 'our' community issues. This included the standards we expected, the advantages of this school community over others, school and individual successes and 'our' values and attitudes. If misbehaviour was mentioned it was in the context of shock that it occurred in 'our' community and that it was atypical of the standards of 'our' students 'our' families and 'our' neighbourhoods. Periodically, and with gravitas, named students would be asked to leave the assembly. They would be escorted away by a member of staff and isolated until parents were contacted and either came in or accepted the student at home. The rest of the students were informed that there was no place in 'our' community for malign individuals compromising the well-being and progress of the rest.

We treated bullying particularly harshly. The relief when certain individuals were removed was palpable. The students and staff responded well to these devices. From time to time, senior staff will be perceived as unresponsive to problems in school for a variety of reasons. Morale can dip badly and the effectiveness and authority of the Head will suffer. The Head must be sensitive to this and redress the situation. **Clearly, the head would want to minimise their interventions as this undermines the effectiveness of others, however, direct action is needed, periodically, to restore equilibrium even in the best system.** This may relate to discipline but could equally relate to standards of teaching, lunchtime arrangements, the effectiveness of reporting, entrance and exeat procedures, and punctuality and attendance issues. In a city school standards can improve rapidly but can deteriorate even more rapidly. **The maintenance of standards requires constant concern and vigilance on the part of all staff,** in a similar manner to the good order on a ship. Standards can slip due to staff being overwhelmed by pastoral issues, changes of personnel, staff absence, staff disaffection, curriculum change, student absence, student movement in and out of school, physical problems with the school building and tensions in the community.

We permanently excluded for unprovoked violence, persistent anti social behaviour -bullying, racism, sexism or relentless disruption, for carrying offensive weapons, supplying drugs and any assault on a member of staff. Some parents rigorously contested the policy of exclusion. In instances where there was equivocation over the facts or we knew there were procedural inconsistencies we would exclude anyway knowing that the Governors would reinstate on appeal after negotiating terms. This is often necessary in order to appease staff. **The importance of dialogue between management and Governors is crucial to supporting the behaviour policy of the school.**

Governors must never have their impartiality compromised but they do deserve a very well presented case. After an unsuccessful appeal to Governors parents invariably appealed to the LEA panel. In eleven years we never lost an appeal either against expulsion or, later, when parents were demanding admission to the school. The school was always represented by the head and the chair of governors and we knew that in the face of legal services, independent legal support, social and educational professionals supporting the appellant, parents and the child we had to be very heavily prepared. This is challenging, given the relatively short notice of some appeals, and we used the intervention record on each child in the school very effectively. Another health warning. **Student behaviour records are only as good as the person making the entry.**

We were still experiencing problems generated by ex governors, in particular around allegations of mal treatment of their children. Every complaint lodged with the LEA was investigated independently of the school and there was never a case to answer. A Liberal Democrat Councillor was still plying the media with false information and the NUT considered the possibility of action over defamation. The Police had undertaken handwriting analysis and fingerprinting on a range of nuisance letters received by the school. The Ombudsman's enquiry, arising from allegations the previous year, had now formally concluded that no injustice had been caused to any child. Nevertheless a huge amount of our time had been wasted. I had more meetings with the police, the leader of the

Liberal Democrat group, the Director of Education, LEA Officers, journalists and unions.

Yet again we had received adverse publicity timed to coincide with parental choices over secondary schools. I proposed a judicial review of the behaviour of the LEA and Liverpool City councillors and asked for Secondary School transfer forms to be reissued to prospective parents with a supporting letter from the LEA. This did not happen. I also decided that we would no longer respond directly to any complaint or enquiry relating to the ex chair or his affiliates. Any correspondent, be it a councillor, the LEA or the Queen would receive a standard response which, politely, informed them that they were part of a wide issue of orchestrated harassment. To date this amounted to 835 incidences of complaint, baseless allegation, unreasonable criticism innuendo and unwelcome visits. In total a record of 2169 pages held in nine files!

In October 94 we experienced overwhelming staff absence problems. This was noted as a post Ofsted feature in many schools. In seven weeks we lost nearly 1000 lessons to a flu virus, bereavements, courses and trips. We introduced stringent tests for out of school activity, which, initially, was an action resented by many staff. On the other hand it was obvious that staff feeling below par themselves were less likely to come to work if their preparation time was to be lost to support the professional development of colleagues. This is an unanswerable problem for schools. In order to develop, the staff need to be out of school, but this affects the core job. Years later when schools were under intense pressure to release staff for examination and KS4 training the supply agencies themselves couldn't cope with the demand. We bought in full time temporary supply in order to deal with the situation.

We were facing huge financial problems and had a deficit predicted at £365,000 for April 95. We started an 'Armageddon file' and our options were fairly clear. We must increase income by – raising student numbers; generating additional non public revenue; applying for grant funding to support existing core expenditure on the back of European projects; attracting sponsorship for any future development activity; retrieving unpaid revenue funding from the LEA from previous years. The latter related to funding arbitrarily with held by the LEA from community activity supported across our two sites.

We had to reduce expenditure by – rationalising the teaching staff establishment through early retirement, redeployment, external promotion, severance or redundancy (we never resorted to the latter two but had to warn staff of the possibility); rationalising the caretaking arrangements onto a rotating shift pattern to remove huge overtime bills; managing our own cleaning contract to reduce payments to the LEA; challenging annual charges to the LEA for unused detached playing fields; putting a moratorium on external appointments and managing the existing budget in order to generate the maximum end of year carry forward.

This latter strategy necessitated the reorganisation of all contingencies, reserves and development funding into other budget lines in order to gain the support of the LEA and the unions. Any level of reserve would have generated union opposition to redeployment and thus guaranteed financial collapse. By under spending during 93/94, shedding staff, reorganising the school, reclaiming missing funds and generating revenue we were able to present a balanced budget in April '95.

While some schools were supportive in respect of redeployment, others, through LEA committee membership, clearly obstructed any level of financial support or development around Shorefields. Repairs prioritised in Council were blocked, applications for LEA grants were blocked, community tenants were poached, use of space in our annexe was blocked, support for social disadvantage, special educational needs and bilingual provision at the school was under relentless attack. The method in this madness was clear. The closure of a 'failing' school, regardless of the community consequences, served the purposes of the remaining schools in the city. This was not mere paranoia as a range of schools in the same predicament faced the same treatment. Shorefields is the only school in Liverpool to have suffered such a collapse of intake and to have survived and thrived. A further seven secondary schools were unable to reverse the trend and closed. Others face uncertainty.

Key elements in the survival of Shorefields were – a willingness to build positively on its key characteristics as a multi racial, inner city, community school. A focus on its geographical and demographic advantages-in a defined area of the city, relatively isolated from other schools, close to a large number of County, Diocesan and Archdiocesan Primaries, able to offer education close at hand to a relatively conservative local population reluctant to travel beyond the area and accessible to a BME population in the Granby and Smithdown areas who had expressed dissatisfaction with much of the county secondary provision, including Shorefields, in the past. Finally, a determination to identify with the struggle for resources and recognition faced by the Primary sector in Toxteth and indeed by many of the local community organisations. We treated the community as a whole, all our parents, governors and many, many, individuals with professionalism, friendship and respect and, in time, this was reciprocated. **A school must identify its own key components for survival, although all schools facing falling rolls may have to address issues of public confidence.**

During our 'downsizing' we stripped out the senior team and myself and one deputy, forwent incremental pay increases. A good idea at the time but a difficult precedent for later. It was nearly ten years before we established an appropriate management team of Head, three deputies and two assistant heads. In the interim the schools development rested, at senior management level, on a couple of people.

Having, initially, faced hostility and rejection from the local SRB and ESF body, which was concerned to promote 'community' activity, we were accepted for involvement having argued that the community, as represented by students in the school, required support beyond the statutory.

We successfully bid for SRB funds to support the employment of our own attendance officer. We employed an ex teacher. This led to the boycott of the school by the Liverpool Educational Welfare Service. This was despite a clear demarcation between roles. We significantly improved both attendance and punctuality and EWO relented and resumed a level of sensible working with us. We did, however, face relentless and quite unwarranted scrutiny of our records over a period of eighteen months. There appeared to be a determination to uncover anomalies. **Never make any assumptions about bureaucrats. There are statuses and power bases and vested interests that have nothing to do with improving standards and everything to do with protecting position.** The various attendance initiatives were successful but any initiative may have unforeseen structural consequences. In our case, while the employment of an Attendance Officer initially improved attendance it also, quickly, led to a decline in responsibility on the part of staff generally. **The advantages of change must be weighed against the consequences and steps taken to forestall a structural reaction and deterioration in basic provision.**

We were, clearly, in a desperate situation over student recruitment and organised visits to primary school by all senior staff. I later recognised **that Primary visits are not worthwhile per se.** Particularly when dealing with a large number of feeder schools, in our case, more than twenty, it is difficult to form a meaningful relationship. Secondary visits can be irritating, patronising and time wasting for Primary Colleagues. You need to exercise quality control over the messages colleagues are delivering or the visits may achieve the opposite of that intended with both students and staff.

Visits work best if there is a good relationship between the Heads. The secondary school should also be providing something tangible, e.g. discussion of secondary transfer issues in general, encouragement to persevere towards the end of year six or the provision of a good quality sponsored competition rather than merely making a marketing pitch. Obviously the curriculum link possibili-

ties must be exploited to the full. On the one hand, secondary facilities are often very attractive to primaries; on the other hand, great
relationships can be formed by acknowledging the huge expertise at
primary level. Genuine cross phase working and sharing of projects
and good practice would be the ideal but is very time consuming.

One thing primary schools are concerned about is the well being
of their children including their progress in year 7. Anything organised around this tends to be well received – feedback from past
students, year 7 taken on visits back to their old schools, exchanges
of information are all well received. We also organised home visits
to deliver invitations to our open evenings and pass on brochures
personally. This was incredibly difficult and time consuming and
we only attempted it once.

We had to announce possible redundancies, as per procedure. A
couple of staff wanted to go to the barricades and couldn't accept
the reality of Local Financial Management. There was simply no
funding to support us in the absence of students. Most of the staff,
fortunately, had little appetite for this. Such attitudes and behaviour
would have been most unhelpful particularly as we did actually
manage our way out of the crisis.

We achieved something of a media coup when the 'TES', 'Times
Educational Supplement', picked up a story from the 'Liverpool
ECHO' about the reintroduction of prefects. The headline was:
'School heads back to a prefect world'. We had excellent coverage and photographs. Similarly, the supportive articles in the local
press, 'Back to basics school praised', were a huge boost to staff
morale.

Never forget the feelings of the staff in a school struggling to
survive. They must endure attendance at courses, feeling like the
poor relations in the face of complacency from oversubscribed colleagues. They face comments from family and friends each time
'their' school receives negative coverage or is lowly placed in a
league table. In these circumstances it is tempting to adopt a siege
mentality. 'After all this is a tough environment, we are doing a

good job, others couldn't cope, the criticism is unwarranted.' This doesn't work. It is negative and protectionist. **The profile of the school and the mindset of the staff must change in order to survive.** No matter how hard staff work, schools get few sympathy votes. The Head must organise relentlessly good coverage in the media. There must also be a drive and purpose within the school, which focuses upon getting the basics right at the same time as harnessing new initiatives. **A measure of success is the reaction of other professional colleagues.** If they have noticed a positive media reaction towards the school and have a perception of the school as forward looking and dynamic then you are on an upper trajectory. Providing these perceptions are exploited to the full the benefits can be colossal. There *will* be an increase in parental interest, staff recruitment, LEA funding, grant funding, DFES initiatives and staff and student confidence.

Chinese New Year was a great opportunity to galvanise the school, affirm our multi cultural credentials and inject some fun and enjoyment. We also used it to gain valuable publicity. One of the local firework retailers agreed to us having £100 worth of old stock. We were overwhelmed by the delivery. Hundreds of display fireworks, which, at that time, were relatively uncommon and very expensive. We laid them out in rows and the display was twenty five yards long and ten yards deep. It was an incredible display! The whole school watched half an hour of continuous explosions. They were all given sweets. A handful of staff grumbled about disruption to the curriculum but the effect on students of being given genuine entertainment is dramatic. **You must create a sense of fun, enjoyment, fulfilment and belonging. It binds students to the school, gives them a sense of ownership and helps them see the school as being 'on their side'.** The students also had the opportunity to give to charity.

We were never able to replicate the scale of this event but, nevertheless, lit fireworks each Chinese New Year. **The students will be entertained by any diversion from the ordinary.** The year after our grand display, and unable to secure the same kind of fireworks deal, we hired a 'pyrotechnician' to run the event. In some respects this was as entertaining despite the display being pitiful. Scaffolding was erected on the field complete with runners and pulleys and the 'pyrotechnician' appeared wearing a boiler suit, wellies, a welders mask and gloves. The first few fireworks performed to plan but the highlight of the display, a huge 'bomb' running up the scaffolding tower to explode twenty feet above the ground, failed badly. The pulley jammed at six feet and the whole school was treated to the sight of the 'pyrotechnician' struggling with the smoking and fizzing apparatus before being blown up like a Tom and Jerry cartoon. Fortunately, his 'specialised' safety equipment saved him and he walked away to cheers and laughter. It was a cautionary experience all round.

Our building issues were a nightmare. The LEA wouldn't or couldn't fulfil their schedule of responsibilities to either the main school or the Annexe. Some of the roof repairs were derisory. On occasions we had a single workman arrive with a bucket of pitch to repair flat roofing that was fundamentally unsound. We would wait weeks for boiler repairs. Council workmen would arrive without the components or the components would arrive on their own. Most of the toilets were unfit for human use and the drainage problems we experienced with the PE showers created a repulsive smell. There was no area of the school without problems. In one wing the wiring was so old that staff made their own extension cables in order to make use of the pre-war round pin Bakelite sockets.

While there were other schools in the city struggling with similar problems and the Direct Labour Organisation were struggling against a mountain of dilapidation, we were undoubtedly being treated prejudicially as a result of the influence of a handful of the larger schools. They had spare management capacity to attend policy committees and working parties and were hell bent on the closure of smaller schools in the most disadvantaged areas. It was common knowledge that council priorities were reordered and manipulated in favour of some areas of the city.

Such a manipulation occurred around the earmarked expenditure to repair the terracotta frontage to our annexe-at the time in a highly dangerous condition. The expenditure was delayed, carried over and finally removed from the budget.

As for relations with the larger county schools in the city – they were diabolical. The Secondary Heads met once a fortnight and a small cabal controlled the group. As a newcomer trying to defend minority funding issues such as SEN (special educational needs), social disadvantage and bilingual grant I was under relentless attack. Without any doubt the Liverpool Secondary Heads were in the grip of a bullying culture, which, unsurprisingly, went beyond unpleasantness to political manipulation and personal advantage. Private companies were clearly in a position to exploit the handful of heads who set the agenda and the tone for business. And part of that agenda was to disempower the LEA and challenge issues of accountability. From the position of Shorefields there was no alternative but to set our face against such behaviour, after all we were in their sights. To do **this I took the view that we did not want to achieve parity with the other county schools in the city. That would have been modelling our aspirations on weakness.** We had to better them. We needed to be *not* 'a good inner city school'; as such schools struggle to survive when there is a demographic downturn. We needed to be a 'good school in the inner city', attractive to a wide range of students from outside our immediate area and leading on educational issues, not following.

We realised that, with only a Head and Deputy in place as SMT, there was a tendency for staff to bring problems directly to us. This was partly because we were trying to cultivate an environment in which staff felt supported but mainly because staff were taking the line of least resistance to where they knew they would get effective support. This was particularly the case where a middle manager was weak or where incidents occurred outside of lessons. This is not a situation that senior staff can sustain no matter how much they like being front line, supporting the troops or demonstrating their ability to handle disciplinary issues. Two common issues, over which we were taking a very hard line, were fighting and smoking. In each case, during 93/94 we would exclude until parents came in and the situation was resolved.

Staff certainly misinterpreted, sometimes deliberately, the role the head played in this. They were very happy to hand over 'the problem' as they saw it. No organisation can work like this. **The only way to achieve success is for everyone to play their part. Unity is strength. Every member of staff must take individual as well as collective responsibility for discipline.** The students themselves know which staff take their responsibility for behaviour and discipline seriously and respond accordingly. This is not necessarily a factor of age or experience. We found it necessary to write down a flow chart for ourselves in order to handle staff who would burst in with a wrongdoer in tow. We would be deadly serious, thank the member of staff, ask them to deposit the student with an appropriate head of year/head of department/ tutor and ask them for a write up of the situation in order that we could consider the matter properly with middle management.

This worked both ways. It prevented us being swamped and, therefore, the leadership of the school grinding to a halt. It also prevented SMT from making inadequate on the spot judgements without the benefit of student files.

Sometimes, of course, the well being of the school depends upon the head taking personal responsibility for a specific issue, particularly in a small school. In Dec. '94 I spent three days dealing with a race related problem between groups of girls. It culminated in some students being removed from the school. Similarly there were many other occasions when I spent exorbitant amounts of time dealing with parents and students. This has got to be done. It is a key way in which a head demonstrates to parents that they do matter and that their concerns are being treated with appropriate gravity. Certainly, whenever a parent was insistent upon seeing me

I saw them. Particularly in relation to any type of bullying, parents can be very agitated and I would, if necessary, ring people at home in the evening simply to placate them and let them know they had an opportunity to come into school. When parents feel thwarted, unsupported and patronised they can behave very badly indeed. **Parents deserve to be treated with respect and fairness no matter how they present themselves. We must remember they are often suffering considerable stress for a complex of reasons.**

It's essential in a school to generate a mass of 'feel good' activity for students and staff. The impact on morale is important but it goes beyond this to the cultural heart and soul of the organisation. If you can make the organisation human, humane and a place people want to be then this is communicated externally to parents and the community as a whole. We generated many examples of 'feel good' activity. The Chinese New Years have already been mentioned. We arranged widespread publicity for our 21st anniversary. It wasn't actually the 21st anniversary but the school needed a lift at the time. We held a prize draw and staff attended a party in the main hall. We had a live band and the caretaker produced the whole buffet himself.

If there was no staff night out organised for the end of term the senior managers organised one. Memorable nights included a grand Chinese buffet, the Turkish meal with belly dancer, an end of term buffet in a hotel on Sefton Park, a Christmas disco at the Adelphi, a meal in a city centre karaoke bar. The widest support, however, is given when staff appear to be organising events themselves and we were fortunate to have a number of non teaching staff prepared to do the leg work of ringing venues and collecting money. Nevertheless, there was seldom a year when we did not start asking questions about the Christmas event around mid October. The school frequently paid deposits up front and always subsidised the event.

One of the big successes of social activity was that it involved all the staff. This generated large numbers for each occasion. It also raised the tone of many events as the non teaching staff, many of whom had never been students, always dressed very well for social occasions. It was most important that the teachers, classroom assistants, cleaners, cooks, caretakers, administrative and support staff and the senior managers were able to socialise together as this cemented the close relationships needed to do a job in difficult circumstances.

We made free drinks and refreshments available to everyone at the end of each term when speeches were made for those leaving. We all gathered in the staffroom and any member of staff leaving was treated in the same way. The retirement of a member of the APTC staff was treated in the same way as a teaching retirement. We did this each Christmas, Easter and Summer.

For a school, or any other organisation to be healthy and thrive it is essential to respect and value *all* the staff and to create a genuine sense of community. In Shorefields there had been a tradition of seeing the school as a special place and this was born out of adversity and of a sense of opposition to the educational mainstream – perceived, rightly or wrongly, to be advantaged. In 93/94, however, there was certainly opposition to shared social events and, in fairness to the teaching staff, the cleaners were still employed by the Local Authority and we had not yet experienced the significant influx of new classroom assistants and para educationalists who were to transform the workforce and change relationships. Nevertheless, the ancillary staff, like the teachers, were working in dilapidated demoralising conditions and in 94 we made a presentation to them in recognition of them achieving the 'Cleanest School in the City'.

They really were working against almost insurmountable odds yet the school did look clean. Visitors were complimentary and the staff needed to know. Later when we tendered for, and won, our right to manage the cleaning contract these same employees became some of the most loyal and dedicated on the staff. Little surprise really. Most lived locally and people, naturally, take pride in where they work and its success. The cleaners always sold the most draw tickets and raised a substantial amount for the school. Later again when we 'sold' the cleaning and catering staff as part of our major Private Finance Initiative some really were treated quite badly. I had to intervene, contractually, on their behalf on many occasions and, ultimately, guaranteed employment to those who left their new employer. This was the right thing to do morally and the right thing for the school. Staff who had, previously, been in catering became superb classroom assistants. Later, we would include student supervision as part of every member of staff's contract and we paid all staff to attend all training days. **Without disparaging the professionalism of teachers, it is very clear that other adults can act as an example to raise standards in schools.** Ancillary staff have diverse backgrounds and wide experiences. They may represent different cultures and beliefs. Their expectations, in some respects such as social behaviour, fundraising or supervision, may be higher than some of their younger teaching colleagues.

In city areas **security and discipline** can be a huge problem. On a day to day basis there are issues around the integrity of the site and whether intrusion is possible. Can the students enter and leave the school in safety and make their way home without trouble? Are the staff safe on outside patrol and supervision? Can equipment and materials be safeguarded against break-in and theft? Will the school be overwhelmed by factional differences brought in from outside? How do the staff impose appropriate norms of behaviour and create a climate in which fighting is taboo and anti social behaviour in the form of name calling, graffiti, theft, sexism, racism and bullying are found unacceptable by the students themselves?

The majority of students wish to be cooperative, avoid trouble and want harmonious relations with their peers. They will respond well to high standards and to respect. However, in a small, unpopular school with a declining roll it must be accepted that a high proportion of problematical students, and an influx of students mid term, make the task of establishing the right ethos more challenging. Certainly, by December '94 we had significant and irresolvable issues between a group of black girls and a group of white girls. This involved a graffiti 'war' in school, the involvement of extended family members on both sides, threats and intimidation at the end of each school day and a permanent police presence. We were the victims of trouble in the community during the evening and at weekends. The behaviour of some of our students in their own time was undoubtedly shocking and families frequently supported this. We had some particularly difficult young women – intelligent and articulate but bitter, dysfunctional and attention seeking. We used counselling, reconciliation meetings, the 'Unit', exclusions, the Governors, the Race Equality Management Team and Expulsion. We had already established an 'At Risk Register' for behavioural cases and let individual parents and all the students in the school know about it. The staff felt more confident that the wide ranging discipline cases in progress were receiving attention from senior staff and conversely they were under more pressure to take effective action at a lower level, rather than merely complain, and to contribute to records and make referrals. Whenever the exclusion of a difficult and intimidating student was announced in an assembly- 'for failing to meet the standards expected at Shorefields' – there was visible relief from both staff and students. **Wrong doing must be named and shamed, but most of our time must be spent upon praise, highlighting the positives, reward, encouragement, clarifying standards and expectations, ensuring safety and security, motivating staff and students and communicating wholeheartedly that progress is being made.**

A significant element in the sense of security enjoyed by students comes from the consistency around them. It took time but once we established our locked gate policy-implying no daytime entry or exit – the sense of security and control within a gated community increased significantly. We also devoted time, early in '95, to whole staff INSET on discipline, clarifying procedures and focussing significantly on rewards throughout the school.

In my experience teachers who teach positively, are well prepared, focus on student learning, mark work constructively, praise effort, are self critical and take full responsibility for the outcome of their work – have the fewest problems. On the other hand, teachers who blame students for lack of progress, fail to provide regular and encouraging feedback, use punishment as a means of control and are prone to rudeness and sarcasm generate endless problems.

Our situation though, at this time, was very difficult. The staff were working in demanding circumstances under the threat of redeployment or redundancy and with senior management expecting a change in outlook from some of the longest serving.

Paradoxically, some colleagues holding most dearly to the 'open enrolment' and 'community involvement' ideas of twenty years earlier were the most authoritarian and unsuccessful in the classroom. **The simple fact is that without a change in ethos, impacting on all aspects of the life of the school, a declining school will close.**

One way of changing the ethos is through grouping arrangements. It was clear that reasonably academic students were succumbing to peer pressure in mixed ability situations and we continued and refined an earlier approach at grouping the more academically able, in one tutor group, and grouping the rest of the year as mixed ability. This is the only way, in the circumstances, of controlling the peer situation and determining the expectations of the more able beyond setting and through the pastoral arrangements themselves. Later we adopted the same approach to two tutor groups and eventually to a banded situation. There are some very obvious social and motivational drawbacks to this arrangement but choices have to be made.

In a small school the pool of traditionally talented students is likely to be very small or non-existent. By this I mean students with sporting talent, artistic, musical or acting ability. This generates a problem with regard to the school promoting itself. It may be difficult to sustain teams, and putting on shows or concerts may be impossible. Nevertheless it is these cultural events, which help define the school in the eyes of the parents and the students. **It is essential to widen participation in sports and Performing Arts, in-house, and to provide opportunities for performance.** Public performance, and I include performance to any assembly of the school, must, however, be of an acceptable standard in fairness to the audience and the performers. There are teachers with a real generosity of spirit who would argue that one should 'take a chance' and provide an inarticulate or musically talentless child with a performance opportunity. This can be humiliating and demeaning to all concerned. On the other hand the transparent overuse of a handful of students who speak confidently or play an instrument can cause irritation and can marginalize the arts for others. Performing Arts in these circumstances can only move forward with talented and committed staff, with carefully structured performance allowing opportunity for wide participation at an appropriate level and with massive practice.

A well – presented but, essentially, simple and undemanding performance piece is better received than if the students are overextended. Two examples of this were our Annual Celebration of Public Speaking, introduced against the scepticism of most of the English Dept. at the time, and the formation of the Steel Band. In the case of the former, the talent of the students improved visibly year on year and we even won the Toxteth Rotary Club Public speaking prize on the first year of entering. In the case of the latter we used sponsorship from Merseyside Police to provide tuition to some musically unpromising youngsters on some dilapidated pans we had found in a cellar and also to purchase new equipment. Within twelve months of their formation the Shorefields Steel Band played at the Liverpool Philharmonic Hall. Thereafter we were able to use 'the tradition' of public speaking and the support of the Steel Band to bolster wider performance and create greater opportunities.

By March '95 the number of exclusions had dropped dramatically due to the changed disciplinary procedures, the use of the Unit, the new powers of Heads of Year and the system of 'at risk' referrals to governors. Promisingly we were engaged in a number of Education-Business initiatives and the school appeared to be running reasonably well. Despite this we had identified the need to lose eight staff to balance the budget and morale was shaky.

A concern for me was that I might have lacked judgement in the In Service training role I had adopted recently. As the Head I needed to take a high profile on issues of standards with both staff and students but I had gone further than this and taken an active role in preparing and presenting Inset on Attendance, Motivation, Discipline and Management. Unsurprisingly, any staff angst and disillusion over these matters was partly directed at me. Meanwhile we were using the 'Armageddon file' to explore any possible ways out of our financial crisis. The collapse in student numbers in only two years meant that the future budget shortfall of £350,000 threatened our survival and was a major obstacle to any possible development at the time. We discussed the 'Armageddon file' at some point every single day. **The major challenges in a school – curriculum, finance, discipline or whatever – need to be wrestled until solutions present themselves. Every decision must contribute to the wider solution.**

In management, change comes very quickly. Only two months later, in the middle of the first National Curriculum tests for 14 year olds, we were called to a JNC meeting in Liverpool to discuss redundancies with employers and unions. Other declining schools had made presentations ahead of us and Headteachers had been given a rough ride over their efforts to resolve their financial problems. We were able to present a sensible budget, a curriculum plan and criteria for selection in the event of redundancies. However, we also had six staff moving from the school on severance terms, redeployment or early retirement and a number of staff with interviews pending. We were confident of avoiding redundancies and were congratulated on the way in which we had handled such a difficult situation.

At the same time we had also been successful in bidding for European funds and had also successfully bid to be one of only five Liverpool schools to launch a new ICT initiative with ICL – as part of the Merseyside Education Superhighway (MESH). This would bring much needed computer resources to the school. **The hours spent attending European Social fund meetings and writing bids had paid off. The optimism relentlessly pumped out at staff was now taking substance.** The school felt less threatened by financial insecurity and indeed other agencies regarded us as worthy of support.

There was, however, a caveat. We found that a proportion of our bidding work was being undermined by approaches to the same funding bodies on behalf of a charitable trust associated with the school. Like many charitable groups in the area, the Shorefields Community and Educational Trust had been more or less moribund prior to the arrival of European funding in the '90s. While, in the past it had been well regarded and had some robust trustees, it now had no funding and limped along on the goodwill of a handful of staff. I was a trustee but, like the others, found the business to be arcane and generally irrelevant to the life of the school. The concerns of the Trust were always around raising funds for drivers and vehicles. The underlying rationale was to provide the basis for a biannual expedition to the Sahara, led by the chair of the Trust and school staff and involving students.

Notwithstanding my own reservations over this high risk project, which I subsequently stopped, the main issue was a failure on the part of the school, and its Trust, to address the same priorities. Despite a period of negotiation in which the Trust had the opportunity to fully represent the School's interests within the Dingle Partnership, and thereby justify its existence, we could reach no compromise. The situation, over the next two years, degenerated into civil war with the trustees, mainly staff in the employment of the school, on one side and me and the bulk of the Governing body on the other. This was an incredibly difficult and acrimonious period of time. We were a school struggling for survival, doing everything to create the right public image and determined to plan strategically for the long term future, yet, the authority of the Head and Governors was being challenged by the sectarian interests of those who wanted to cling to the priorities of the past. Eventually, our only option was to close the Trust and I relied heavily on my experience of organisational procedure, protocol for meetings and standing orders, derived from years in tedious union and political meetings, to bring this about.

There is no doubt that charitable status should carry a health warning. It is easy to establish a charity. It is easy for a charity to shift from its original objectives. It is easy for self-interest to emerge. It is exceptionally difficult to close down a charity if there is any measure of dispute over its continuing existence.

We achieved a quorum of supportive trustees. The chair resigned and took retirement. We resolved to disband the Trust. We agreed to the return of unspent grants and the disposal of remaining funds to similar charities, including one the ex chair had recently established, and we wrote off remaining assets. This, in fact, included a fleet of trucks and buses around which there was disputed ownership. We could have spent the next decade arguing whether ownership lay with the school, the Trust or an individual. It wasn't worth it!

What I did have to endure was a campaign of letter writing and vilification on the part of supporters of the Trust and supporters of previous Desert expeditions. These ventures had been going on for twenty years. They had, understandably, attracted genuine acclaim, but they had also been expensive and disruptive at school level.

Despite a number of burdensome long term absences, and developing issues around the Trust, staff morale was positive. We had a good HMI inspection towards the end of term despite huge pressures surrounding the recent killing of a well known gangland figure. The pressure on the school at that point was phenomenal.

A white gangster shot by a black gangster and we had members of both families in the school. Many of the black students absented themselves for fear of reprisals, Liverpool was beset by copycat gun crime, there were armed police around the whole area and we were in contact with their control centre on a daily basis.

The press were portraying the situation in Dingle as all out gangland warfare, which was not helpful. Life in school was in fact surprisingly peaceful at this strained time. There was a strong concern amongst all communities that social life did not degenerate into violent reprisal. Liverpool did not perform to media stereotype.

Again this had been a year of tremendous activity. In addition to dealing with a mass of disciplinary issues, we had introduced a student charter. **The charter outlined student rights and responsibilities and detailed precisely what they should do in the event of encountering problems at school.** Direct physical action was not one of the options! The charter was also useful when dealing with parents. Disappointingly, there was no support for any of our behaviour modification strategies from our assigned Educational Psychologist.

To strengthen procedures we had introduced a number of 'protocols'. These were direct instructions to staff over procedure in certain situations such as the conduct of assemblies, handling disciplinary problems and managing pastoral responsibilities. Again, **protocols are a way of making expectations clear and provide a point of reference in discussion with staff.**

In relation to publicity we had enjoyed extensive free coverage during the year. A particularly successful piece dealt with the 'discovery' of Ringo's desk and this brought national attention. We, subsequently, received surprise visitors from the Netherlands and Japan eager to be photographed with this piece of history. We had also launched CQEC (the Centre for Quality in Education and the Community). This was to be an independent body reflecting and publicising developments at the school, and in the area, to an external audience. There were a number of action research projects underway, in the school and these were highlighted. Similarly, we reported the publication, by staff, of teaching aides, particularly through Chalkface Publishing and the involvement of staff with BERA (the British Educational Research Association).

There was more optimism on the financial front with the additional resources provided by TVE and Compact having an impact. We were also now generally accepted as a partner in Dingle 2000, the local body overseeing European and Single Regeneration Budget funding. My involvement with the Granby Toxteth Development Trust gained funds for raising attainment and we had received huge support for our Arts and Music Festival, in the form of instruments and specialist musicians, from Rushworths, a leading Liverpool music store. We had, also, prepared a room adjacent to the library to receive computer equipment as part of our MESH (Merseyside Super Highway) involvement.

Finally, as we came to the year end, it appeared that we had moved beyond the governance problems that had plagued the school for years. The refusal to respond to correspondence, the very public highlighting of the ex chair of governors in our standard letter and an insistence that the LEA play an appropriate role had ended the matter.

LEARNING POINTS YEAR TWO

- Be prepared to rally the staff when there is a serious set back.
- The calendar is a crucial management tool.
- Look very carefully at marketing and PR. Your current efforts may be counter-productive.
- Form a personal relationship with Primary headteacher colleagues.
- Use the local media – carefully.
- Work with staff to identify and name your problem students. It raises morale.
- Use assemblies to build a sense of community.
- Name and shame wrongdoing.
- The majority of students support action, which maintains discipline.
- From time to time the Head may need to act directly over any organisational issue.
- In a city school standards can improve rapidly and can deterio-

rate more rapidly.

- Constant concern and vigilance are required in order to maintain standards.
- The Head and the Chair of Governors must be in complete accord over handling individual disciplinary cases.
- Be rigorous and demanding over the quality of pastoral records.
- Always responding to a vexatious complainant – be it a member of the public or a member of staff – may fuel the problem.
- Exercise firm control over staff time out of school.
- Be clear over your options for raising income and reducing expenditure.
- Be selective in the financial information you release to outsiders.
- Do not anticipate or rely upon any help from competitor schools. That would be naïve. Schools exist in a marketplace.
- You must identify your own key components for survival.
- 'Downsizing' can create problems of management capacity.
- Do not expect employees of a Local Authority to necessarily support progress or share a concern with raising standards in your school.
- New initiatives may undermine the quality of existing provision and an existing sense of responsibility on the part of staff.
- The profile of the school and the mindset of the staff must change in order to survive.
- You must get the basics right as well as considering new initiatives.
- Exploit any positive change in external perceptions of the school to the full.

- It is essential to see the students as both partners in, and beneficiaries of, school improvement. This is *their* education and the more engagement and fulfilment they experience the greater will be their contribution.

- Professional organisations exhibit the same in fighting and corruption as any others.

- Do not allow yourself, as the Head, to be overwhelmed by problems more appropriately handled by others. Direct staff accordingly.

- The Head must be available to parents. Any request to see the Head must receive a swift response. This gives parents confidence and can resolve potentially serious problems.

- A school must develop a mass of 'feel good' activity for everyone.

- It is important to develop a sense of community amongst *all* the staff.

- Show the APTC, ancillary, professional, technical, clerical and manual staff that they are valued. A school cannot function without caretaking and cleaning staff!

- Adults other than teachers may also present excellent role models.

- Security and good order require relentless concentration and effort and the application of highly effective procedures.

- Always 'talk up' the school to the staff – they need that from the Head.

- Spend time developing the whole staff, together, in order to create a community focussed on rewards and positive approaches to discipline.

- Without a genuine change in ethos a declining school *will* close.

- The school must develop capacity in Performing Arts and Sport to have credibility in the community.

- Public performance *must* be of an acceptable standard.

- Managers need to maintain a healthy focus on financial problems, interrogating every possible solution.

- Beware of establishing charitable trusts.

- There is the need for a student charter in order to highlight the boundaries of acceptable behaviour.

- Creating 'protocols' makes performance standards clear to staff and helps to establish consistency.

- The school must be represented on any funding bodies locally. The head must, however, continually evaluate the time spent.

START OF THIRD YEAR OF
HEADSHIP SEPTEMBER '95

W E ENJOYED A BUOYANT start to the year with a big improvement in exam results and 7% gaining five or more good GCSEs. These results sound meagre now but in the context of the time they represented real improvement. Our record of exclusions the previous year had fallen to 91. We also celebrated a major improvement in intake with the enrolment of 84 year 7 students. This was, however, accompanied by some familiar community problems as soon as the students themselves returned.

Geographically, the school was in an awkward position in relation to its catchment area and this was compounded by the racial characteristics of South Liverpool and by the presence of a gang of anti social white youths in the Dingle.

In terms of geographical position, we were in the extreme south of Dingle, Liverpool 8. Our active catchment area at the time ran roughly North to the Pier Head, East to Smithdown Rd., then North again to Lime Street, thus encompassing the whole of Toxteth (L8) and a large portion of the city centre. We had few students from the

South, Aigburth, or from the West, the River Mersey! This situation was compounded by the pattern of main roads and the dense terraced housing in the area. In effect the bulk of students leaving the school each evening were travelling in roughly the same direction. Between the students themselves this was not an issue. It was an issue, however, between a handful of white delinquents in the Dingle and our black students making their way home to the Granby and Smithdown areas. The Dingle, historically, was perceived as a white area with other areas of Toxteth being more racially mixed and cosmopolitan. Ironically, while substantial numbers of black and minority ethnic students were travelling into the Dingle, to Shorefields, for secondary education there were also large numbers of white students travelling out. In particular, at that time, this included many Roman Catholic boys for whom there was no provision in the area. Catholic girls had the rapidly improving and, ultimately, outstanding St. Mary's/Bellerive on their doorstep.

While many Catholic Dingle boys would undoubtedly have been successful travelling to Everton, Garston, or to one of the premier Catholic Colleges, a small minority became school refusers, or were excluded, and were the nucleus of long running problems for Shorefields.

The simple presence of youths on the corner of the road created huge anxiety amongst students and staff. The spitting, swearing, jostling inevitably led to confrontation and created a situation in which we issued a blanket instruction that our students must not congregate. They had to be moving home or we directed them back into school. This was a nightly occurrence. Furthermore, the inadequacy of public service buses hugely exacerbated our problems. While most of the white students could walk home, living in close proximity to the school, many of the black students waited at local bus stops and were very vulnerable. Our supervision arrangements were, nightly, stretched to the limit. The slightest incident or even suspicion that delinquents were around caused the students to congregate and behave defensively. On occasions, this 'defensive' behaviour was on the offensive. Buses frequently drove straight past groups of black students at bus stops. The bus routes themselves were wholly inappropriate for the needs of the school as they wound through some challenging areas of the Dingle before black students actually embarked on a route out of the area. We had numerous incidents of fighting at bus stops, abuse and spitting as the buses passed along Mill St., bus windows being smashed, fighting on buses and, on two occasions, youths with bull terriers boarding buses to terrorise the students. We were doing everything in our power to protect the students and to change the situation.

I was on duty outside every night of the week. On occasions we would detain the entire school or call most of the staff out onto the street. We travelled on buses, broke up fights at bus stops, faced down local hooligans, complained to the police daily, petitioned Merseytravel, officers of the Authority, councillors and our MP to provide a dedicated bus service, and dealt with countless complaints from parents. In all of this, the trouble, while it appeared to be about generalised racist behaviour, invariably concerned a handful of black and white youths or girls. As ever this centred on gang activities in the evenings and at weekends.

The school itself was relatively harmonious and relations between students of all backgrounds were, on the whole good. This could, however, be challenged very easily by the arrival of an import from another school. All we could do in the face of these multiple problems was try to see matters as they really were rather than becoming hysterical and counter productive. **We used the ethos and rules of the school to maintain a sense of order and direction.**

There were certainly some staff and parents who wished to characterise our problems as evidence of NF/BNP activity. There was in fact no evidence for this. Local residents themselves were at their wits end over the anti-social behaviour of a minority, buses did not run through areas of the Dingle at night due to stonings by youths and one of our head boys, who was white and a piper in the local Orange Lodge Band, was threatened with a knife by one of the hooligans because he was Protestant and could stand up for himself. We were suffering from a more generalised problem that was easily being characterised as racist.

Dealing with some black parents was very difficult particularly when they defended increasingly politicised behaviour on the part of a minority of students. For example, we had incidents in which students would deliberately walk home through some very difficult estates indeed. In effect looking for trouble by asserting their rights. On a personal level I could understand this but practically and professionally it generated huge problems. **We really were trying to maintain order and sanity on the edge of potential chaos.** If any young person had been seriously hurt the consequences for the school and the area would have been grave. I won those arguments. Particularly as I was able to demonstrate to black parents and students my overriding concern for their welfare and multiple instances where I had physically intervened to defend them.

The situation, however, was not sustainable and this was reflected in the strength of our campaigning. Thus, by the end of that half term, October '95 we had a police presence outside the school each night and had finally persuaded the Local Authority and Merseytravel to provide a dedicated school bus service.

In reality we faced a further half term of significant problems, now generated by the failure of the school bus to arrive on time or sometimes even at all. Some evenings presented us with more problems than we had previously experienced as the late bus left us with around 100 black students anticipating transport and therefore requiring supervision on the street. The presence of local youths in these circumstances created great tension, as we were unable to disperse the students home.

The police presence, often in force, students milling around and the occasional fracas were all bad for our image at this time. Unfortunately, it appeared that officers were present to police Shorefields students whereas, in reality, they were there to protect them. We had recently established a student forum and this was a good vehicle for discussing the problems with the people who mattered. Head Boys and Girls, prefects, reps from each year and anyone else who cared to turn up, attended it. In later years the forum would be involved in redesigning the school and in developing plans for expanding the school site and providing community sports facilities.

Staff morale was poor due to the serious problems at the end of each day, the extent of short and long term absences and the necessity to cancel external courses and activities in order to keep staff in front of classes. We were also continuing to deal with staff performance and capability and conduct issues. During the year we tackled competency with a middle manager (with remarkable success), falsification of time sheets with an administrator, mismanagement by a supervisor, conflict between a teacher and a parent, gross insubordination, a failure in departmental leadership, poor punctuality, minor financial mismanagement on the part of two staff and the mismanagement of our primary liaison programme. A natural reaction to this might be that the Senior Staff were the problem and that we were overcritical and too quickly jumped into procedures. Nothing could be further from the truth.

I had inherited a school in which there had, for many years, been a real lack of consistency over standards. In fact, the consistency and rigour introduced by the National Curriculum itself was a challenge to some. There were, also, staff who could not accept that informal corporal punishment was a thing of the past. Furthermore, we had introduced serious financial accountability at all levels and trained the staff accordingly. **The exceptional detail in the new staff handbook and the creation of additional protocols were an indication of how much this school, at this time, required a clear and assertive style of management.** The bottom line was still about survival and while dealing with problems generated by staff was a time consuming distraction it was a vital part of this process. As a rule we would do our best to prioritise issues of performance while, generally, providing support to everyone. **Fortunately, or**

unfortunately, there are many staff conduct issues, which force themselves to the top of the agenda.

We ended the term, Christmas '95, with a Staff night out, which I organised, and with a Christmas Assembly with carol singing for the school. We had tried the carol singing previously and it had been a disaster. It would take years before this event was well organised and had the dignity and spirit it warranted. The key problems early on were lack of staff confidence, a failure to conceptualise, simply, how such events can work, lack of adequate planning and preparation and a reluctance to take responsibility. The event was also marred by the political correctness of some staff who objected to carol singing in a multi racial/cultural school. Nevertheless the Assembly for '95 was passable and the night out, and drinks on the last day, were very enjoyable. **If staff end the term well that carries them forward into the new term.**

1996 started very positively with excellent press coverage for the school. We were releasing weekly stories, not press releases, but fully worked pieces ready for publication. The number of exclusions continued to drop dramatically due to the use of the Unit, restricting exclusion to myself and, finally, a determination to make much earlier contact with parents. Parents were much more supportive if we avoided exclusion and sent for them immediately. The atmosphere was changing appreciably with a sense from most parents that we were 'on the same side'. **Parents must be treated as partners in the enterprise of giving their children an education.** Too often they are kept at arms length, receive lack of respect or are blamed for their children's shortcomings. All pointless.

Our resourcing situation continued to improve and we were now receiving funds that had previously been top-sliced by the LEA for central services. This led to the creation of a further range of Service Level Agreements in order for us to buy back services and we were in a better position to demand value for money. We were successful in gaining Single Regeneration Budget funds to pay responsibility points to staff for running motivational activities for students. The

Toxteth Cluster was asserting itself and we submitted a bid to the LEA, via the new Assistant Director, to employ our own Attendance Officer. We were also involved in negotiations to purchase places in independent Pupil referral Units in the Toxteth area. The standards of some were so low that we would have been at professional risk had we contracted with them.

Meanwhile, we were pursuing increased rents from our community tenants and had engaged in a pilot scheme in relation to the education of bilingual students. This evolved from the closure of the Liverpool Language Centre and the inevitable absorption of first stage English speakers into mainstream. The scheme involved partnership teaching between our staff and those from the Language Centre and a significant group of staff involved themselves with great enthusiasm. It brought additional staffing and additional funds.

It was disappointing that we were making such progress, in most respects, yet were under constant pressure to justify the use of our community staff. We, rightly, regarded this as an attempt to cut central costs. We repeatedly provided comprehensive details of timetables, deployment, our additional resourcing, beneficiary numbers and management arrangements to different officers in the Community Section of the LEA. We spent hours in discussion and negotiation over refocusing the work of our staff onto an area level and addressing new priorities – yet we always came full circle to cost cutting. The stress on the three community tutors was awful and they had lived with this atrocious approach to people management for years. Subsequently, we capitulated and absorbed one of the tutors into our own budget. This was no way to do business.

In terms of the wider world, outside of the school, we were obviously making good progress with the Toxteth Cluster and with local funding bodies. We had supported a black learners project at the local Elimu Study School, from which many of our students benefited in the evenings. We had also found regular translators for our newsletter and been successful in creating a number of 'chaplaincies' associated with the school. These were representatives of the major faith groups in the area – Church of England, Methodism, Islam, Judaism, and Roman Catholicism. The only group demonstrating reluctance was the Roman Catholics and, initially, this was a big stumbling block. The local Priest took the view that Catholics should be in Catholic schools and that was where the Church would provide spiritual support and guidance. He was not persuaded by the fact that 20% of our students were from Catholic families and, frankly, our discussion became heated. I challenged him to explain why black boys from the recently closed Nugent School had transferred to Shorefields en masse rather than move to another Catholic Boys School in the City. If these other schools could not guarantee their wellbeing at least he should provide a measure of ongoing support. Fortunately, I was dealing with a strong minded but fair man. He accepted the argument and came on board.

The influx of new students did give rise to a number of problems. The number entering Year 10, aged 14 and 15, swamped the available options offered by our curriculum. At Christmas we added two more options, both vocational, and reorganised our new and existing students into appropriate groups. As we were very short of teacher time, I timetabled myself with one of these options. I had, previously, reduced my classroom teaching, to a single group per week, I now had a brand new Year 10 course to teach in which half the students were new to the school.

We had also taken a number of students from Liverpool Special Schools (EBD) and were assimilating them into mainstream.

While the progress in lessons and behaviour in class of these new students was reasonable the situation outside of lessons was volatile. **A group of people arriving simultaneously tend to be more cohesive than the population they move in to.** We experienced a resurgence of petty gangsterism and fighting. This led to the removal of a number of newcomers for unprovoked assaults. We also had to intervene in a number of street fights between new students and youths from outside the area who had, essentially, followed them to Shorefields intent on trouble. This was a difficult and dangerous time, particularly on the end of day duty. We were dealing with students we knew little about and outsiders we didn't recognise at all. Yet again neighbourhood rivalries threatened our stability.

All this trouble wasn't even worth it financially as we had great difficulty extracting the transfer funding for the Nugent students from the LEA.

In March '96 the shocking 'Drumlane Massacre', in which a madman gunned down children at a Scottish Primary School, generated great concern and sympathy amongst the students. We collected hundreds of pounds in donations in a matter of 20 minutes. This was significant as an example of the general moral fibre of the area. A strong sense of right and wrong and natural justice and great sympathy for those bereaved or in misfortune. **We constantly drew on the students own inherent qualities and their sense of family values** in identifying their responsibilities, their place in the school community and the significance of their school's reputation to the area and to Liverpool. This was bolstered by relentlessly representing their achievements back to them. In the same month, for example, we highlighted a student's GCSE Maths success, at 13, a student winning the 'Plain English Competition', 6th form success in the Merseyside Industry and Commerce Awards and our own successful Celebration of Public Speaking, which had been a highly polished event.

We were presenting a range of certificates in each whole school assembly for both academic and social successes and this culminated at the end of the year in a graduation ceremony for years 11, 12 and 13. This annual event was, in many respects, the highpoint of staff and student efforts. Every student in full uniform, the hall packed with parents and each student called up to be eulogised upon receiving their record of achievement. Culminating in a buffet, photos, signed notebooks, shirts etc. **The graduation ceremonies, which we later extended to all year groups, were about**

expectations, reward and respect. They were also about education being a cooperative rather than an oppositional venture. At the same time, across the county, there were other, more prestigious schools, dismissing students a day early to avoid trouble. We knew of an example in which a headteacher informed year 11 half way through a lesson that they should leave school immediately. This creates a feeling of alienation and disappointment on the part of students.

We had growing reasons for optimism. We had achieved an Investors In People Award and a very positive assessment of our Post -16 GNVQ work (this would progress to being a major strength of the school). The plans for the Summer Fair were well advanced and well supported by a wide range of staff. Finally, a major gangland funeral had passed off without incident. It seems strange to mention such a thing but we were constantly watching our environment trying to maintain an awareness of potential problems. I reacted quite brusquely to attempts by a BBC crew to highlight the underside of life in the area and insisted upon talking about regeneration, the important role played by sport and the successes of the school.

The year ended in good form. The main school Parents Day, when students received their reports, was always well attended. It had been a good tradition in the school for many years and guaranteed a high turnout of parents to collect the reports. We had decided to combine it with two, previously, highly unsuccessful events – The Annual Governors Report to Parents and the new year 7 Induction Evening. A tremendous success. While the number of new year 7 pupils had increased yet again, the sense that the school was full and buzzing with activity was inescapable. The message, as ever, to the New Intake parents was that they were lucky to have obtained places at the school and that we could not guarantee places to late applicants. **Always exude confidence**. Exactly what parents want to hear. We held the Governors Meeting in the open Reception area and simply closed the doors when it was full of parents and addressed them, briefly, on school issues. Rather than the paltry 2 or

3 parents of previous years we actually had around 100 in forcible attendance.

We also received a request from the LEA to take 30 more students. That would take us to an intake of 160. This was incredible news for the staff as it meant we had gone from threatened closure to over subscription in two years. I was also asked, surprisingly, by our most prestigious local Primary School, to present the annual prizes at their Speech Day. This was a remarkable PR opportunity and I made the very most of it.

LEARNING POINTS YEAR 3

- The behaviour of students leaving school has a big influence on the perceptions of local people. A Head needs to exercise responsibility and control in this respect.
- Constantly reaffirm the ethos of the school and be very clear over what *you* are trying to achieve.
- If at first you don't succeed in lobbying the authorities (education, police, transport) to effect change then lobby harder.
- A school in difficulty probably needs clear and assertive management.
- Certain staff conduct issues are forced to the top of your agenda at the most inconvenient times.
- If staff end the term well, it carries them forward into the new term.
- The press respond to well-written articles rather than 'press releases'.
- Parents must be treated as partners in their children's education in order to achieve their full cooperation.

- Be sensitive to the needs of all groups in the school and try to make appropriate provision. The different communities served by the school will appreciate this.

- Beware of the impact of new students, particularly groups of new students, on the stability of the school.

- Frequently praise the students and re-present to them the best of their inherent qualities.

- You must make education feel cooperative rather than oppositional.

- Combine activities on the site to create a busy atmosphere.

- Always exude confidence.

- Grab good PR opportunities with both hands.

START OF FOURTH YEAR OF
HEADSHIP SEPTEMBER '96

DESPITE THE TOTAL ASSURANCES from the LEA of extra students they did not materialise on the first day. **Never make assumptions. It is best to trust what is actually in front of you.** We had 127 Year 7 students enrol. Additional students, not necessarily those indicated by the LEA, did, however, arrive over the course of that half term and we were organised into six forms of entry. This was a situation we endured for years and each September we had a 'real' and a provisional backup timetable. This was not ideal by any means. Nor was it helpful that young people were completing their Primary education without knowledge of the secondary school they would attend. **A student entering secondary school in October, after failing to gain entry to other schools on appeal, is significantly disadvantaged in relation to their peers and may present real challenges to staff.** One of our worst cases was a young girl instructed by her aunt to write down everything she disliked about the school on an hourly basis. This was a poor recipe for integration.

The increased number of Year 7 students was immediately of

concern to staff. The intake for several years had been very small and staff were now experiencing larger class sizes in year 7 and many students who, in effect, had expressed a negative preference for the school. The ability intake was seriously skewed with significant numbers of children scoring 70 – on cognitive ability tests, at or below level 2 NC scores or as first stage EAL learners. A proportion of the intake had clear behavioural difficulties and three were sent home on the first day. One child had to be removed from classes within an hour of arriving.

Again the school performance for the previous year had been promising and we had met all our targets for attendance, GNVQ, A level and GCSE success. We had also seen a really dramatic fall in the number of exclusions to 17. This was one of the best performances in the city. We had 11% of the students gaining five or more good GCSEs and this was an indication that all curriculum areas were developing the capability to teach to the higher levels. Nevertheless, these were still extremely low levels by national standards and we were bumping along near the bottom of the Liverpool league table.

A group of year ten students had performed well at GCSE a year early and, as ever, this was highlighted in the newsletter and through awarding certificates.

The school log for Sept. '96 records such an award to a young man who subsequently died in a shooting incident at the age of just 19. Killed by another ex student. This was a desperately sad but routine experience for the staff and reflected the growing problem for families as the prevalence of guns in the area increased. In less than ten years I knew of around twenty young men who were the victims of gun crime and a couple of cases were they were the perpetrators. Most of these young men had very good qualities and in some cases had been popular with staff while at school. It was depressing.

There were also dangers for professionals working in the area. One example occurred prior to the start of this first term, towards the end of August, when I attended a meeting over 'Pathways' funding at an organisation called Southern Training on Park Road in Dingle. They were housed in a dilapidated building and the premises were gated and barred. Leaving the car beside the adjacent pub, I walked to the rear of the building following signs to the entrance. On the path behind the pub there were three youths toying with a large hunting knife. I walked between them and into the Southern Training offices. An hour later, I left, having brokered support for a number of our community projects.

Returning to the car, I started the engine and was about to pull away when the tailgate was forced open and one of the youths from earlier flung himself over the rear seat towards me. The car was in gear and I accelerated throwing the youth into the pub car park. I stopped and jumped out of the car but all three had made their escape. There was some damage to the car but the situation could have been a great deal worse.

By the end of the first term that year we realised that **the growing numbers of students warranted a formal induction package.** We were already sending home material to be completed during the previous Easter and Summer breaks, organising parental visits, hosting Primary classes and providing an Induction evening in the July. We also invited in parents on the first day in September. All this was inadequate in providing for the many students we were taking who, clearly, were unsuited to a Secondary environment and the organisation of a Secondary curriculum. It was an indication of the low level of maturity of some students, and of family relationships, that parents delivered and collected them for a full 12 months. Had our later initiatives around induction failed to work, we would certainly have considered reorganising the staff and the curriculum to reflect a Middle School arrangement.

While staff were struggling with the larger year 7 intake they were also working very hard indeed to improve year 11 results. Each student had targets and had been allocated a mentor. The students academic and pastoral performance was intensively monitored and staff were providing additional lessons in all curriculum areas. Across the school there was an emphasis upon planning, preparation, clarity of objectives and marking and feedback.

We were conducting regular whole school checks on attendance and felt that this increased the focus on standards. We were also involved in laborious negotiations around guarantees of Higher Education places for our post 16 students. We had introduced specialised Science programmes, mentoring, University visits, parental meetings and, collectively devoted hundreds of hours to motivational and collaborative working. The exercise was a failure. We found that **16 was too early to track students onto an undergraduate programme** and that, despite realistically having severely limited options, neither students nor parents wanted to restrict their aspirations to a single institution.

Lower down the school we were faced with some really difficult students who had recently transferred in from a Roman Catholic school. Two of these boys, in particular, appeared irrational and unmanageable. When we met parents it was clear that they presented the same problems for their families who were guilty of spoiling and indulging them and being entirely inconsistent over standards. It was quite remarkable to see a thirteen year old boy have the sort of tantrum one would associate with a two year old. Following placement in our Unit, they ended formal education in an Independent Pupil Referral Unit. This, however, absorbed a great deal of our time, and detracted from the education of others, over a two year period.

We also experienced serious problems with another transfer student, a 14 year old girl. She generated huge tension in every class she attended and was the focus of much aggression during breaks and lunchtimes. She was a very troubled individual, in the care of the Local Authority, and we were ill equipped to deal with her range of problems. In the space of a matter of weeks she had fought with other students, truanted from school, absconded from her carers, been arrested for shoplifting, been the victim of an alleged sexual assault on a public service bus and attempted to cut her wrists. Very, very, sad indeed. We had to declare, though, that we could not cope and that the girl needed to be in a place of safety.

We had an equally serious incident around a boy of the same age. He had become increasingly uncooperative with staff and violent towards other students. This culminated in a confrontation with a member of staff, following which, the youth absconded. He returned, swinging a plank of wood, intent on causing injury. We were able to chase him from the site but required the police to make an arrest as he had gone berserk in the local area.

Finally, in respect of some of our more memorable disciplinary cases at the time, the Chair of Governors and I had to battle our way through a series of appeal hearings over my expulsion of a student. He had brought a large knife to school, shown it to other students and some girls had been threatened. The boy was not a hooligan and was well supported by his family. The Appeals Panel was sympathetic and the family had strong legal support. Our problem was that we were trying to raise standards. Staff, in particular, demanded and deserved protection and assurances over the action that would be taken over those standards. It seemed incredible that we were repeatedly challenged by councillors over whether we made it clear that possession of a knife, suitable only for jungle warfare, was an excludable offence. Did the parent, or the child, realise that this was what we meant by 'offensive weapon'?

After dozens of hours of preparation, appeals and serious contention in front of councillors, we won the case.

Despite the difficulties presented by some of these disciplinary cases, there was a strong sense that standards were improving and that team leaders were exercising influence over those standards through the regularity of meetings being held. In directed time we held a Curriculum team meeting on a Tuesday and a Pastoral team meeting on a Wednesday. Staff with responsibility met once a month in the Staff Council. Senior staff met on a Monday. **There is no doubt that this amount of time devoted to teamwork paid divi-**

dends in terms of relations between staff, development activity and support for weaker colleagues. It also enabled the entire staff to be involved in complex consultation over the development of the school as a whole. The team leaders made use of the time to monitor work, discuss planning, scrutinise attendance, reinforce standards, deal with problems and arrange additional support where necessary. No one in the school could claim to be unaware of the priorities. In terms of achieving the badly needed consistency required in our difficult circumstances, the time was invaluable. A few years later, when the union position was antagonistic to 'meetings' in general we lost impetus. The better curriculum leaders found time to work with their teams in an informal manner and made progress. The weaker ones floundered without the directed time structure.

Without regular meetings Pastoral work for some staff becomes little more than register marking and the hard-pressed team leaders can use up colossal amounts of time communicating the same information or undertaking the same development work to each individual. While this became part of the workload and bureaucracy debate it was frustrating to see staff actually working harder and less effectively due to the restrictions.

To support staff in better fulfilling their roles I started revising all job specifications in the school. We had also organised In Service training on assertive discipline to improve classroom management generally and to reduce the number of avoidable confrontations we were experiencing. Meanwhile we were focussing our attempts to improve performance on specific staff. These included an administrator, regularly working below standard; the long-term absence of a classroom assistant; an incompetent teacher; a reorganisation of caretakers and a teacher with a drink problem outside of school.

We were aware that weak teaching on the part of a minority was undermining much progress. The main complainants were other staff followed by students, then parents. However when senior staff tried to deal with issues of Performance and Capability or Conduct on the part of colleagues the staff closed ranks behind the union's

aggressive defences. **The only way to deal with staff performance problems is on the basis of firm evidence.** Fortunately we
had introduced a system of light touch monitoring which generated
hundreds of superficial observations on staff performance annually.
The system enabled Senior staff to record impressions of a dozen
or more lessons in a fifty minute period of walking the school. It
also put Senior staff where they were needed – on corridors and in
lessons all around the building. Although we never used the expres-
sion we did, in effect, have a traffic light system for monitoring
staff performance. Green represented the staff performing well.
They were lightly monitored and could be used to improve others. Amber represented staff causing concern. They were monitored
more intensively, would be alerted to any issues and perhaps be
the subject of discussion with heads of dept. Red represented staff
with Performance problems. They had a specific improvement plan
under the direction of a head of department and a senior member
of staff. They had targets to meet and were formally observed by
outside consultants and the LEA. We were very serious about raising standards indeed. Even in these fairly stringent circumstances,
however, **it is very difficult to increase the competence and improve the performance of seriously weak staff. In fact formal
monitoring and support arrangements frequently have the
exact opposite effect.**

It is true to say that you 'cannot make a grafter'. If staff are
unmotivated and have little concern for the students for whom they
are responsible then all the supervision and short term targets in
the world are unlikely to raise performance above the mediocre.
**Personal motivation is of great importance in teaching – the
motivation to do the best possible job in a professional manner.**
There have always been teachers with their own interpretation of
what constitutes 'success' and with their own idiosyncratic expectations of what they should achieve with students. There have even
been teachers who argued that student failure, whether to produce
coursework, perform in exams or just be punctual to school was

the responsibility of the students alone. These attitudes guarantee failure in disadvantaged areas. Children in such areas need and deserve the highest expectations from school. Other than a lack of motivation and drive to be successful **the other key characteristic of failing staff is that they suffer from distorted perception.** In other words, the belief that the problems they encounter are being experienced by everyone else. They are, therefore, not to 'blame'. The logical extension of this view is that, in singling out such an individual for support, management are engaging in harassment. We were always very careful not to act on superficial judgements about staff performance and always ensured that all senior staff had a concern before discussing issues with a head of dept.

Competent staff providing a listening ear or sympathising with a struggling colleague may actually be compounding the problem. Even when observation of colleagues is arranged in order to observe different teaching styles or different subject approaches the experience of seeing successful teaching can be dismissed as irrelevant. After all the colleague being observed is 'older', 'more experienced', 'charismatic' or even 'works too hard'. It is very difficult to impact upon an individual's perception, their self image and their belief system about the world and their place in it. **Successful teachers tend to be self-motivated, dynamic, assured and altruistic with a strong sense of self-determination.** Weak teachers tend to be more shortsighted, fatalistic, selfish and reactive.

Anybody can experience an alarming dip in performance and it can be a personal struggle to maintain your level of motivation and drive. Teaching is a very demanding job. Sometimes change is needed in order to refresh professional commitment and there is no doubt that a change of job, changing aspects of ones role, a new syllabus or a complete change of teaching area can be transformational and give a new lease of life.

Early in '97 the Managers and Governors were demonstrating increasing frustration with the LEA's inability to meet its repairs and maintenance responsibilities. Our Annexe building, once Toxteth

Technical College, was fully tenanted to a range of community groups under our general management. An entire floor was occupied by The Park Children's Centre, sponsored by save the Children. The ground floor was occupied by Liverpool Compact, Help the Aged and the Riverside Pensioners Group and the basement was tenanted by Artskills, a European funded anti drugs programme. We controlled the tenancies and provided overall management, caretaking and cleaning. In return we received income directly from the tenants or from the LEA 'essential user' funds. Unfortunately, the Annexe was in a state of dilapidation with leaking roofs, faulty boilers and an unstable terracotta facia to the front elevation. While internal aspects of repair and maintenance were our responsibility, and could be negotiated with tenants, the capital works were clearly the responsibility of the LEA at that time. Despite prioritising the Annexe frontage in the Councils minor works budget from April '96 the work was never undertaken. We believed that the influence of a handful of larger schools in the city was distorting the programme of expenditure by influencing the ordering of priorities at working party or committee stage.

It was also a matter of extreme frustration to us that Health and Safety legislation was more stringent in respect of the pre-school children tenanting the Annexe and, therefore, demanded immediate responses and ad hoc expenditure on the part of Shorefields as landlords. Much of this expenditure masked an absence of LEA responsibility and detracted from the position on our main school site where the conditions for the secondary age students, and staff, were often appalling.

The conditions on the main site, affected staff, students, Adult Education users, the full time Youth Club and all our main site community groups. We had leaking roofs, rotten windows, rising damp, defective wiring, falling plaster, unsanitary toilets, bad drains, uneven floors and relentless heating problems. We produced a dossier of photographic evidence to share with Officers of the Authority and Councillors.

Despite problems with the fabric of the building we were still trying to make progress over other resourcing issues unrelated to the LEA. We were in receipt of a Grant for Educational Support and Training (GEST), which represented the new wave of funding coming straight to schools, and gave us significantly greater flexibility. We had, also, entered into an agreement for CCTV cameras to increase our security.

At Easter we launched a 'Grand Easter Draw' in order to boost our non-public School Fund and were also in negotiation over ICT equipment for the Resource Centre and LEA support for the Unit.

In relation to the Resource Centre we had found ourselves with only a dozen PCs as part of the MESH deal. This created hopeless problems for whole class use. The later phases of MESH had allowed for whole suites of PCs for the host schools. We were informed that the only obstacle to our equipment being similarly upgraded was the opposition of a small number of Liverpool headteachers. A disgraceful situation.

Similarly disgraceful was the refusal of the new Assistant Director of Education to provide any funding for our Unit, while funding places in unregulated, private, Pupil Referral Units and to refuse development funding for the Toxteth Cluster to directly employ an Attendance Officer. **All of this concern with resourcing the school was absorbing a significant amount of time.**

One problem, of course, was that **a successful application for funds brought a new monitoring regime and process of accountability.** In relation to our existing SRB projects we were under careful scrutiny, at this time, as a full scale evaluation of funding was underway across the Dingle. It was, however, through my links with Dingle Opportunities (the SRB/ESF base) and community leaders that we received a remarkable boost to our fortunes.

I was offered sponsorship by the Littlewoods organisation, based in Liverpool and famous for philanthropy. This was an incredible deal. £30,000 per year, for three years, with unlimited in-kind support, in order to assist in moving the school forward. Obviously, there were negotiations and we required a delivery plan but there was an immediate impact upon our ICT programme and the facilities available in the Resource Centre. Furthermore, the general impact of this sponsorship – the Littlewoods name publicly associated with the school and the confidence that this suggested -were incalculable in terms of PR value and staff morale.

All these premises and resourcing issues recede in the face of tragedy and in June '97 we returned after the half term break knowing that a student had died during the holiday, as a result of an accident while playing at the Edge Hill railway sidings. It had been a deeply unpleasant and traumatic experience for family and friends. The students and staff knew of the event and, as well as visiting the family, we were able to organise a very dignified memorial service in school. **People of any religious persuasion and of none respond well to traditional and universal symbols** at such times – a covered top table, candles, lectern, eulogy and period of silence. The student response, as ever, was considerate and sympathetic and there was a strong sense of communal grief and shock.

Unfortunately, the very next day, we were plunged back into crisis. The dedicated school bus, the 681, had a window broken by a stone throwing youth as it turned away from the school. While nobody was hurt the driver, unfortunately, stopped the bus and the students thought they were in danger of violent attack. The single stone thrower had disappeared by the time the bus emptied but the passengers, nearly all black students, had already committed themselves to defence and set off home en bloc. They were agitated, noisy and belligerent. Traffic came to a halt on Park Rd and a group of white youths were chased into a local pub. It was a bad situation. I received complaints from both black and white parents and from the general public. We contacted the police. Having established the full story, which we always managed to do, I had to take action against some of our own students. This was not popular but everyone conceded that the white youths attacked on Park Rd. were also victims. **I was always, openly, concerned that a single incident**

such as this would set back our attempts to build the image of the school but I was more concerned that it might trigger a cycle of violent behaviour.

The following evening I was anxious about the possibility of trouble and left the school early to check the local streets. Reaching the end of our side road I was shocked to find a cavalcade of seven cars parked against the kerb on the main road itself. There were around thirty white males, all big built and between 25 and 35 years of age completely blocking the pavement along which most of the students would have to pass. Despite realising they were being observed and that I was very obviously on a mobile phone the group made no attempt to move off. Their demeanour was entirely threatening. It was clear that some influence was required to marshal such a large group and this reinforced my view that we suffered from the tail end of gangsterism in the area. Having contacted the police I stayed in position and rang various colleagues in the building to alert them to the problem. While doing this the bell rang for the end of the day and the students started spilling onto the street. I was stationary on the corner and was joined by a couple of colleagues. We were able to observe our students in one direction and the group of adult males in the other. We were on the brink of violent chaos. Then the police arrived in force. We were able to contain the whole school in the road while the police dispersed the men. **The message really is to be exceptionally vigilant and attuned to what is happening.** The consequences of that particular confrontation would have been dreadful.

Understandably, I yet again faced a flood of telephone complaints, for which there were no answers and the following evening the dispersal of students was the familiar nightmare of expectations, posturing and threats. I made an urgent appointment to see the Director of Education and the Race equality Management Team.

We were plagued by one small group of youths right up to the summer break. They should have been attending a Catholic school, out of the area, but managed to appear nightly. One produced a knife one evening and threatened one of the older students. On another occasion two youths aged about 18 approached the school bus wearing brass knuckles. This was despite the nightly presence of both uniformed *and* plain-clothes officers.

Throughout the academic year I was wrestling with the problems created by the Shorefields Trust – mentioned earlier. This was a strange state of affairs, as **I had to compartmentalise business in order to sensibly run the school.** While some staff were causing real difficulty, as members of the Trust, they were, in fact, working very well in other respects. One day I would be locked into an acrimonious dispute between Trust members and Governors while the next I would be discussing community management, the introduction of the Junior Sports Leaders Award or school security with the same people.

We continued to invite into school as many useful visitors as possible and this included, councillors, the MP, local Primary headteachers, community leaders and officers of the Local Authority. It was during one such visit that I proposed the creation of a Lifelong Learning Campus for the south end of the Dingle. This would include Shorefields as an 11-18 High School, our Youth Centre, our Adult Education Centre, all our community activity on the main site, the Dingle Swings Play Centre, The Park Children's Centre and Riverside Pensioners Group (both in our annexe) and Matthew Arnold JMI School. All these institutions were struggling for survival at the time and the general idea was that there was strength in unity. Having held meetings with all the parties we publicised the idea of a 'crescent' of educational activity on the South Liverpool Educational Campus and talked of a unique 'cradle to grave facility' raising standards for the local community. We certainly formed some excellent relationships at the time, not least with our main feeder Primary school, and maintained the rhetoric for a short while. The truth was that, without resourcing, we could never make the concept a physical reality. Interestingly, by the new millenium, we had more holistic thinking about educational and community development, a greater commitment to regeneration and genuine moves towards the kind of interagency working implied in the 'campus' idea. For the time being the 'campus' was a useful notion. **It suggested forward thinking, could be referenced in newsletters to parents and, as a big idea, fitted with the revivalist rhetoric about Shorefields, which had become my stock in trade.**

Our Summer Fair was a great success that year despite trouble caused by a handful of local youths. I had to eject one for theft of alcohol and subsequently managed to obtain a banning order as he had attempted to hit me with a bottle of champagne. It would have been a waste. The same youth later gained local notoriety for stabbing a fellow delinquent with a Japanese sword.

I had a further problem outside the school the week after the Fair. This was, strangely, unrelated to any of the 'corner' difficulties with which we were familiar. It did, nevertheless, occur on the 'corner'. Two young men, aged about nineteen or twenty, had been waiting outside the school. When the students emerged it was obvious that they had come to collect a young girl in Year 7, presumably a younger sister. The two men and the girl walked away from the school along with many other students and adults moving in the same direction. As ever there was a good deal of noise and laughter. Suddenly, completely misinterpreting the situation, one of the men rounded on a group of Year 11 girls and began threatening them. I was about twenty feet away. One of the Head Boys intervened and the man pulled a knife. I had to step in. I told the man to back off and came between him and the students. He had moved into the road and was issuing threats. This was an awful position to be in. The students were milling around in increasing numbers because of the drama. This, in itself, was unhelpful, as the man needed the space to back out of the situation without being forced into a confrontation. Anybody could have been stabbed. After this stalemate had endured for too long he turned, crossed the main road, and disappeared.

My relief was tempered by the fact that I had completely forgotten about his partner. He had circled behind me and, fortunately, run foul of some of the older students. I was most appreciative. This could have ended very badly. It was most traumatic.

As ever this problem, due to its seriousness, led to a significant amount of work. The Police took a report that night and I was delayed in leaving work by about three hours. We had been able to identify the two men very quickly and they were, apparently, local heroin addicts. Unsurprisingly, they could not be located. Weeks later I spent hours with the Police at an Identity Parade waiting for the culprit to arrive. He didn't do so. The Police saw this as commonplace. A tactic to wear down the Police and the witnesses. I never heard of the matter again.

In terms of curriculum developments, we had received external recognition of the quality of our Records of Achievement, were strengthening our bi-lingual provision and had undertaken a thorough review of our GNVQ and City and Guilds courses post 16. We had also questioned the value of Liverpool Compact – the quality of coordination with schools, arrangements for a Careers Convention and an Options Evening, the suitability of the graduation ceremony and the success of the programme in student terms. A preoccupation with progressing equality of opportunity is apparent from the sheer number of occasions it appeared on agendas for meetings, as a discussion item with senior staff or as a priority during the year.

For me each day was a whirlwind of activity. A typical Thursday in February involved a full morning meeting with the Liverpool Secondary Heads, lunchtime meetings with representatives of Dingle Swings followed by a meeting with two Pastoral leaders, a meeting with a Senior Teacher, a meeting with one of the Governors, a meeting with a languages teacher followed by meetings with the Head of History, the Head of English and the Community Manager.

Obviously, I set out what I wanted to achieve. For a typical day in April I had the ambitious agenda of – organising staffing for August's exam analysis, chasing administration over Year 5 home addresses, initiating an attendance check, reviewing the Year 6 Primary Liaison Programme, dealing with SRB returns, considering staff development issues, ordering raffle tickets for the Summer Fair, reviewing a number of senior roles, progress chasing the new school database and discussing the location of the 'Girls Club'.

There was no doubt that our management structure was inadequate and that we also had weaknesses in operational and functional roles within the school, hence all the progress chasing. **In an improving school, in our circumstances, the Head must accept wide responsibility, set high expectations and constantly challenge the quality of delivery.**

In order to improve teamworking and collective responsibility for development we arranged for the Curriculum Team Leaders to meet regularly with the Deputy Head and for the Pastoral Team Leaders to meet with the Senior Teacher. We also devoted In Service days each year to school development planning and had a well organised exercise of review and development, department by department, based on 'top level' priorities for the school.

Despite the problems 'on the corner', as we called it, that final half term was a staggering success in PR terms. I had by chance been visiting our most prestigious feeder school, St. Michael in the Hamlet, which was in Aigburth, Liverpool 17. It was a day of torrential rain at the end of June and their roof was leaking like a colander. They had buckets down the middle of every corridor and pans, bowls, basins, cups in fact anything to catch the water in each classroom. The situation was impossible. I heard the following day that St. Michael's was being closed and evacuated. But where to? I rang the Director immediately and offered to accommodate the whole school. The matter was left in the hands of an officer who was favourable towards us and within days we had every Junior school child and member of staff on site. We provided offices, a staffroom, free refreshments, unlimited photocopying, porterage, everything. They were with us for a month and held their annual sports day and annual prizegiving on site to which all their parents were invited. We could not have paid for that much publicity. The children, staff and parents loved it and this was reflected in the dramatic increase in children choosing to transfer from St. Michael's from then on. **When an opportunity presents itself it is necessary to make a decision and to act very quickly indeed.** Fortunately the Junior children and Staff departed twenty minutes before the rest of the school each day.

The year ended well with the successful Fair, a Summer Show, foreign trips and visits and a Sports Day. I committed myself to reducing my involvement in external fund raising bodies, as there were issues of internal standards, particularly attendance, which needed addressing.

LEARNING POINTS YEAR 4

- Don't make assumptions about the quality of information you receive. It is necessary to evaluate its effectiveness.
- A growing school can experience disproportionate problems.
- Schools should consider a full programme of induction for all students.
- 16 is too early to track students onto an undergraduate programme.
- Mainstream schools are inappropriate for some students.
- Regardless of the time involved, the Head must *strongly* represent the school in the face of appeals.
- Regular meetings between a team leader and their staff contribute to raising standards.
- Job specifications are an important starting point in discussing performance and in determining the relationships and lines of accountability between colleagues.
- Staff close ranks when managers attempt to deal with individual performance problems.

- The only way to deal with staff performance problems is on the basis of firm evidence.
- Weak staff need a specific, and agreed, improvement plan.
- It is difficult to improve seriously weak staff. Procedures often have the opposite effect to that intended.
- Changing work roles can bring a new lease of life.
- Beyond a certain stage of dilapidation in school buildings the education of students suffers badly.
- Each successful grant application introduces a new layer of bureaucracy.
- Tragic events require the dignity and respect afforded by traditional symbols.
- A single incident can undo months of effort.
- The Head should have 'big' ideas and be able to articulate them.
- In a small school it may be impossible to delegate many areas of business.
- When an opportunity presents itself it is important to make a decision and to act very quickly indeed.

START OF FIFTH YEAR OF
HEADSHIP SEPTEMBER '97

T HE YEAR STARTED WELL with improved results for years 11 and
12. We now had nearly 15% of students gaining five or more good
grades at GCSE. A number of Curriculum leaders were becoming
very confident, were competitive with each other and were driven
to succeed for the sake of the individual students. Our Year 12 intake was good and we had 130 Year 7 students enrol on the first day,
fractionally up on the previous year. We had also maintained our
standards in respect of discipline, again only excluding 17 students
the previous year.

The induction package for year 7 worked very well. The entire
first half term was planned around the assimilation of year 7. Every
teacher and every subject emphasised the same common rules
and expectations, behavioural issues and disciplinary responses.
Each subject laid out their programme for the half term and this
was sent to parents. The departments then concentrated upon the
basic academic requirements for working in their area with the aim
of achieving a common standard for all by the half term break. It

worked well and was backed up by a very quick 'pager' response from SMT. Later we established an 'Early Intervention Unit' solely to deal with the students failing to make the transition to Secondary School and who had been identified as 'at risk' by the Head of Year 7. An important element in the success of the induction arrangements was the use of student mentors to guide the newcomers from a to b. This helped the new students settle quickly and also cut down on the colossal loss of time experienced in year 7.

Equally important, is the induction of new staff to a school or the development of staff new to a post. While we provided the clearest guidelines for staff, in the form of the Handbook, it was also necessary to lay out the expectations of the school to newcomers, to ensure that Heads of Department were playing an appropriate role in the development of their staff and to provide those new to responsibility with structured support. It would be a number of years before we had the management strength to guarantee an effective job in these respects but during this academic year we had a real focus on staff development and staff performance.

A key way in which the Head can impact upon the performance of senior staff and middle managers is through mentoring or management supervision meetings. We now had one Deputy, two Senior Teachers and a number of middle managers with whole school responsibility in areas such as staff development, premises and equal opportunities. I met with most of these staff weekly.

A danger with management supervision, however, is that the Head may be endlessly progress chasing and in the position of micro managing colleagues. Due to shedding staff, and being restricted in our later pattern of recruitment, we had some excellent classroom teachers joining the school but were still weak managerially. While all faculty heads had been given an additional school wide responsibility they did not necessarily have the strategic ability to develop these roles coherently nor, in some cases, were they motivated to do so. Furthermore, with a headteacher and one deputy, we only had two people exercising 'executive' responsibility.

In a school as complex as Shorefields this was not enough. The inevitable result was that I had too much personal responsibility for all our community issues, for the pastoral system and for staff development. **Excessive operational concerns militate against the head developing an independent strategic role.**

During the year we had performance concerns in relation to fifteen staff. This is not a situation one would choose as it necessitated a raft of observations, discussions and, in six cases, formal improvement plans with targets. There was, however, no alternative. If an administrator fails to conduct themselves professionally, it undermines the progress of the school. If a teacher is failing to cope in the classroom due to a lack of control, failure to adapt to curriculum change, stress or incompetence then something must be done. Unfortunately, this view was not shared by one of the main teaching unions in Liverpool who mounted a campaign against our improvement programme, which was entirely unhelpful.

We were, in every respect, the most disadvantaged and deprived school in the city. We were still struggling to survive having endured a collapse in confidence and a collapse in numbers five years earlier and it was remarkable that we were all still in employment. **The only way to guarantee the continuing survival of the school was by developing higher standards.** The fact that many Liverpool schools were loath to address issues of performance, capability and conduct could not be our benchmark. This reluctance, though, made it easier for unions to characterise our approach to professional development as aggressive.

I was completely resentful of the fact that this was further manipulated to generate union militancy in the school as a spearhead for union campaigning in the city. This should not have happened and was an abusive use of vulnerable staff in a vulnerable school.

The proof, anyway, was in the outcome of our work in the school. Of the fifteen staff causing concern that year, three eventually left and eleven improved dramatically. Of the eleven, nine went on to gain promotion. This seems like a reasonable vindication of our procedures.

In management terms these performance problems added to the weight of operational concerns I had at the time. While my role was concerned with leadership of the organisation, and providing challenge and support for colleagues, I found that the extent to which I was fulfilling these roles personally was worrying. Firstly, in an institutional sense, it was unhealthy for these roles not to be more diffuse. Secondly, the scale of the concerns I had around our improvement and school development needs was almost overwhelming.

I was micro-managing large areas of the pastoral system and the primary liaison programme. I had responsibility for our SRB and ESF returns, for negotiations over community funding, for much of the preparation for our forthcoming Ofsted inspection the forthcoming May, for dealing with the Trust, for reviewing post 16 provision and updating school policies – behaviour, homework, health and safety and appraisal. **In a sense, progress chasing demeans all concerned yet it seems unavoidable in the context of improving an organisation.**

I found myself 'chasing' the calendar to guarantee that our plans actually materialised. These included – exams, identifying In – Service needs, primary liaison, tenant invoicing, preparation for training days, our monitoring arrangements, our next induction month, duty lists, the exam timetable, production of revision lists, Youth and Community timetables, plans for the Summer Fair and Summer Show, administrative cover for holiday periods, arrangements for 'results days' and examination analysis, the transfer of pastoral records and the provision of coffee and biscuits for staff.

In addition I was involved in activities from which most sensible headteachers would have stepped away. These included oversight of the prefect system, my teaching commitment, arranging substitution work in Media Studies for an absent colleague, running a Year 9 football team and managing the steel band in the absence of the music teacher. This latter issue arose as a result of an earlier

promise to the Caribbean Centre that the band would play in the
Empire Windrush anniversary celebrations in the city and nearly
degenerated into farce. I found it almost impossible to coordinate
the band, who all knew what they were doing anyway, and to get
any sensible level of cooperation from this little group of prima
donnas. I now have the utmost respect for music teachers.

My naïve assumption that they would be able to play a few tunes
led me into a nightmare of negotiation over who played which pan,
changeover of players between tunes, the choice of tunes, availability on the day, transport arrangements and catering issues. I had to
refuse permission for the band to play atop an open flat-back truck
as the organisers had no idea how to secure the equipment, or the
students, on the vehicle and the forecast was for torrential rain.

Our scheduled interview on Radio Merseyside was jeopardised
by the loss of the bass beaters. The bass drummer was dispatched
to the local pet shop from where he obtained two round dog chews.
These objects, forced onto sticks, were, apparently, essential to
achieving the correct bass sound. And they certainly worked.

The following day, in the rain, the Shorefields Steel Band provided the only musical entertainment at Liverpool's Pier Head. We
extended our planned slot from twenty minutes to three hours. As
they only had four tunes the band played them repeatedly and, in
order to avoid changeovers, I had them play 'Can't find my brother'
for half an hour at one point. They were a huge success, appeared
on television, radio and in the press and I was very grateful to them.
In addition to the PR value of this exercise we also enjoyed a good
buffet at the Caribbean Centre.

Involvement in such activities was not frivolous. At the time it
was necessary to generate the maximum good publicity. I could have
dropped my other extra curricular activities – the football team, the
prefects and the Media Studies – but, **by personally supporting
activity 'on the ground', the head gives a clear commitment to
the sort of development needed in the school.**

Strategically, we needed to develop highly effective approaches to teaching across the school. We also needed to audit the effectiveness of our work on an ongoing basis. Examination results are an inadequate reflection of the quality of teaching and we needed a robust system of monitoring and tracking students in order to actually know more about the quality of delivery and how it could be improved. We were also encouraging a wider review and testing of progress in departments.

It was from this point that we made a heavy investment of time in creating a school wide database to log academic and pastoral progress.

As ever, I was engaged in a struggle with myself to create the time to manage effectively. I did succeed in creating blocks of uninterrupted time in order to concentrate on specific projects but these were few and far between. Other than that, **I relied upon the discipline imposed by the calendar, on reasonable time management each day, upon regular meetings with colleagues and upon a constant reassessment of priorities in order to move forward.**

Each day was as busy as the last. A typical day in October involved – an early morning management meeting, the staff briefing, teaching a year 11 class, an off site meeting at the Granby Toxteth Development Trust, Year 9 football training at lunchtime followed by a meeting about the Trust, a meeting with the manager of the Park Children's Centre, a meeting with our Staff Development Coordinator, a meeting with the site manager, bus duty and our Senior Management Team meeting.

It became clear that **systems and people require constant maintenance and reinforcement if they are to remain effective.** In some respects this appeared a bigger challenge than the achievement of many of our earlier objectives. **In order to reach a position in which the organisation is functioning well, permanently, there must be arrangements for monitoring and reviewing all key functions.** More importantly, there need to be people in post at every level who understand what they are doing and care about it. Schools cannot afford to have incompetent or disengaged members of staff at any level and particularly not holding management responsibilities.

I was in the embarrassing position of dealing with a senior colleague in respect of performance and capability over an extended period of time. This only serves to demoralise colleagues and feeds the disaffected. We certainly had a number of disaffected staff. In fact many colleagues avoided the staff-room in order to rise above the wearying negativity of the 'disruptive provocateurs'. As ever, I felt that it was the responsibility of management to address this problem. We ensured that a senior member of staff took time to sit in the staff-room each lunchtime simply to banter with colleagues and try to raise the tone. I also spoke directly to one viciously undermining colleague and requested more professional conduct. **Headteachers can, and should, take action over any shortcomings likely to detract from the purposes of the school.**

Governors were still dealing with residual problems related to 'expeditions' and the Shorefields Trust but the school was moving on far more positively in respect of raising development funding. We continued to benefit from SRB (Single Regeneration Budget), ESF (European Social Fund) and GEST (Grant For Education Support and Training). Our profile was becoming dynamic and forward thinking. We had a large number of staff on courses, had successfully changed our Year 12 curriculum, had a healthy intake, improving relations with the Primary sector and Shorefields was the only secondary school in the city continuing to pursue the Community Comprehensive ideal. We now had a mass of community tenants in both the Annexe and on our main site and our Youth Club maintained the highest attendances in the city. In addition we hosted a wide range of sports clubs under the auspices of the Youth Club and these included basketball, a range of football clubs, the Golden Gloves Boxing Club and various keep fit and martial arts groups. The regularity of our appearances in the local media, press, radio and television meant that we had a high profile. **There is no doubt that by this time we had created an essential ingredient**

of success – confidence. The sense that the organisation was in the ascendancy and was worth supporting.

An example of our own confidence was the organisation of a series of meetings with local councillors over repairs and maintenance issues and over the loss of LEA funding. We were able to demonstrate that each increase in grant funding, obtained by our own efforts, was matched by a diminution in the resource available through formula funding. This related, particularly, to our community, special needs and social disadvantage funding but also to specific items of planned maintenance and to the loss of ICT funds. We produced a dossier of photographs showing dilapidation and had constructed a database of our efforts to communicate with the Council over their responsibilities.

The result of this lobbying was a series of meetings with Council officers. In one memorable meeting we were promised an entire new roof in corrugated steel. Neither the roof, nor any other appreciable repairs materialised and the officer concerned retired soon after. Apparently he had promised every head teacher in the city a new roof!

Meanwhile, we continued involvement in a range of developments from the simple to the highly sophisticated. We were now using community service offenders to pick litter and this was improving the site. I was pursuing the idea of a South Liverpool Educational Campus although this was more conceptual than realistic. We were engaged in discussions over the closure of EBD schools and the assimilation of children into mainstream. I was also pleased to be invited to speak at a conference organised by the Race Equality Management Team on 'Effective Approaches to Race Equality'.

At Christmas we arranged a special assembly and carol concert for our neighbouring Primary schools. This was the first and only time we attempted it. We were well organised and all the schools had accepted invitations in advance. On the morning of the concert we were concerned to receive a number of messages indicating the non attendance of a number of schools. As a precaution we rang to check with the remaining schools only to find that none, *not one*, could attend. Some had staffing problems, others had rearranged events at the last minute and created a clash and some headteachers had simply forgotten. This was disastrous as we had a choir, musicians and staff all rehearsed.

I contacted each school personally and cajoled headteachers into sending the students accompanied, if necessary by classroom assistants. One school, Tiber Street, could spare no staff and, rashly, I offered to collect all the students and walk them the twenty minutes to Shorefields. This was a mistake. Even accompanied by a number of our prefects it was obvious that some of these children were determined to be uncooperative and objectionable. I found, subsequently, that they were the most difficult youngsters many of the Tiber Street staff had ever encountered. It was a bad experience for me and, due to their behaviour, for those unfortunate enough to be nearby in the carol concert. The only silver lining was that we obtained the names of the most difficult youngsters and succeeded in dissuading them from applying for places at Shorefields for the following September.

In school we continued to have more than enough challenges from our own students. We had rivalry and fighting between a group of black and a group of white girls in Year 8. A teacher was assaulted, in my office, by the parents of a sixth former. There were disciplinary problems with a Somali, a Yemeni and a white boy all involving me in repeated meetings with parents and we excluded a Chinese boy, a black boy and a number of white boys all for general behavioural problems. We also had a growing problem with two of the older black boys, the most intelligent and promising students in their year group, demonstrating all the characteristics associated with gang culture. Our systems were failing to contain these youths and their influence was pernicious. Ultimately, working very cooperatively with parents, with the forbearance of a portion of the staff and with me accepting personal responsibility for them, they both left the school at the end of Year 11 with excellent qualifications. But it was very challenging.

The new Labour government had introduced the idea of Education Action Zones to raise standards in city areas. The plan was to form a zone from a couple of secondary schools and a range of Primaries in the same area as a vehicle for encouraging collective working and innovation. We had already been involved in a number of meetings between local schools and the LEA and the initiative held opportunities for us. **Anything that binds a Secondary School into a partnership with Primary School colleagues is helpful in securing the future.**

That future was already looking brighter as a result of the sponsorship from Littlewoods and I had regular meetings to discuss the nature of the support. An example of that support was the removal from our site of outdated and hazardous chemicals. Years earlier, Shorefields had been the recipient of chemicals and laboratory equipment from five secondary schools. We had a potentially lethal collection of proscribed substances on site for which, without Littlewoods help, the specialised removal and disposal would have cost many thousands of pounds.

During one of our many meetings a Littlewoods manager said that **he tried to appoint self developers and self motivators rather than command and do people**. It summed up one of my own key concerns at the time.

Throughout the year the teacher unions nationally had been stepping up action over bureaucracy and meetings. The Liverpool divisions had been pushing for a hard line on the issues. This came to a head shortly before our Ofsted inspection and I was informed by one of the union representatives that members would not be attending their usual meetings during the inspection week. We had already sent details of the school programme to the inspectors and agreed an observation schedule for meetings. The timing could not have been worse. The union rep was militant and provocative and determined to ignore the 'no prejudice' clause, which normally accompanied guidance over action. This, in effect, meant union members could avoid self-harm.

I went to the staff as a body and explained the dilemma and the consequences of a poor inspection. I proposed cancelling all meetings for a period of time following the inspection providing staff carried on as normal during the week. Fortunately common sense prevailed.

We had a further obstacle prior to the inspection with the resignation of a senior administrative officer. While we undertook some rapid restructuring, ultimately to the benefit of the school, this move undermined support for senior staff during the inspection process itself, which was unfortunate.

Despite these setbacks, our Ofsted inspection in May '98 was a big success and we gained excellent publicity. We were becoming adept at managing the Inspections and, again, established a great rapport with the team and treated them with courtesy and respect. This certainly does not guarantee a good report or a trouble free inspection period but it does allow for negotiation and compromise and for the Head to honestly feed back any concerns generated by the presence of the inspection team. This is particularly important when discussing the report itself. It is remarkable that some schools overlook the importance of reading the draft inspection report and exercising their right to challenge the phraseology. This is not about altering judgements but the way they are expressed. It is crucial that a minor reservation does not take precedence over a substantive positive judgement. In my experience inspection judgements are, invariably, perceptive and fair. On the handful of occasions where I think there have been errors of judgement they have always been towards leniency.

My main concerns during the academic year had been the success of the Ofsted Inspection, the maintenance of links with the Dingle SRB/ESF partnership and improving our relationships with Primary colleagues. We were now hosting the monthly Cluster meetings, between Primary and Secondary colleagues in the school.

The Toxteth Cluster, as we were known, was becoming increasingly assertive. There had been some changes in personnel in the primaries and they brought high expectations of what could be achieved when schools cooperated. They, also, now, had the huge support of one local secondary, ourselves. We were using our reprographic facilities to produce their newsletters and, on occasions, lending out our secretarial, caretaking and maintenance staff. In the last twelve months the Cluster had organised staff development for the heads, residential conferences and, importantly, bids, into the LEA, for additional resources to support the work being done in our neglected area of the city.

It is interesting to note that by the date of the Toxteth Cluster residential on June 26th, we still had no clear idea how many students would be attending Shorefields the following September. It really is shocking that this situation endured for so many years.

In school, the Ofsted Inspection had helped considerably in tightening up procedures, particularly around attendance. This was a bonus as it had been a concern from the previous year. The Registered Inspector was highly complimentary over our efforts. As ever, the Inspectors had approached their task of inspecting a secondary school in the notorious Toxteth, Liverpool, with real trepidation. They expected anarchy and low standards. What they found was courtesy, good behaviour, high standards, dignity and respect. They found it remarkable and felt that we were on the cusp of creating a quality school with lasting success. I found this incredibly motivating and a spur to greater efforts.

LEARNING POINTS YEAR FIVE

- There must be an induction and development programme for all new staff and, importantly, for any staff new to a post of responsibility.

- Management supervision is an important element of the Head's role.

- There is a danger of drifting into micro-management.

- Excessive operational concerns militate against the head developing a strategic role.

- Tackling teacher underperformance may receive little support from either the Local Authority or the teacher unions.

- In a small school in challenging circumstances the Head can expect to take on multiple roles.

- Never try to manage a steel band.

- The Head may have to lead over basic developments in order for the school to improve.

- The Head needs to operate within a clear management framework of planned business, effective communication, meetings, responsibilities and review.

- Systems and people require constant maintenance and reinforcement if they are to remain effective.

- All key functions need to be regularly and systematically monitored and reviewed.

- Staff, at every level, need to understand what they are doing and care about it.

- Heads can and should take action over those who would undermine and demoralise colleagues.

- An organisation must be seen as being in the ascendancy and, therefore, worth supporting.

- Anything that binds a Secondary school into partnership with Primary school colleagues is helpful in securing the future.

- Try to appoint self developers and self motivators rather than 'command and do' people.

- Nurture your own motivation.

START OF SIXTH YEAR OF HEADSHIP SEPTEMBER '98

W E SUFFERED A DETERIORATION in the percentage of students gaining 5 A-C grades at GCSE –down to 9.5%. This left us still bumping along in single figures, but we had seen an improvement in results in other respects. The previous Year 11 had of course been the students who entered the school at around its lowest point, when, five years earlier, other parents were opting to send their children elsewhere. We also had a disappointing turnout of year 7 students, 125 on the first day, but this grew quickly to around 150. Our exclusion record was again very promising, only having excluded 14 students the previous year. One of our head boys was Palestinian and one white British. One of our head girls was Yemeni and the other white British.

We had significant problems in the second week of term with our Year 9 students, the ones who, two years earlier, had prompted consideration of full induction for new students. We called in ten sets of parents immediately in order to forestall further problems and in order to set out school standards unambiguously.

We then embarked upon a very busy term indeed with post Ofsted work and an avalanche of consultation from the new Labour government and from the LEA under the new Liberal Democrat administration. We made an enthusiastic response to many of the review exercises underway such as those relating to Youth and Community and Post 16 provision.

The Education Action Zone initiative had now moved from the LEA, as lead agent, and clusters of schools were being encouraged to submit bids to form zones. Two of our Primary colleagues arrived one morning to suggest we submitted a bid but we had minimal response time. I read the bid documentation overnight and contacted our local Regeneration Partnership manager the following day. There was no time for consultation. As a school we had the administrative resources to tackle this quickly and I wrote a bid based on what I knew, at the time, were the Cluster priorities – support over attendance, increased teaching and ancillary staffing and access to resources, particularly ICT. This was later couched in Government Office language by our Partnership Manager and an officer seconded from the LEA – both highly motivated and dedicated professionals. We submitted the first draft in advance of consultation then set about appealing for support via the Cluster, partner organisations and public meetings.

On one level this was fairly straightforward. The key aims of reducing social exclusion, raising standards and improving employability found no disagreement. There is, nevertheless, a tendency for such grassroots initiatives as ours to be overwhelmed by individual interests. A big advantage for me in presenting the bid, and leading the early consultations, was that I disclaimed any financial advantage for Shorefields. The plans we presented would give overwhelming support to the Primary sector while the bulk of the actual work was, currently, being done by ourselves. My motivation was, as ever, to secure the support of Primary colleagues for the long term.

Secondly, I realised that the government had committed itself to creating a specialist college in every zone. We needed no more incentive than this to make the effort worthwhile. **It is necessary to look beyond short-term gains when involved in the long game of school survival.**

Back in school there were union rumblings, as ever, over this latest attempt to move forward. Our highly unionised staff were under tremendous pressure from their local secretary to lead the opposition to Education Action Zones and there was a great deal of scaremongering. They were told that it would mean changes to their contracts of employment, that we would be overwhelmed by bureaucracy and that the initiative would not lead to raising standards. It was very much to the credit of headteachers and staff throughout, what became, the Dingle Granby Toxteth EAZ that they relentlessly focussed on the issue of raising standards. The Primary heads were absolutely tenacious in pushing for the best possible support for their schools and for the area in general. A small group of Primary heads gave up an exhausting amount of their time in working up the bid, cooperating with our LEA lead officer and representing the case to the DFES.

At this time we were embroiled in a dispute over our caretaking arrangements. Again this was partly an issue of authority. The caretaking staff had been engaged to undertake minor repairs and, in this, they were very effective. Our caretaking bill for the four caretakers across our two sites was, however, very high indeed. This was partly due to outdated working practices, in particular the distinction between 'casual', 'regular' and 'contractual' overtime. As 'regular' overtime undertaken over a couple of months became 'contractual' the individual caretaker would receive payment whether or not the overtime was undertaken. This situation was compounded by our site manager requiring the caretaking team to be on site, together, to carry out repairs, maintenance and minor works. This work included the installation of a new kitchen in the staffroom, the construction of concrete steps from the field and new flooring to the reception area and corridors. We had a real clash of priorities. It had been advantageous to have a site manager with the vision to sort out many of our day to day maintenance problems and we had created this post ahead of many other schools. **A problem for any organisation, however, lies in the struggle to maintain budgetary control over a motivated, highly independent but divergent manager.** Our caretaking staffing costs were unreasonably high and we had two further problems. Firstly, the site manager had embarked upon modifications to parts of the building without authority. Secondly, there was friction between the site team over shifts and overtime and over caretaking duties, which were less popular than maintenance work.

Fortunately we had access to a vastly experienced consultant in supervisory issues. He interrogated our work sheets and overtime claims, interviewed staff, reorganised contracts, arranged notice and provided reports for Governors. One of the caretakers left, we moved the manager and established better working practices. It was hard and acrimonious.

We had been running our own cleaning contract for a number of years and this was highly instructive in respect of people management. We now had three large groupings of staff – the teachers, the site and cleaning staff and, finally, the clerical and technical staff. Our cleaner in charge was outstanding and we had a very straightforward relationship. She took full responsibility for and managed that entire area of school life. This included recruitment, deployment, deciding upon working practices, completing timesheets and chasing payments. Obviously our expectations were high and, periodically, we had additional urgent work to which the cleaners responded well. Obviously the cleaners were 'supervised' staff as opposed to 'professionals' but the job required training, a clear performance standard and the integrity and motivation to work alone. The staff had pride in the areas for which they were responsible, formed good relationships with the teachers, were loyal to the school and were exceptionally well managed by someone committed to delivering a quality service. I wanted to replicate this successful model in other areas.

In terms of administration we were manifestly inefficient with staff working in a fragmented and unfocussed manner. In fairness to individual staff this was due to an absence of effective management in this area and this compounded the problems inherent in school offices generally. We found that new staff, with a background in commercial organisations, were quickly overwhelmed by the range of tasks expected of them and by the scale of the interruptions. Shorefields was probably an exaggerated example of its type with extensive typing requirements, thousands of financial transactions, phones constantly ringing, mountains of letters and parcels delivered daily, a busy community foyer, students requiring attention, parents arriving for scheduled and unscheduled meetings, a huge demand on reprographic services and teachers requesting registers, forms, certificates, typing, extracts from the database and photocopies.

Repeated attempts to establish quality office management had failed due to the paucity of the post holders and we only moved towards resolution when, years later, we physically separated out the administration functions from each other. Nevertheless, **in order for a team to work effectively there must be general oversight of the work and an ability to order and prioritise tasks.**

At one point in the year we were overwhelmed with complaints from teaching staff about the admin arrangements. Neither the school brochure nor the options booklets were produced on time; typing relating to governors, heads of year and the PTA had been ignored; pastoral review papers were not produced; a report on attendance had gone astray as had information relating to SRB returns; the database was inaccurate and the daily bulletin mocked the English language in its inaccuracy.

I imposed a work schedule on the admin staff, discussed time and task management with the Senior Admin Officer and included her in all Senior Management meetings in order to create a better awareness of forthcoming calendar events. We also introduced regular meetings for the admin staff. Despite the criticisms, above, this was not their 'fault'. The system did work better and everyone seemed happier. We continued, like other schools, to search for quality management in this area.

While we had a high level of accountability amongst the site staff this was not the case across the teaching force-the professionals. This is common amongst groups of workers who have a broadly collegial relationship with each other and consider themselves to have professional equality and individual discretion. This is one reason why team leadership in education and, indeed, running schools is so challenging. **Professionals, in any sphere, tend to be very difficult to manage.**

Historically, the pastoral staff had overshadowed the department leaders at Shorefields. This compounded a common problem in schools, whereby heads of department tended to see themselves as managers of resources rather than managers of people. With an increasing number of young teachers joining the school and with continuing performance problems on the part of some of the existing staff I realised that we needed a 'theory of skill learning' even to have a dialogue with some of our colleagues. This, in effect, was a way of empowering the heads of department, engendering some humility in new staff and encouraging reflection generally. It predated both the NQT Career Entry Profile and the Threshold process for experienced staff – both of which emphasised the importance of development and growth during a teaching career.

I published a set of descriptors for – novice teacher, advanced beginner, competent performer, complete proficiency and expert performance. At least I felt confident that, in school, we had a clear model through which we could consider teacher improvement.

We supported the developing role for heads of department with the introduction of departmental reviews. The first two we conducted were in Design Technology and Personal and Social Education. Support and challenge were the key themes and the department head was invited to consider all aspects of departmental performance. We created proformas from Ofsted and HMI documents and produced a biannual rotation of department and year group reviews. **Team leaders, whether curriculum, pastoral, admin or site are crucially important in school effectiveness. They deserve tremendous support as individuals and the problems they identify should be resourced.**

In November the international news was dominated by appalling devastation and loss of life in Honduras. This was a result of torrential rains and mud slides destroying whole communities. A number of staff asked that the school make a response to the appeal for aid. Obviously this was absolutely appropriate and they were told to discuss the organisational practicalities of this with the deputy before informing staff and students. This did not happen.

What ensued was a textbook example of how not to manage an event and of how teachers can make grossly unreasonable assumptions of those around them. There were no arrangements for handling finance. Tutors were not briefed on dealing with donations in kind. No on site storage had been arranged. There were no transport arrangements for goods collected and, crucially, there had been an assumption that our admin section would handle the situation despite their existing workload problems.

It is understandable that creative people with a moral mission sometimes become frustrated by organisational detail but **a good idea is not the same as a good deed.** This appeal quickly degenerated into public criticism of senior management and acrimony from and between the organisers. I instructed the deputy to take responsibility for the whole affair.

This is only one example of the poor events management that can occur within an organisation. **We suffered, as all large organisations will, from the curse of staff making assumptions.** Those assumptions are *always* that someone else will take responsibility for an element of the event or that arrangements are, somehow, automatically in place. Examples include – arranging meetings without booking rooms; booking rooms without providing instructions for furniture and equipment; failing to arrange refreshments; failing to arrange car parking or security; failing to request late opening of the premises; poor cash handling arrangements; failing to make banking and cheque payment arrangements; failing to appreciate full overall costs; creating clashes with other events; ignoring the reception/greeting/master of ceremonies roles; an absence of signage for visitors; failing to book transport; requiring cheques in advance of receipts; publicity and communication problems; failing to arrange work cover; late requests for reprographics; ignoring health and safety considerations; failing to issue guidance and reminders to all involved; lack of clarity over dates, times, duration, contact details and principal responsibilities.

It is certainly the experience of many in education that organising activity with professionals from other sectors is terribly difficult. Teachers are, understandably, focussed on time and supervisory issues and experience bitter frustration at a lack of reliability on the part of some in the private, voluntary and other areas of the public sector. Consequently, the organisation of activity in schools, including having provisional standby arrangements, needs to be of the highest order.

Ironically, we were having great success with students managing events. The sixth form, as part of their GNVQ course, were involved with a music promoter and, annually, invited an up and coming group into school. The students were treated to performances by 'Another Level', 'Clock' and 'Fierce' and all aspects of these events were handled by the sixth form. A buffet lunch was arranged for the performers on each occasion and the sixth form handled publicity, ticket sales, door management and so on.

The Honduras debacle was certainly instrumental in formalising our 'project management' arrangements. While schools tended to be good at arranging trips and visits, and had adequate policies and procedures in place, there was insufficient recognition that much school activity can be broken down into projects. Again this is reflective of the inherent problems involved in managing professionals. **It is easy to assume that a professional knows how to do things properly. This is unwarranted.**

We investigated industrial models of project management and combined these with the good practice from education to produce a general model applicable to all activity. We piloted this with a number of our staff, highly experienced at arranging trips all over the world, and with those organising on site events. After two years the arrangements were widely accepted and staff reported that organising activity was in fact easier! Crucially, it released senior staff from firefighting problems. It also provided training in responsible and fully accountable management each time an activity was arranged.

It had been a busy term and we were all looking forward to Christmas when, in late December, I suspended a teacher for striking a student. If life had been a popularity contest I would have been losing badly. The staff were angered by the suspension but, as ever, were not party to the facts and there was comment about how distressed the teacher's family would be prior to Christmas. There are many schools where no effective action is taken in these circumstances. Such schools cannot be on an incline of improvement. **There is no doubt that serious issues of performance and capability or misconduct require a principled and consistent approach.** We had procedures and we used them and the key reason for this was that to do otherwise, in a difficult working environment, could involve making separate and inconsistent judgements. Ultimately this is unfair to staff, undermines the ability of management to take effective action and contributes nothing to raising standards.

The reality was that, although suspension was used on a number of occasions, it only involved a handful of staff, principally from the same department and with the same flawed attitude to their relationship with young people.

Interestingly, staff with performance and capability or conduct problems very seldom acknowledge the situation. **It is essential that**

managers record perceived problems and complaints in order to even have a dialogue with a colleague. For example, a parental complaint that a child has been shouted at by a teacher is relatively easy to dismiss. This sort of complaint annoys teachers particularly when they see themselves as involved in a struggle to raise standards. If, however, there have been five such complaints, comments about abusive or humiliating language and concerns raised by colleagues over demeanour in the staff-room, then this is evidence of genuine concern and it is necessary to open a professional discussion. It must also be remembered that an abusive member of staff will come into contact with an awful lot of children. In a secondary school this may be two hundred each week on timetable and many more on general supervision and other duties. **Not only do young people deserve protection, but we must also understand that the whole image of the school can be distorted, in the eyes of parents, as a result of the behaviour of an individual teacher.**

In relation to other personnel matters, I had to address the poor attendance record of a technician, who subsequently, left the school on good terms. The Council also instructed me, to remove a member of the ancillary staff for benefit irregularities. This was, apparently, Liverpool Council policy and Council officers pursued me vigorously over the matter. We managed to achieve a dignified resignation and relocation to the private sector. We also lost a good lunchtime supervisor due to a conflict between herself and another family in the area. This is obviously the downside of employing so many local people. We made it clear that conflicts affecting the life of the school would jeopardise employment and I intervened in, and managed to resolve, many neighbourhood disputes over the years. On any occasion that we parted company with an employee it was by mutual agreement.

We had had a long-standing problem over the punctuality to lessons of a particular staff member. In a very short meeting he was informed that this was not a matter of 'professional judgement' and that he was in breach of a contractual obligation. The situation improved.

Interestingly, one of our cleaners retired that year and we held up her attendance and punctuality record as an example to all students in the school. Never absent and never late for work in over forty years. The story was featured in the Liverpool Echo and we created an annual prize, 'the Amy Grice Award', for the greatest improvement in punctuality and attendance. The students thought this quite remarkable and gave Amy great respect.

I had, earlier, made an error of judgement in becoming involved in a dispute over attendance at In Service days with a number of part time teaching staff. This was going nowhere and caused bitterness on each of the five statutory days throughout the year. We now agreed to payment for those staff and all term-time only classroom assistants and ancillary staff in order that all staff could be in attendance and work together.

This was important, as the time spent was invaluable in communicating key issues around the development of the school. One contemporary matter concerned the 'Use of Force' policy each school was obliged to draw up. It was still shocking to me that a tiny minority of staff held to the view that manhandling students should be acceptable. The policy agreed, and supported by the overwhelming majority, made it clear which line must be followed.

We had an ongoing improvement plan, from the previous year, for eight of the staff and were trying hard to support two very experienced colleagues suffering from stress. One ultimately retired, a loss to the profession, and the other found a new lease of life, took on additional responsibility temporarily then gained a substantive promotion. We did find over the years that a change of role could have a huge impact upon staff motivation and performance – almost as though old baggage was left behind and the world viewed through fresh eyes.

In order to create the possibility for staff movement and promotion we published a new structure for the school. This described both academic and pastoral responsibilities and made clear that promotion could be achieved by moving between these two broad areas of professional experience and by having a concern for both. We also indicated that specific responsibility over and above teaching was an expectation of all staff, with or without remuneration, and encouraged staff to see their own profiles in this manner. An example was our identification of senior tutors in each year group, capable of acting as Head of Year in the event of absence. All of this predated later, national, moves to establish key stage coordinators to oversee the entire experience of students at each level of their schooling.

In addition to the pastoral and academic strands of the structure we described the 'third strand'. This was all the support elements required for the organisation to function well. This strand was characterised as of equal importance in the life of the school and was to be under the direction of a bursar. In order to make the support more transparent we assigned specific admin staff to the upper and lower school respectively.

For the following academic year, we advertised for a Head of Lower School, a Bursar, an additional Deputy Head and staff in Maths, English, Special Needs and Design Technology. There was a determination here to increase our management strength. We had reached a point, financially, where this was possible and, if the school was to take advantage of developing opportunities, we needed to make some very good appointments.

There was a mass of activity in the school requiring management oversight. After Ofsted we were concentrating upon literacy and numeracy strategies and had undertaken a full post-16 review. Curriculum leaders were still focussing on issues of assessment and planning as an entity and were working on departmental action plans. The role of Senior and Middle management in driving up standards was becoming more sophisticated and we were interrogating our schemes of work, conducting our most detailed exam analysis from the previous year's results and setting well – informed targets for improvement. We had, in particular, more refined targets for students on IEPs (Individual Education Plans) logged on the school database. The quality of data available was improving dramatically with the adoption of refined predictive tests (Midyis and Yellis) allowing for better pupil forecasts. We were also reviewing all attendance and punctuality procedures and our entire marketing strategy.

In the latter case we were considering two proposals. Firstly, that **there were significant benefits attached to marketing the school to the students themselves, both those presently in the school and those in the Primaries.** This built upon the earlier idea of the fireworks displays, the quality graduations, the daytime Youth Club, student responsibility and the recent pop concerts. It meant creating genuine ownership for the students through identification with the school and its activities.

Secondly, and linked, was **a proposal to market learning.** We found ourselves in a favoured situation here, as our newly enhanced computer facilities were a huge attraction to visiting youngsters. We also genuinely believed that we were developing good quality learning experiences across the curriculum and that these should prove to be inherently attractive.

The students were benefiting from a Breakfast Club and a Homework Club – both of which were popular – and the Girls only club, at lunchtimes and in the evenings, was a runaway success. A small group of girls made a presentation of their work at Westminster. This was fitting, as there was significant work around equal opportunities underway in the school.

While problems generated by students in a secondary school are relatively monotonous, we were concerned about the racial undertones to many of our issues at the time. We had a particularly aggressive group of black girls in Year 8 and 9 and they were causing problems in and out of school. Their parents were very concerned and had been quite effective in curbing the poor behaviour in the evenings. There was, however, friction on the school bus between this group and groups of Muslim girls who, quite rightly, wished to travel without threats and interference. We had a series of complaints and parental meetings, involved the Race Equality Management Team – who were always highly supportive, and stepped up our supervision of the buses.

While we could not realistically travel on the buses we did inspect them nightly before they departed. We had a rule that only girls were allowed on the top deck and encouraged drivers to return to the school in the event of problems. We also, periodically, stopped the buses en route by driving ahead and flagging them down. Any boys on the top deck were put off the bus as were any students creating problems. Finally, we controlled access to the buses at the school and prevented unreliable students from travelling.

We took all complaints very seriously indeed. There were enough problems for our students travelling away from the school at night without jeopardising the only transport we had available. We expected, and generally achieved, a good standard from our students travelling on these overcrowded buses and we gave great support to the drivers. We received a collective letter of appreciation from the drivers employed by one contractor.

Problems are often unexpected and we found that a completely innocuous white boy in Year 10, from a decent family, was becoming aggressive and that some of this was directed at black students. Much of his behaviour appeared attention seeking and self-destructive. We quickly exhausted any remedies we had on site and exclusion was inevitable.

Unfortunately, for a school in our physical position, exclusion did not necessarily mean that a problem had been removed. Far from it. This boy appeared, nightly, on the street corner accompanied by other youths with dogs. This behaviour was hugely intimidating and, yet again, warranted a permanent police presence. The situation remained volatile for months.

Two other student behaviour issues stood out that year and both concerned inappropriate behaviour. In the first case a 14 year old boy had touched a student teacher and she had, rightly, made a complaint. This was a very difficult situation in which other students required interviewing, there was strong representation from the family, who made a counter complaint, and there was some division amongst the staff over whether the teacher's naïve overfamiliarity with students was an issue. We achieved an untidy solution by excluding the boy and using the Unit to keep him out of mainstream education for an extended period. As with many issues we had to gauge whether a permanent exclusion was appropriate and whether it would survive an independent appeal.

The second serious issue went to a Governors Appeal, an LEA Appeal and an Independent Appeal. This concerned another 14 year old with a record of aggression and violence including sexually aggressive behaviour towards girls. We permanently excluded the boy for an assault on a female member of staff when she became caught in the middle of a fight. This assault had been quite deliberate and, in my experience, was very uncommon.

Yet again the Chair of Governors and I were shocked at the extent to which we had to go to 'fight our corner' and protect both staff and students from the behaviour of such individuals. As ever, we were treated quite roughly by the panels who insisted upon the boy being allowed back into the school – despite us informing them that he was absent from the Appeal meeting due to being on remand for a rape in the neighbourhood! I declared that staff would not teach the boy and we won the case. Again the total cost of dealing with this one individual had been huge.

The cost is significant. **On the one hand, difficult students take time and resources from the majority. On the other hand, this is a necessary investment in the creation of a decent environment and a respectable community.**

While I was concerned to deal with problems and to maintain systems and standards I was also concerned to move forward emphasising our ethos – Hard Work, Achievement, Respectability, Personal Fulfilment – and to ensure that the majority of students were gaining substantially from the experience of being at Shorefields. I took the view that they deserved the best. The majority of students exhibited high standards of decency and respectability and I found dealing with them to be very fulfilling. They deserved loyalty and hard work from me and from the staff in their school.

The Good Citizenship Award, sponsored by John Moores University and a local Housing Association, was entirely in tune with the ethos we were promoting in the school and we received excellent publicity when we presented the annual award.

This was also featured in our weekly newsletter, which, by the end of 1998, had reached its 200th edition. Given that our distribution list included all students and staff in Shorefields, all councillors and all local Primary Schools we had probably, by this time, produced around 400,000 of these self congratulatory and promotional newsletters. They were of course only one element in the marketing strategy. A strategy, which, above all else, revolved around images of confidence and organisational improvement.

An element of our strategy in desperate need of change was the Primary liaison programme. Firstly, because it was outdated and, in some respects, damaging and counter productive. Secondly, because Liverpool, as a whole, had been experiencing a very low birth rate and our area of the city recorded the lowest numbers entering reception classes. If we were to survive we needed to be in the strongest possible position to handle this demographic problem.

I was spending an increasing amount of time with the Primary Heads dealing with our common issues and developing the message that Shorefields was the natural secondary school of choice for their pupils. We were sharing common concerns over attendance, benchmarking issues and the progress of the EAZ. Meanwhile, on every occasion that I stepped away from direct involvement with the programme of promotional visits into the Primaries, it degenerated into a dry as dust, half hearted, world weary, 'jobs worth' of an exercise. This was seriously undermining, particularly when the Primary Heads started making complaints. One thing they hated was being taken for granted and patronised by secondary colleagues.

I produced a summary of Primary Liaison activity including all our standard points of contact and dates relevant to the LEA's Admissions Section. It also included a menu of activities around which we could develop a meaningful relationship with our feeder schools. This encompassed the organisation of curriculum work, the delivery of newsletters, competitions, assistance with reprographics, use of our facilities, motivational talks to Year 6 and personal contact with staff. Thereafter, my role should have been to monitor the effectiveness of this programme and provide support. In reality, I spent too much time micro-managing and much of our primary liaison at the time was relatively ineffective. **Micro-management is exhausting and, generally, fails to produce results.**

The extent, to which the relationship with primary schools was a concern, is indicated by the number of visits I made to our local schools at the start of 1999. These visits were in pursuance of EAZ business, for marketing purposes or by invitation and included – Windsor St., Park Hill, Beaufort St., Matthew Arnold, Tiber St., St. Michael in the Hamlet, Smithdown, St. Silas, Granby St., St. Finbar's, St. Hugh's, Our Lady of Mount Carmel and St Malachy's. The last four were significant in that they were Roman Catholic schools with whom we, previously, had little involvement. The final school on the list, St. Malachy's, was of great importance in that the headteacher believed Shorefields should be the school of choice for her Year 6 boys rather than any of the available Catholic schools. This was unprecedented.

While we had always taken a handful of children from the Catholic sector, the turning point had come when the head at St. Malachy's realised that we genuinely had a concern for the welfare of students. Furthermore, as the head, I was prepared to have a dialogue with anyone – parents, students, Primary colleagues – over creating the best situation for any students transferring to the school. It was not uncommon for a Year 7 parent, with concerns about their child's progress at Shorefields, to speak to a teacher, or the head, at the Primary school. That was an indication of the closeness of some of the relationships. Periodically, I received phone calls from Primary colleagues asking me to deal with problems and **the PR value of demonstrating effectiveness was tremendous.**

The relationship with St. Malachy's progressed very rapidly indeed. I was invited to meet the Chair of Governors and the parish priest and **we generated further momentum by nominating members of the Shorefields staff as 'teacher advisors on faith issues'.** We had advisors from Anglican, Muslim and Catholic backgrounds. None of this was popular with the Archdiocese and we caused further upset when I met with large groups of Catholic parents in order to discuss secondary transfer. **The simple truth is that most parents want a reasonable school, relatively close by where they believe their children will be secure.**

During the year I met regularly over the issue of funding for our Youth and Community staff. Again, this involved a pointless amount of repetitive work as LEA officers used the device of repeatedly 're-viewing' the deployment of staff as an opportunity to explore cost cutting opportunities. Despite agreeing, over and over again to joint planning, to helping deliver the Youth Service strategic plan and to an area wide responsibility for our youth workers nothing ever materialised. This was an unfair, insecure and unhealthy environment for the youth workers.

Having experienced a poverty of educational resources, both before and upon taking up headship, I was determined that **we would find financial security by accessing multiple funding streams.** Unfortunately, this involved dozens of meetings around the Education Action Zone, Excellence in Cities and our SRB/ESF projects.

In the latter case we were accessing funds to run the Unit, to pay for a librarian, to provide study support, to pay staff to run motivational programmes and for foreign trips. I was a member of the SRB/ESF evaluation group in the area and was appreciating the protection of a 'closed shop'. This is not a criticism, nor a comment upon the integrity of the hard working social professionals in the area. It is simply a practical and historical fact. In order to even be aware of funding possibilities one needed to be in a 'loop'. In order to understand the demands of the bidding processes one needed experience of effective bid writing to arcane criteria. Finally, a new bid would need to be extraordinarily well constructed, and avoid duplication, in order to succeed at evaluation stage, against ongoing projects.

The wider scene, involving developments across Liverpool, included discussion and negotiation over a Private Finance Initiative (PFI) to handle our desperate premises issues. We had repeated meetings, with the Clerk of Works, during the year and, when governors and councillors were present, we appeared to make progress. The problem, however, was that no appreciable work was ever undertaken and, therefore, the time devoted to these meetings was broadly misspent.

We had also established a governing Forum for the Education Action Zone and had a heated meeting with the Assistant Director of Education and Chief Inspector at which we demanded LEA support in developing the project as a legitimate element of Liverpool's Education Development Plan. We needed a timetable of planning activities between December '98 and March '99 in order to qualify for a grant of £30,000 development funding that May. This would enable us to 'work up' the bid to the point where real development funding would be available from September '99 for a January 2000 start.

As an individual school we were pursuing a mass of individual funding ideas. Littlewoods was, of course, a highly significant sponsor and we attempted to capitalise on the status of this support at every turn. We were also involved in a relatively bizarre series of discussions over a possible transfer of funds from the Liverpool Institute Trust. This prestigious school had closed down leaving, apparently, significant wealth and assets in the Trust. It was alleged that the wealth of the Trust had been dissipated but a local community activist claimed to have traced the missing fortune, particularly missing art works. I was offered the Trust funds providing I agreed to Shorefields becoming 'The New Liverpool Institute', demolishing the school and dismissing all the staff. In the proposal I could, generously, keep my own job and the new Board of Governors would guarantee permanent membership to our activist benefactor.

Despite the strangeness of this offer we did hold a number of exploratory meetings. We were never shown provenance for the existence of the funds and quickly backed away. This did not prevent some awkward press releases and hysterical debate on the internet between old boys of the Institute. Our 'benefactor' also generated unrest in Dingle pubs and a number of Governors felt compromised by our unwillingness to pursue the matter. **Be careful who chooses you as a friend and beware of strangers bearing gifts.**

Still intent upon pursuing sponsorship, I contacted Mohammed al-Fayed, the owner of Harrods. He had supported a number of Muslim projects. We had a large number of Muslim students. He was bound to help!

I was very surprised to be able to contact his office so directly. He was away at the time but his PA was more than happy to discuss the issue. It transpired that Mr al-Fayed had pledged support for an entire school and was focussing his educational support in that direction. Despite this being, effectively, a rejection it was a nice response and, therefore, quite encouraging.

Following this, our newly established PTA produced an appeal letter and the deputy and I competed to see what response we could achieve by canvassing businesses. The response was relatively poor. We did, though, receive some 'in kind' support and free publicity.

An odd example of publicity arose when the manager of a city centre building society contacted me to ask if we would like to be the recipients of free second-hand computers. He had a scheme whereby his branch would collect unwanted business machines from Liverpool offices then pass them on to us. We were both interviewed on local radio and were animated in our enthusiasm for this latest education/business link. To my knowledge no computers were ever collected by the building society but the publicity was of greater value to us than outdated hardware.

We had three additional sources of unofficial income within school. Firstly, the school tuck shop, which was being run as a mini-enterprise by students under the direction of the Head of Maths. Open twice daily, the profits were mounting rapidly and we agreed that a large percentage be paid into school fund. Secondly, the Youth Club tuck shop, which was competing with the canteen in the volume of snacks served daily. We could rely upon this to resource and update much of the equipment in the Youth Centre, including the purchase of televisions and computer games. Thirdly, the school levy, collected termly. This should have produced around £3,000 annually which, at the time, would have supported a variety of trips and visits. The variation, between tutor groups, in the amount collected was enormous and this reflected the enthusiasm, or lack of it, on the part of the tutors.

Finally, we had two highly questionable schemes. The first involved the sale and distribution of scratch cards to parents. For this we would receive a high percentage of the return. While this was ethically unsound, due to the promotion of gambling, it was also organisationally difficult and we did not pursue it.

The second involved McDonald's who proposed to build a diner, opposite our Annexe on Aigburth Rd., on the site of a derelict petrol station. There was significant opposition to this from local schools who felt that it would encourage truancy. Sensing a sponsorship opportunity, I wrote in support of the development. I genuinely saw no problem and felt that McDonald's would improve the site, provide employment opportunities and create a local amenity. We didn't achieve sponsorship as such but did receive endless vouchers we could use as rewards. As far as I am aware the diner had no impact upon truancy whatsoever.

All this activity was contemporary with a move towards 'value for money' in education. The questions we were asking internally were around the impact of spending upon attainment and we were concerned to generate the funds to support heads of department in planning development. **Access to money is power.** Without 'spare' funds we would not have had the capacity to respond to, and to influence, the outcome of our departmental reviews. These reviews were effective because middle managers were able to demonstrate to their teams that there was tangible support for change. To classroom teachers this generally manifested itself in more books, stationery, materials and equipment. The things that matter! While our annual budget was carefully constructed and incorporated development funding, a capital sinking fund, and so on, we really needed as much capacity as possible to respond to in year developments.

The academic year was very busy indeed with an explosion of meetings and initiatives. These included meetings with – governors, staff, parents, police, EAZ, EIC, the student forum, Friends of Shorefields, PTA, pastoral and curriculum meetings, LEA, Headteachers, SRB/ESF, the Law Centre, community groups and tenants. In total I recorded 550 formal meetings. These lasted a minimum of 45 minutes and many were full days. It was helpful that our calendar was far more detailed and prescriptive and that a better framework of business was emerging than previously. I had a schedule of individual and collective management meetings with the deputy, two senior teachers, the site manager, the Chair of Governors, LEA Advisor and the Governors Executive group.

I was still teaching and found that this conflicted with the demands of off site meetings. **Being out of school also detracted from a fundamental aspect of management – WTJ – walking the job.**

Meanwhile, there was a flood of correspondence relating to the major new projects we were engaged with and in the form of consultation over proposed new government initiatives. It was not possible, administratively, to 'field' much of this material firstly, because we had an inadequate management structure and secondly, because much was on the level of Headteacher and governance. I had an ongoing triage system for quickly prioritising administrative tasks and this saved me from becoming overwhelmed. **It is essential to maintain a perspective and a control over administrative workload.**

I noted, in June '99, that the school needed a capacity to respond to future initiatives. I was certainly hoping that our new appointments for September were going to help with this. My ideal was a school of self developers and self motivators. We needed colleagues efficient in operational routine and with strategic foresight. Fortunately, we had a core of highly professional colleagues who, as a group, were now the 'critical mass' needed to move the school forwards.

We had new staff joining us from two Liverpool schools facing closure. We were pleased to take these colleagues for themselves but also because of the 'bumping' arrangement in Liverpool at that point. This meant that by helping to avoid a redundancy we would be supported in gaining a pre-mature retirement for a member of our staff. The retirement terms, for staff over 50, were very generous indeed with up to 10 years enhancement of pension. There is no doubt that, without this scheme, we would not have achieved the staff turnover necessary to improve the school. Subsequently, when any such arrangements ceased, there was a core of staff who had lost their expectation of leaving the profession in their early 50's. More importantly, there was no negotiable route out in respect of those staff who had exhausted themselves during a career in an inner city environment and were now ineffective.

By the end of the academic year we felt very much part of the mainstream of educational development. In fact we were at the cutting edge. The development of the Education Action Zone initiative had been very successful and we were working closely with all our neighbouring Primary Schools. Our involvement in the EAZ had, ironically, lifted staff morale considerably. We were in receipt of substantial Ethnic Minority Achievement Grant funds, to the displeasure of other city schools with predominantly white populations.

The new and overarching Excellence in Cities programme, of-fering substantial additional funds to Liverpool was looking very promising and, as a school, we had been heavily involved in the development of the framework for this.

We had persuaded the Governors that the school needed in-volvement in the new PFI, Private Finance Initiative, available to Liverpool to rebuild or refurbish schools. Despite the condition of the building there was some concern about this, mainly around the terms and conditions of ancillary staff who would transfer to the chosen contractor. In effect we were opting to mortgage ourselves for thirty years and agreeing to pass over responsibility for facilities management and catering. We would pay an annual premium and, in return would have the school rebuilt or refurbished.

At this important time for the city, however, there was chaos at the level of the Local Authority. There had been a poor Ofsted re-port and the Director and most of his senior team had departed. We had a temporary Director and consultants were advising the LEA and the DFE. This upheaval had put real pressure on schools with an extraordinary number of meetings and with a decision to draft in heads, temporarily, to fill officers roles the following term. This was not an easy time for us as an organisation, generally judged to be something of a maverick, and with vested interest in relat-ing directly to the LEA rather than through the Heads organisation. Nevertheless, despite another challenging year, Shorefields ap-peared to be in the ascendancy. We believed that we had confirma-tion of 185 year 7 students for September and were benefiting from excellent publicity around the EAZ.

LEARNING POINTS YEAR SIX

- It is necessary to look beyond short-term gains when engaged in the long game of school survival.
- There is a tension between encouraging self-motivation and independent action, on the part of managers, on the one hand and maintaining appropriate accountability to the corporate plan on the other.
- Always involve experienced consultants in disputes around caretaking and cleaning.
- Where possible engage with professional personnel services in cases of performance and capability.
- Professionals can learn from models of management relating to manual or supervised staff.
- In order for a team to work effectively there must be general oversight of the work and an ability to order and prioritise tasks.
- Professionals, in any sphere, tend to be very difficult to manage.

- We need 'a theory of skill learning' to conceptualise the professional journey a novice teacher is undertaking.

- Each department in the school requires a detailed and thorough review – preferably annually.

- Team leaders are critically important in school effectiveness and deserve maximum support.

- A good idea is not the same as a good deed.

- Organisations suffer from the curse of staff making assumptions.

- It is easy to assume that a professional knows how to do things properly. This is unwarranted.

- Staff need training in project management and this requires the application of highly consistent procedures.

- Serious issues of performance and capability or misconduct require a principled and consistent approach.

- It is essential that managers record all problems, perceived problems and complaints in order to even have a dialogue with a colleague.

- Not only do young people deserve protection but we must also understand that the whole image of the school can be distorted, in the eyes of parents, as a result of the behaviour of an individual teacher.

- Punctuality, to work or lessons, is a contractual responsibility for teachers.

- It is worth paying part-time staff for attending In-service days.

- Schools should create the widest opportunities for staff to gain management experience.

- A supportive 'third strand' within school structures – not academic and not pastoral – is a vital element in the success of the organisation.

- There are significant benefits to marketing the school to the students themselves.

- A school can market 'learning'.

- Schools should assert control over the quality of the experience students have travelling to and from school by school bus.

- Exclusion does not necessarily remove a problem.

- The cost of dealing with problems is a necessary investment in creating a decent environment and a respectable community.

- A marketing strategy should revolve around issues of confidence and organisational improvement.

- Schools need to plan a strategy in advance of demographic changes.

- Micro-management is exhausting and, generally, fails to produce results.

- The PR value of demonstrating effectiveness to Primary colleagues is tremendous.

- Most parents want a reasonable school, relatively close by, where they believe their children will be secure.

- There is greater financial security through accessing multiple funding streams.

- Beware who chooses you as a friend and beware of strangers bearing gifts.

- Access to money is power.

- You must find time for WTJ – walking the job.

- It is essential to maintain a perspective and a control over administrative workload.

START OF SEVENTH YEAR OF
HEADSHIP SEPTEMBER '99

T HE START OF TERM could not have been more upbeat. The predicted number of students, 180, had arrived and our exam results had improved dramatically, from 9.5% gaining 5 A-C grades at GCSE to 21%. We had only excluded 10 students the previous year, which was remarkably good. We were also looking at the implications of involvement in the educational PFI, Private Finance Initiative, involving a number of Liverpool schools. This offered the opportunity, at some future point, to deal with our dreadful premises problems.

The formal approval of our Action Zone status was imminent and we had been selected, under Excellence in Cities, to be the site of a City Learning Centre (CLC). Apparently we had demonstrated the ability to work with grant funded projects and were seen as sufficiently entrepreneurial to make things happen. This was a multi million pound initiative around information and communication technology and innovative approaches to teaching and learning. As ever the announcement of our CLC status was greeted with hostility and serious challenge from a handful of other schools in the city. We did, nevertheless, set about, planning the new CLC in order for the overall Liverpool proposal to go before the DFE. We read all the available literature, understood the principles and were clear about the expected outputs. We produced an initial plan which modified and improved our existing buildings, provided a substantial range of computer hardware and related technology, outlined the anticipated curriculum usage, enabled full community and partner access, was staffed and managed and crucially was closely budgeted. Privately we had also considered an exit strategy for the funding and management of the CLC beyond the life of the project. The curriculum leaders in the school did an outstanding job of working through the possibilities for their areas and helping to create an initial map of how the new technology would raise standards.

As part of the Excellence in Cities, subsequently Excellence in Liverpool, submission our CLC plans were accepted by the DFE.

Early in the year behaviour in the school and the quality of discipline were both very sound and we were considering keeping all students on site all day. While this was generally the case, there were exceptions. We were still allowing students out at lunchtime with an 'exeat' which, in effect, was a contract with individual parents for them to take responsibility for their sons and daughters at home. There were numerous problems with this arrangement and, of course, **even the best system can be subverted.**

Due to the location of the school the only students able to walk home and back in the lunch period were white. This seemed inherently unfair and also produced a distorted and unhelpful social situation on site during the lunch hour. Staff were working well at creating a harmonious racially mixed educational environment during the day and this was being undermined by a degree of unplanned segregation between twelve thirty and one thirty.

The second problem with the 'exeats' was that parents failed to keep their part of the deal. We were frequently finding students around the area when they should have been at home. Withdrawing 'exeats', and the ensuing argument with parents, was immensely time consuming.

Strangely, even the very best students and the most support-ive families generated problems around this issue. Understandably, some youngsters would go home, eat and then become bored and want to return to see friends. The very fact that they returned too early was a significant problem. Our system for guaranteeing the welfare of everyone on site involved all exits from the site being locked or controlled. It also involved major areas of the school being locked down in order for staff to be concentrated around the canteen, youth club and sports areas. If staff wanted to run a club or see a group of students then they had to collect them from the can-teen quad and arrange access back into the locked building. In these circumstances, any individual presenting themselves at the main entrance and being allowed in during the lunch period would need the services of a caretaker or key holder to negotiate the building.

Finally, administering an 'exeat' system was time consuming and detracted from other business. The distribution of 'exeats' via tutors was always inefficient and the database needed constant modification. The staff time required to monitor exit doors, check passes and control entrance at one thirty was exorbitant.

We gave substantial advance notice and informed all parents that 'exeats' were being withdrawn and most were very coopera-tive. As ever, their main concern was that we might allow some students out and therefore enable their sons and daughters to com-plain and to pressurise them. **Parents need protecting against the demands of their own children.**

A minority of parents and students were, unfortunately, incred-ibly difficult. We heard every conceivable argument for retaining the 'exeat' – eating disorders, bullying at lunchtime, special diets, vague medical reasons, agoraphobia, supervision needed while eat-ing, caring for siblings, caring for parents, dislike of school meals, an inability to eat school chips, an addiction to lunchtime televi-sion and, finally, recourse to the European Convention on Human

Rights.

We challenged all of this and, in time, prevailed. There were obvious risks to unsupervised young people in the area and there were considerable educational and social benefits to staying on site. **We dealt with opposition by accommodating it** – offering to produce special meals, providing one to one supervision, creating the 'Girl's Club', providing large screen televisions and computer games.

It was apparent that any child or parent arguing over an 'exeat', in the face of the new school policy, had a significant range of problems. We never, for example, managed to persuade the anorexic, who could only eat McDonald's food, to stay on site but she was rarely in school anyway and left a short while later. Girls like her were really colluding in a form of domestic abuse whereby they provided companionship to their relatively young mothers, helped look after siblings and existed in a limited world of daytime television, the supermarket and visits to family and neighbours in the same street.

As with many other successful initiatives it was necessary to think through the reasons for and the implications of change, to plan it carefully, to communicate clearly and well in advance and to convey the complete conviction that it would be successful.

Within twelve months we had won over even the most intransigent and had only one remaining parent demanding access to their child each lunchtime. In order to maintain the policy we refused an 'exeat' and insisted on a daily request for the child to leave the site.

While an issue such as lunch passes might appear trivial it is an example of the mundane life of an organisation, which serves to define the experience for the participants. Other examples may be toilet breaks, canteen facilities, car parking, office space, access to photocopiers, telephone use, dress codes or working hours. When we, eventually, improved the facilities the advantages of all students being on site all day were really significant particularly for access to a wide range of clubs and activities and, crucially, for Year 11 to prepare for exams. We also eradicated the interminable off site problems which had previously arisen during the lunch hour and which had dominated our afternoons.

It is easy to see why some schools have opted for 'continental day' arrangements whereby they abandon the lunch period and end the day earlier. This may avoid significant issues of supervision but, in my view, is educationally, socially and morally unsound. **The spaces between activities may be as valuable as the activities themselves in a general educative and social sense.** Not only are schools with 'continental days' abandoning the opportunity for informal and semi formal development to take place, they may also be significantly disadvantaging children from the lowest socio-economic backgrounds by denying the time for an adequate meal. They also risk exhausting the staff and limiting the work opportunities of all the parents.

Our buoyant start to the '99-2000 academic year was helped by the fact that we now had three buses dedicated to transporting children from and to the Granby and Smithdown areas each morning and evening. This was a significant boost to the long-term stability for which we were struggling. **There was no doubt that parental confidence was greater with a school bus service than with the prospect of using the public service routes.** Furthermore, it offered the potential for us to have much greater control at the end of each day.

Without doubt our exit and bus duty had the characteristics of a military operation. We had abandoned the arrangement, familiar to many schools, whereby different staff supervised the students leaving the school each day on a rotational basis. This simply didn't work. While there is generally, and quite reasonably, a reluctance amongst teachers to undertake duties, that was not the core of the problem. **It was always apparent to me that good order depended upon expectations, routine and vigilance.** All of these are undermined by a rotational system of supervision.

A teacher undertaking an infrequent duty is disempowered.

They can have very little sense of ownership or responsibility. **It is difficult, even for a highly experienced person, to confidently demonstrate the knowledge, skill and field of perception required for good supervision if they are unfamiliar with the duty area. Young people are intuitively aware of this.**

In addition, staff on infrequent rotas regularly arrive late or forget the duty altogether. It can be demonstrated that for schools in challenging circumstances the absence of supervision leads to trouble. **This is an 'iron law'. Where there is no supervision, albeit briefly, there *will* be trouble.** While we had already made the case, years earlier, for staff punctuality to lessons and duties even going as far as providing a definition of 'being at post', this expectation failed where the arrangement for allocating duties was poor. In these circumstances frustration is a wasted emotion as the problem is systemic.

While we had some very strong and reliable staff on supervision in the middle of the day, undertaking the same sessions each week, the exit and bus arrangements proved too difficult to manage in this way.

It was now habitually the case that our handful of senior staff were on duty outside the school every day at 3.20. In fact we were always outside earlier than that scanning for potential problems and speaking to anyone in the vicinity of the school to establish their identities. Two of us would walk, immediately, to the corner of the road, where most friction was likely to occur, and one managed the loading and departure of the buses – a huge undertaking in its own right. We were in constant contact by mobile phone.

The aim was to secure the welfare of our students with low-key vigilance and immediate intervention where there was a real problem. The objective was to identify any potential troublemakers loitering in the area, let them know they were identified and diffuse problems. We needed the students to move away from the immediate area of the school as quickly as possible. We tried to do this quietly, with encouragement and, where necessary, only dealing with small numbers at a time. As we were the senior staff we achieved cooperation from the majority of students. Neighbours came to know us well as did parents collecting children from the local Primary school.

Interestingly, a greater staff presence actually made the situation less manageable and less secure. On those occasions where we had asked for emergency help from colleagues we sometimes found that a difficult situation had become a drama. Unfamiliar with the duty routine outside and, understandably, intimidated by the huge numbers of students and the presence of strangers some staff resorted to shouting and bawling. This amplified any ongoing problem, entertained the students and actually slowed down their dispersal. In fairness to staff we occasionally had the same problem with Police officers.

Over a period of ten years there were hundreds and hundreds of occasions when we had a police presence. This was always to protect the students from attack. These officers tended to be either from the Merseyside Police Community Section or from an Area Unit very familiar with our issues. They were all excellent people and hugely supportive. Occasionally, however, a new officer would present difficulty. One particular example was the occasion when a pregnant policewoman waded into a minor scuffle between a group of Year 10 boys. We had to rescue her from the consequences of her own enthusiasm. She lacked the authority and the power to do anything constructive in that situation.

There were clear advantages to having the senior staff undertaking these external duties. We had a complete consistency of approach between people who trusted each other. We were always present on duty and came to know local issues very well indeed. Understandably, it was crucially important for the image of the school that the students were able to come and go without interference. **The sight of large numbers of happy, well dressed, well mannered young people carrying bags and equipment is the best advertisement a school can have.** We had to support their right to travel without interference. Because we were there every night we could name dozens of youths from the area should it be necessary to invoke police action. We had the authority and the power to control difficult situations and make immediate decisions such as calling emergency services or imposing an exclusion from the school.

The consequences of using the senior staff in this manner were significant. While we maintained better order than any alternative arrangement it was at a huge cost. Our attendance at meetings held at the end of the day was easily compromised. If, for example, the buses were delayed we had a supervisory and welfare problem until they arrived. On occasions we travelled on the buses or intercepted them en route in order to check behaviour. Any indication of trouble in the neighbourhood led us away from the school, usually on foot, to ensure the dispersal of the students. This could be very time consuming. We still had a handful of students using the public service routes and were still dealing with problems around the bus stops. We were frequently threatened by local youths but seldom challenged.

We occasionally ordered taxis to guarantee the safe return home of individual students. There were many occasions when parents arrived at the school, before we had finished our duty, in order to report incidents on the route home. They had to be dealt with as did any students we had sent back into the building while on duty. Finally, any matter involving the more formal involvement of the police such as an assault, external damage to one of the buses or the presence of offensive weapons, required a report, which was a lengthy business.

Undoubtedly, again, it is better to be proactive, to prevent problems occurring rather than deal with the consequences later. While there was huge personal satisfaction in seeing our students leaving the school and the area in good order, good spirits and in safety it really was regrettable that we were, in effect, struggling with a wider societal problem. Our issue, 'bus duty', sounds parochial and immature. In effect it was a key defining feature of our lives. The good order of the organisation, day to day, depended upon the previous evening's evacuation being satisfactory. Long term it was a significant marketing issue. We were not, however, able to budget for this use of staff time at this point. In comparison to schools without these problems, our lives were distracted and organisationally this high level of supervision was exhausting. I wonder what we could have achieved as a school had our circumstances been different.

We had experienced an inter regnum in the LEA with a Senior Assistant Director acting up followed by the secondment of a neighbouring Director and then the appointment of Liverpool's own Head of Education and Lifelong Learning with three new Heads of Service. At school level it was a very difficult period of time dominated by uncertainty, lack of clarity over central support and anxiety over the role of the Secondary Heads, in particular. The voices of the largest schools in the city were increasingly dominating the debate over educational funding to the frustration of Primary colleagues, of whom they were almost entirely dismissive, and any school representing a minority concern such as ourselves. The news, in the first term, that a handful of these headteachers had been seconded to senior officer posts in the LEA was greeted with dismay. A number of Secondary headteachers were widely regarded as self-centred, rapacious individuals, devoid of objectivity. It seemed inconceivable that any such person could now be in a position to determine aspects of our funding and support.

By November '99 we had made the appointment of our EAZ Director. This had been a complex process and we were assisted, principally, by the Dingle SRB/ESF Partnership. Having requested help from the LEA over the organisation of interviews and personnel support, in the event of contractual issues being raised, we received none and, as a school, we organised and initially paid for hotel bookings, catering, the interview procedure and the clerking of the event in which all schools in our area participated.

It is fair to say that the Toxteth Cluster of headteachers had, by now, exhausted themselves over the EAZ application. While it offered the only opportunity to gain resources in order to raise standards, the whole process entailed a punishing cycle of meetings and, worryingly, took key staff out of their schools.

Having appointed our new EAZ Director, there was a communal sense of relief that the process of developing the EAZ would now continue in professional hands with heads contributing at a non-executive level.

This was not to be the case and the principal members of the cluster found a further significant increase in workload. We were victims here of our own optimism and also of the 'grass roots' nature of our submission. At the time Liverpool was successful in gaining two EAZs. Ours, the DGTEAZ (Dingle, Granby, Toxteth EAZ) and the larger Speke-Garston EAZ in the far south of the city. In the latter case the model of development had been entirely different and the local Partnership had driven the submission, taken full responsibility for organisational matters and had invited schools to participate in the educational programmes. There was, of course, consultation in Speke but the significant difference was that our EAZ was actually generated by the schools themselves.

Having appointed our Director we really had no lead organisation to fall back upon. We approached the LEA over office accommodation in anticipation of this being a foregone conclusion. Informally it had been indicated that the approach would be welcomed as part of the new School Effectiveness/Raising Standards agenda. Clearly, shared accommodation would enable our EAZ Director to work closely with LEA officers. Our approach to the LEA over accommodation was, however, rejected by the same seconded head, now in charge of accommodation, who had objected to our CLC status.

The role of EAZ Director in these circumstances was very challenging. The organisation of office space, furnishings, ICT, staff, payroll, financial management and oversight and the negotiation of the EAZ programme and targets with the DFE were the dominant concerns. All of this involved heads from the Cluster. Furthermore the new Director had to make sense of the priorities we had lived with for several years and could articulate strongly but which were less clear in the codified language of our submission. More meetings, more negotiation around targets, more heated debate over genuinely **trying to bring about improvement in the face of an increasingly bureaucratised initiative as it moved from political sound bite to over regulated delivery.**

In addition to spending an extraordinary number of hours on ongoing EAZ business, as the chair of the new Executive, I was also committed to the development of the City Learning Centre on our site. There were three nominated sites in the city at that time – ourselves in Toxteth, Speke in the south and Croxteth in the east. The Excellence in Cities coordinator arranged for the appointment of consultant architects to assist in drawing up the next stage of plans for the DFE and to manage each project through to completion. We organised further consultation with our staff and with other schools. Even at this early stage we were nervous about the architects. Having become very familiar with the DFE documents on City Learning Centres and having drawn up the initial plans on the basis of the educational benefits we could derive, with the widest access for everyone else, we had some immediate concerns.

Other than a handful of conceptual words, such as spatial and kinaesthetic, the architects could contribute nothing to a genuine impression of how the new CLC would raise standards. They were determined that the bulk of the finance available would be spent on a 'flagship' development with 'state of the art' architectural features. They, and they claimed the DFE, wanted the CLC to have a social and political as well as an educational impact.

Initially, our discussions focused on the development of an existing large space within the school. This ran contrary to our plans to refurbish and equip a range of spaces and to generate significant curriculum 'ownership'. It also, frustratingly, meant that we had to mount a vigorous defence of areas of the school required for curriculum delivery, such as the sports hall! The DFE were, of course, paying for this and we accepted that if they wanted a dramatic space then that was what they were going to get. It was clear, again, that **there is frequently a significant change in message from the initial policy idea to the practicalities of implementation. Furthermore, essentially good ideas can be hijacked for wider political purposes and can always suffocate under the weight of a mistrustful bureaucracy.**

A more important problem concerned the proportion of funding spent on buildings as opposed to equipment. The architects were determined, again, that they were going to create a large space, which would have dramatic impact. They envisaged soft furnishings and fountains leading to an environment with a semi industrial or commercial feel. The equipment available for student use would be minimal, perhaps thirty computers, as the 'space' was intended to be flexible and creative. Our own initial plans and costings, which had already received DFE approval, focussed on curriculum needs and, at that time, recognised the real shortage of IT in schools. Furthermore, we emphasised the remarkably low level of PC ownership in the area, probably the lowest in the country. If we were not careful our students, and those in similar schools, would be doubly disadvantaged in comparison with their middle class counterparts. Having no access to computers and the internet at home we judged it essential that the greatest access should be provided through the new CLC. **It is vital that professionals have the courage of their convictions, are clear in arguing for resources to raise standards and are unambiguous in how that can be achieved. Politicians and local and national government officials need this. Professionals in education, health, housing and welfare have a responsibility to be vigorously proactive.**

In the spirit of creating the greatest possible access for students we persuaded the architects to plan a development in the very centre of the school. This would involve the wholesale demolition of the existing reception lounge, caretaking facilities, secretarial offices, reprographics rooms and storage areas. This created a very large space indeed. With the architects we planned for this space to include five fully equipped work areas on four levels including an additional CAD/CAM (Computer aided design and manufacturing) suite built in one of the quads. We also planned two remote areas for Science and Music.

The plans were put out to tender and received a poor response from a number of firms who were more interested in building to a clear specification than entering into a design and build arrangement. Nevertheless, one firm (A) tendered for both CLC sites, negotiated a deliverable design with each school and the LEA and a date was set for a presentation meeting. At the eleventh hour we were asked to meet with a new builder, newcomer (B) to the process, in order to increase the sense of competition. We duly met, discussed the plans, and received a proposal back, which bore no relation to the needs of the school. In fact we were presented with the antithesis of what we regarded as educationally sound – a large prefabricated shed on the far end of the site, remote from the main building, inaccessible to students and staff and requiring its own entirely independent management and maintenance arrangements.

Furthermore the provision for extensive PC and internet access had gone. It was clear that a brisk desktop modelling and costing exercise had been undertaken with no regard to local requirements.

We were unperturbed by this as we understood the late bidder was merely a 'stalking horse' being used to extract best value for money. Furthermore, we had a written acknowledgement from earlier in the process, that each CLC host school would be able to choose the design most appropriate to its needs.

At the presentation meeting neither firm performed particularly well and, regardless of this, we chose our original developer. The LEA, the architects, the Excellence in Cities Coordinator and the other CLC host school opted for the 'stalking horse'. That was their prerogative.

We were then informed that one developer was being chosen to build both CLCs and that we must accept the last minute and wholly inadequate plans of the late entrant. Despite ferocious argument on our part, the panel was not for turning. We registered our total disagreement and left.

I spent the following morning attempting to persuade my colleague CLC headteacher, for whom the change of developer made only a marginal difference, to support our case. I was wholly unsuccessful. I then rang the DFE.

Fortunately, we had established excellent relations with the DFE advisor for Liverpool during the difficult process of gaining acceptance for the EAZ. The response was immediate. She was catching the first available train from London to Liverpool and asked for an emergency meeting with the Director of Education and ourselves.

Neither the Director, the new Head of Service nor the Coordinator had been involved with the EIC/CLC process as long as us and we had retained every scrap of correspondence. We presented our case very persuasively. The Director was told very simply that the DFE believed Shorefields was effectively raising standards and they expected our professional judgement to be supported on the matter of the CLC. A victory! **If you are working hard and doing the right thing it will be recognised when it matters and you need to call upon support.**

The following day the Head of Service rang to say that our preferred developer would not build on our site alone, for economic reasons, and that his plans were unacceptable for the other school. Furthermore, the alternative developer was not prepared to build to the plans we wanted. We were very deflated.

Fortunately, we had built a good relationship with developer (A) and I rang to implore them to continue. They simply could not do so. I rang again and asked for a meeting. They agreed to rework their figures. They then, however, declined to take on the job. I rang and spoke to their directors and, eventually, received an undertaking that they would take the work and that our CLC would develop as we had planned.

Work on the CLC began very quickly and it is a tribute to the staff, students and the builders that the school was able to operate at all during this process. We lost our main entrance, moved our reception, administration and reprographics to temporary accommodation and had to reroute students around the building site for more than a year.

It was, indeed, a substantial building site to have in the middle of a fully operational school. The whole front wall of the central block was removed to enable access for bulldozers and diggers. The side walls were enhanced to support new steelwork prior to the entire central block roof being replaced. The building of the new CAD/CAM rooms in the quad was particularly challenging as this was, in effect surrounded by a two-storey building. The only access was over the rooftops or by breaking through from the new CLC area. The use of the road outside the school was limited by all the work and we did have some issues with neighbours. On the whole, though, they were very supportive. The buses coped the parents, students and staff coped, but it was undeniably a very stressful period of time.

The general atmosphere in the school was good and there was a sense that genuine physical improvement was underway. Parents and other visitors were impressed and probably amazed at the high level of order in the school and the manner in which students were working despite the disruption. **Strangely enough, when the circumstances are particularly difficult, everyone can be very accommodating and people during adversity tend to rise to the occasion.**

Our relations with the press were extraordinarily good at this time. We had achieved excellent coverage in the Liverpool Echo, Daily Post and Merseymart since September. Later in the year, when the national school performance tables were published, we found ourselves named as one of the top performing schools in the country in a value added report produced by the Observer. We were feeling very buoyant.

While this was an exciting time educationally, there were serious challenges, at every level, around the development of strategies to use the new information technology flooding into schools. In a sense the technology itself was not new. What was different was the growing availability of PCs in schools, the use of the internet for educational purposes, the development of more sophisticated educational packages and the the use of peripheral equipment – digital cameras, interactive whiteboards and CAM machines. On a local, regional and national level the challenges were around resourcing in the first instance and then around the benefits of connectivity, innovation and on-line curriculum.

The development of the CLC obviously put us in the forefront of this debate but we were also, like other schools, struggling to reconcile the ICT developments, underway, which depended upon different funding streams. Our Resource Centre, funded by MESH and Littlewoods stood alone with slow internet access. The CLC was yet to come on line. Our computer rooms, for curriculum use were desperately outdated. We had two new lines of funding we could use to enhance provision generally. These related to 'social inclusion' and the National Grid for Learning, NGFL. We decided to rationalise the equipment we had on site and lease three new suites of PCs with an upgraded internet specification. The installation was to be completed during August for a September start. This was typical of the independent and somewhat ad hoc solutions schools were arriving at. The pace of development in the city was generally poor, schools were making their own strategic decisions and the secondary heads spent too much of their time challenging and criticising the role of the LEA.

Despite the huge influx of resources onto the site, it would take us years to establish connectivity between the equipment we had in school belonging to Shorefields and the equipment, in the same building, belonging to the CLC. This was partly to do with paranoia over corrupting systems and partly to do with paranoia over how much use we, as the host school, were making of the CLC.

The development of the CLC as a resource was hampered by the slowness of the Excellence in Liverpool team, the LEA and the Council in appointing a manager. In fairness, confusion around some of the new governmental initiatives was rife. There was a clear suspicion that new money placed straight into the hands of LEAs would be dissipated. This gave rise to a 'partnership' model of control and development in which new Boards were required for initiatives such as the EAZs and Excellence in Cities. The governance of new initiatives left tremendous financial control with the DFES, obscured issues of responsibility and accountability at local level and generated a steep learning curve as, in Liverpool, existing LEA services were simply being duplicated. Ultimately, the assimilation of all of this back under the control of the LEA was inevitable. There could be no other exit strategy. Meanwhile, however, we were faced with more unnecessary hard work.

Having agreed to advertise the managers' posts for the two CLCs, 'Liverpool Direct' as an agency of the Council was hopelessly ineffective. The posts were advertised late, no record of enquiries was kept, information packs were not available, application forms were not sent out and, initially, there were **no** applicants for either post.

After an emergency meeting with the Senior Assistant Director we took responsibility for the process at our own CLC, organised the production and distribution of brochures, information packs and applications, collated all responses, organised the shortlisting and hosted the interviews. The LEA was to provide a projector and interactive whiteboard for the day and technical support. They failed to do so.

Despite these setbacks, we appointed an outstanding manager for the CLC and we spent many useful hours through May and June bringing him up to speed with the CLC programme. This was a very exciting time. We had a visionary manager completely committed to the new educational agenda and absolutely clear over the huge potential of the CLC to raise attainment not just in Shorefields but, also, across the whole Dingle/Toxteth area and with a range of partner secondary schools. Even at this stage, prior to the installation of any equipment, we saw opportunities for progress – by giving access to Shorefields facilities in the name of the CLC, by building curriculum content under the name of the CLC on the Shorefields web site and by publicising an action plan detailing milestones over the coming months.

This was, of course, dependent upon the time of our staff, the use of our Resource Centre and curriculum rooms and our funding the publicity material. At this stage the CLC had no revenue budget. We also drew up outline arrangements for Service Level Agreements to support the work of the CLC and canvassed for members of the, necessary, CLC Board of management. We found some excellent recruits.

Our new manager had negotiated some time from his employer and, while awaiting confirmation of his appointment and contractual details, had the opportunity to formulate plans for the CLC, meet with the new Board and discuss issues of procurement with the LEA and Excellence in Liverpool team.

In June, six weeks after his appointment and still awaiting confirmation and an outline contract, he withdrew. His courteous letter to me cited the obvious contractual problem and, also, the turgid, stifling unimaginative arrangements between the LEA and the Excellence in Liverpool team, guaranteed to depress the effectiveness of this remarkable initiative, and under which he would not work. This was a tremendous disappointment. The saddest thing was that he was absolutely right.

Under pressure of time, we agreed with the LEA and EIC people that another candidate from the shortlist would be appointed.

What was quite fantastic about all this technological development, on the back of highly focussed funding streams, was that it was taking place in buildings fit only for demolition. Our refurbishment of the Resource Centre, for example, was delayed by the collapse of the ceiling in the room above. The flat, concrete, roof of the languages block had been carrying eight inches of standing water and, after years of neglect, had finally given way. We were also very limited in our location of new interactive whiteboards, purchased through the EAZ and the CLC. It was inconceivable that such equipment should be located in rooms with 1930s two pin Bakelite sockets and leaking roofs. Rewiring for new technology in these circumstances was completely hazardous.

It was also hazardous simply moving around the building due to ingress of water and the general dilapidation. Our records showed that we pursued the manager of Liverpool's Direct Labour Organisation, DLO, from October to January in an effort to resolve roofing problems. It took extraordinary persuasion to even achieve a site visit and all this work was the responsibility of the Council. In respect of our dilapidation issues we were achieving virtually nothing. Even with the intervention of Governors and Councillors the response was pathetic. On one occasion, after eight weeks of pressure to repair a badly leaking corridor roof, we received a twenty-minute visit from one labourer with a bucket of tar. Again we were forced to spend money, delegated to the school for staffing, materials and equipment, on emergency repairs due to an absence of capital investment.

The DLO appeared to be in a hopeless situation. The condition of Liverpool schools was so bad that the planned maintenance budget was invariably overtaken by the need for emergency repairs. We had learned that the only definition of emergency that counted was one threatening school closure. This did not, apparently, include falling masonry, corridors awash with water, the loss of a first floor window into the quad, condemned wiring, boiler breakdowns, loose parapets, rain water running freely down internal walls, innumerable roof leaks, contaminated water tanks, blocked drains or a host of other entertainments during the year.

That a brand new City Learning Centre should arise right in the middle of all this neglect and decay was a wondrous idea for us.

For the builders it must have been their worst nightmare. Working inside an existing dilapidated building, maintaining all services, tolerating a fully functioning school and having to marry up new brickwork, new roof lines, new drains, new wiring and plumbing to the existing atrocious facilities. It must have been demoralising. I'll always be grateful to them.

The LEA, following the upheavals of the last twelve months, was engaged in a further struggle over identity and aspects of its own survival. This arose as a direct result of the greater delegation of funding to schools. We were now in a position to negotiate service level agreements (SLAs) for central services, including catering and music provision. The secondary headteachers played a significant role in this process and were under considerable pressure from within their own organisation to buy into this or that SLA. This was an undignified and vicious period of time in which the careers of many officers of the Liverpool Authority were made or broken on the basis of favour and cronyism.

It became clear that the government was determined to pursue Performance Management arrangements for Teachers. I had real misgivings about this, as it appeared to undermine much of the work we already had in place. We had been recognised by Investors in People a number of years earlier. We had already introduced professional portfolios for all staff, teaching and APTC, and these were working well as one vehicle for professional development. We also had a clear Staff Development structure, which supported progress in the school and complimented the Development Planning process. Through all this we were able to identify a range of training needs and do our best to fulfil them. Our annual Development Plan always included reference to identified training needs and how we had met the needs from the previous year. We also had robust performance and capability and conduct arrangements.

Given the enormous progress the school was making the staff were unimpressed by the idea of crossing performance 'thresholds' as a means to access higher pay. Generally, they wanted the higher pay but without bureaucratically having to demonstrate their worth to get it. In the end much of what emerged, as Performance Management was similar to a theme we had had for a number of years around the issue of professional skills development. This had regularly been discussed with both individuals and groups of staff and had been a recognition, at school level, that there were different levels of professionalism even amongst staff on the same scale and that professionalism was developmental. **Despite some significant problems with implementing Performance Management at school level, and it arriving at the wrong time for us, it was, generally, a good initiative continuing on from the NQT framework and being fairly prescriptive about the characteristics of a good teacher and good member of staff.**

Despite all the work undertaken around induction and staff development, and extravagant levels of support for some colleagues, we still had a handful of performance and capability problems resistant to any solution. These were obviously time consuming and in all cases became fractious. There emerged a significant difference in attitude between heads of department charged with assisting the development of colleagues. In all cases they gave their time generously but some were deeply reluctant to point out serious faults or shortcomings. In effect, to be appropriately critical. This may or may not have helped performance but a failure on the part of a head of department to be robust had a devastating effect on the process of improvement at senior management level. There were a number of occasions when union discussions revealed a failing colleague who had no idea they were exhibiting significant performance problems. This effectively returned us to square one of our procedures. We also suffered from one head of department who failed to separate the personal from the professional and was completely wrongheaded in their defence of an appallingly incompetent teacher.

We addressed these inconsistencies of approach and continued to focus on the things that mattered – staff performance through which we could raise attainment for our students. Two colleagues

left the school. One had a significant change of role, which improved attitude and performance dramatically. One continued as a
rumbling, intractable problem – one of those cases where it was
difficult to discern whether they were RIP or DIP. Resting in post
or dead in post.

With the school growing we were appointing new staff and
these included – classroom teachers, technicians, a bursar, a new
head of lower school and, in January 2000, a second Deputy Head.
We had also received EAZ funding to appoint classroom support
staff and supplemented this with social inclusion money to make a
number of appointments in this area. Furthermore, the new support
staff and the Learning Mentors had an immediate effect upon the
culture and climate of the school. They were obviously adults other
than teachers to whom the students could relate but they were also
a tremendous additional support helping to provide a genuine team
approach to education in the classroom. Relations between the new
staff and teachers were excellent. We also received requests from
across the city for copies of our Learning Mentor contracts.

The new money in schools created real opportunities. We increased the number of laptop computers available to staff encouraging more efficient work between home and school and around
the site. We also established a second Unit, the 'Early Intervention
Unit', to cater for those youngsters failing to make an effective transition from primary school. We recognised that a proportion lacked
the self-discipline to move from task to task and from lesson to lesson. Some struggled to relate to more than one adult in a day. The
Early Intervention Unit was exceptionally disciplined and provided
supervision throughout the entire day, including the, often problematical, breaks and lunchtimes. It was a huge success.

**There was no doubt that a combination of strategies was
having a positive effect upon discipline in the school.** The first
was around raising the expectations of the staff and there was a relentless concentration on standards and upon performance. During
the year we were, again, questioning the adequacy of our own les-

son observations as a means of exercising quality control in the school – so there was little complacency.

The second strategy concerned the ubiquitous presence of senior staff around the school and the availability of the pager system as an immediate response to problems.

The third involved the paraphernalia of responses we had available for dealing with disciplinary problems. These included a hierarchy of 'assertive' measures used by classroom teachers, clear responsibilities for heads of department and heads of year, the new Early Intervention Unit and the well established, and hugely successful, Reintegration Unit.

Finally, there were the expectations of the students themselves. On the whole, the staff were excellent at creating a good classroom climate, establishing their own control and setting standards. This was bolstered by a 'can do' message from every school assembly, from the graduations, from the 'Student Charter' and from the school internal reward system. Most students genuinely enjoyed coming to school and achieved a reasonable level of fulfilment.

Despite all of this there were issues during the year. In January we held a Lower School 'At Risk' assembly which was our version of a show trial. Any students clearly bucking the system, absorbing significant amounts of staff time and undermining the work of the school were ejected from the assembly with real gravitas and theatricality. There followed immediate meetings with parents and, in a tiny minority of cases, the students never returned. Understandably, both students and staff were impressed by this.

We also had a long running dispute between two groups of girls emanating from rivalries in the community. A number of these girls spent time in the Unit and others left the school voluntarily. Similarly, we struggled with a number of boys whose behaviour outside school was completely intolerable and with whom there was little parental control and regular police involvement. These youths caused us significant problems outside the school towards the end of the year.

On a positive note, the sixth form organised for a 'Changing Rooms' TV team to renovate their common room, there was an excellent school trip to Italy and the whole school enjoyed the annual 'It's a Knockout' tournament.

We were also involved with the Liverpool Race Equality Management Team in producing a series of motivational posters for schools. They photographed some of our black and minority ethnic students undertaking various academic exercises – laboratory work, art, musical performance – and created a series of stunning posters. We were very proud to have been involved and it was a great success. The 'Liverpool Echo' ran a story about the exercise and we had more good publicity.

In terms of our determination to raise standards we were encouraging staff to display targets and student performance figures around the school. We also embarked upon an initiative to ensure that staff were 'marking for improvement' by providing constructively critical feedback to students. Finally, we introduced 'Navigator'. This had been a major plank of our original EAZ submission but had been quietly forgotten in the process of working up the bid. It was intended to be an interactive guidance system applicable to all ages, child and adult, throughout the zone. In the absence of any other development we introduced a junior version of our professional portfolio for the students. It worked reasonably well but had to be taught – and with enthusiasm!

The use of ICT to enhance learning was, of course, the direction in which the school was travelling and, early in the year, I arranged to visit Thomas Telford School – nationally famous for raising standards and for the development of 'on-line curriculum'. Our CLC architects were keen to promote this as an example of the way forward for Shorefields. In particular, a use of flexible spaces for teaching purposes. The visit was most interesting. I saw many very decent young people, dedicated staff and a decent school.

The school was, undoubtedly, a success but there appeared to be an element of selection in the intake, albeit comprehensive, the on-line curriculum was already somewhat dated and, finally, teachers did what they do everywhere with open plan rooms – they partition them using bookcases and filing cabinets. It was, however, heartening to see the spirit of commitment and enthusiasm permeating the place.

We were, at this time, having severe problems with our Annexe building, which was fully tenanted. While we had no success in persuading the LEA to fulfil their repairs and maintenance responsibilities we were, if anything, even more frustrated by our main tenant, The Park Children's Centre, supported by Save the Children. They were well aware that the school itself had been in a dire financial situation for many years, that the relationship with the LEA over funding was fragile for all of us, and that the school had gone to extraordinary lengths to keep the Annexe in order to maintain their good work. Nevertheless, there were too many occasions when we were subject to veiled threats and brinkmanship in respect of their status as tenants and our statutory responsibility to pre-school children. The tap water was too hot, the tap water was too cold, there were insufficient paper towels, they had run out of toilet rolls, the heating was inadequate, it was too hot or cold, the windows were draughty or leaking or unstable.

Despite allocating a full time caretaker to the job, we still received complaints. We realised that around thirty pre school children were using more paper towels than 800 teenagers and sixty adults combined! We didn't lack sympathy, quite the opposite, but we realised that the very high level of support being given was unappreciated. We reached a crisis when, during torrential winter rains, the Children's Centre was flooded. A deep lead box valley between two areas of the roof became full of water and burst sending hundreds of gallons through the ceiling into the Park Centre on the first floor.

The response to this crisis, on the part of our caretaker, was extraordinary. In fact it was heroic. She attended the building, at night, in appalling weather accompanied by her family. With people on the roof clearing the gutters and more inside with mops and buckets they did an outstanding job of preparing the Centre for the staff and children the following day. When I attended in the morning there was barely a sign that there had been a problem. Damp carpet had been moved, the heating had been on overnight and the Centre could have functioned normally. It was what we had been doing in the main school for years following flood damage, arson, break-ins, leaks and boiler failures.

The staff in the Centre refused to allow children to be present and demanded a full Health and Safety inspection before resuming business. They had taped up all the light switches and said the building was unsafe. Despite me repeatedly turning lights on and off and warning that a full Health and Safety report may see the building condemned and them evicted they were insistent. This was the beginning of the end of our relationship. I had been under pressure for years to relinquish control of the Annexe and this was a turning point. There was also a realisation that we could no longer sustain an involvement when there were likely to be further significant problems with the roof. Running the main school was a complex task in itself.

We had already been told that under any PFI arrangement we would have to self fund the capital and revenue costs of the Annexe as it fell outside any financial scheme for PFI. As we were struggling with financial issues around the City Learning Centre we agreed, soon after, to hand over the Annexe to the LEA in return for the refurbishment of three areas of our building to support the CLC – an admin area, music room and Science lab. Should the Annexe ever be sold we were promised that the assets released would be ring-fenced for the benefit of the school.

By Easter, we felt that the school was making very good progress. With Excellence in Cities funding, we had appointed two Learning Mentors, one from the Somali community who was a huge asset to the school. Unlike other schools, complaining of a lack of clarity over the roles and expectations of the Mentors, we were delighted over the performance of our new colleagues. We had, initially, been quite prescriptive over the job we wanted done and every effort was made to engage the Mentors with our Pastoral teams. They responded with generosity and professionalism. We had also bid for an additional ESF grant for support in the Library and this had been favourably received. Finally, we had defeated an appeal against expulsion by the mother of an extraordinarily aggressive boy. The appeal Panel were persuaded by our detailed submission and by the strength of the argument presented by the Chair of Governors and myself. This news was well received by staff.

The new financial year, in April, saw a remarkable improvement in funding, of the order of £500,000. We were benefiting from the increase in student numbers but there was also a real impetus behind government promises to put more emphasis on education. Additionally our European bid for library staffing had been successful and we anticipated an influx of resources via the EAZ and CLC.

We were, however, struggling with managing the school during the building works and, unfortunately, the permanent exclusion of a student in late March had led to more problems than it solved. Having undertaken the permanent exclusion as a result of the youth's extremely aggressive behaviour we were then victimised for months as he showed up outside the school at the end of each day. We had groups of delinquent youths, bull terriers and motorbikes creating an atmosphere of menace and threat.

In June a group of black students were chased on their way to school, which was highly unusual, and we had a serious attack on a Turkish student at the end of the day. We were, undoubtedly, in the midst of wider disturbances in the community as the evenings were lighter and we moved towards the summer months.

In early June the Police intervened directly to stop abuse and threats towards students travelling by bus. The youths gathering on the street corner had become an unmanageable problem as their rude and unpleasant behaviour provoked confrontation. There were occasions when up to four separate gangs would congregate. In those circumstances it was often hard to know which way to turn and which group was likely to cause trouble on any given night. We were dealing with the problems, aided by the Police, while, simultaneously, other officers were chasing stolen cars around the area. This was very much a concern of ours, as the car thieves would attempt to 'perform' for the students leaving the school. We had occasions when car thieves lost control of the vehicles in the street, drove onto the site executing hand brake turns in the car park and even drove stolen vehicles into the bollards at the end of the road in order to destroy the cars before escaping from the police on foot.

Our constant worry in these circumstances was that a vehicle would plough into the hundreds of students crowded along our narrow side street or clustered on the pavements of the main road. I recorded, at this time, that the situation was 'extremely difficult'. We had one bizarre incident in which a black cab mounted the pavement at speed and tried to run down a young man. This was in front of around two hundred witnesses. It was a completely disproportionate response to a refusal to pay, on the part of the cab driver, and was an indication of the climate these delinquent youths were creating at the time.

Our problems of supervision continued through until the end of term. This was now a familiar pattern to the year. We had no problems in the mornings but they surfaced at the end of each day. We made the assumption that our delinquents never arose before mid afternoon. They did not go outdoors if it was cold or wet hence the relative quiet of the winter months. The summer and the light nights were a huge problem for us, at 3.20, and for the police in the evenings.

In late June we had a strange incident in which a group of white youths with an English Bull Terrier arrived to seek a confrontation. A number of black youths also arrived accompanied by two Pit Bulls. The students leaving the school were polarised by this situation and we had to intervene in a very unpleasant stand off between two large groups. We found it impossible to disperse the students. Eventually the solution lay in providing a taxi home for the English Bull Terrier, and assorted friends, who had in fact been the original aggressors.

Perhaps surprisingly, I recorded, at the time that the school was continuing to run well internally. This was despite the problems on the streets and the hugely disruptive building work around the CLC, which was a long way from completion. I taught English for the final term in order to support a supply teacher who was simply not coping. I found it very fulfilling. I had also been reenergised through the management support sessions I had enjoyed with Littlewoods. We now had a new vision for the school to take us through to 2010! In addition to this I had developed a clearer view of the structure the school would need in order to move forward and had considered ways of embedding performance standards into the daily routine of the school through the application of 'trigger points' for pastoral and clerical staff action.

During June and July, I had struggled with arrangements for a trip to Alabama, on behalf of the EAZ, to attend a Black Roots Study School. The project was very interesting and very time consuming. I would miss the end of term and use most of the summer break. Nevertheless, the programme was, apparently, intensive and involved serious academic study. It seemed really worthwhile. I could, however, make no headway over travel arrangements with Liverpool University – the organisers, and, in early July contacted Alabama directly for details of the programme, accommodation and so on. Nothing was forthcoming. Having pressed the matter it transpired that no travel arrangements had been made, no accommodation arranged and, as yet the programme had not been finalised. This was ten days before departure. Furthermore even when the programme was finalised I would have no place on it. Alabama had never heard of me nor had they received any funding from Liverpool.

Colleagues in the EAZ and at the University were surprised that

I withdrew and obviously regarded it as truculence on my part. I was surprised that they were surprised and, yes, I felt very truculent indeed.

Every cloud has a silver lining and the abandonment of the Alabama trip meant that I could attend a Somali Education day held at the Somali Community Centre in late July on a Saturday. All the headteachers in the city with Somali children in their schools had been invited and the aim of the day was to outline aspects of the English educational system and to show parents how to best support their children. What a great idea and an unmissable opportunity to meet parents.

On the day I was the only headteacher to turn up. There was one representative of the LEA and me. It was a disgrace. There were around three hundred people present at the meeting, many coming straight from Saturday prayers in the nearby mosque. Fortunately, the Somali organisers made some well-informed and enthusiastic speeches, the LEA rep spoke and I made an extended speech on behalf of *all* Liverpool schools. This was well received, particularly when I challenged the LEA to monitor and report upon the general progress of Somali students over the next twelve months and then invited everyone present to Shorefields for a meal and an introductory session in the CLC.

LEARNING POINTS YEAR 7

- Even the best system can be subverted.
- Parents need protecting against the demands of their own children.
- Try to deal with opposition by accommodating it.
- For an initiative to be successful it is necessary to think through the reasons for and the implications of change, to plan carefully, to communicate clearly and well in advance and to convey the complete conviction that it *will* be successful.
- It tends to be mundane issues, which define the experience of organisational life for the participants. The mundane therefore becomes very important.
- 'Continental' days are educationally, socially and morally unsound.
- The spaces between activities may be as valuable as the activities themselves in a general educative and social sense.
- There was no doubt that parental confidence was greater with a dedicated school bus service rather than with the public

service routes.

- Exit and bus duties, in fact *all* supervisory duties, should have the characteristics of a military operation.

- Good order depends upon expectations, routine and vigilance.

- A teacher undertaking an infrequent duty is disempowered.

- It is difficult, even for a highly experienced person, to confidently demonstrate the knowledge, skill and field of perception required for good supervision if they are unfamiliar with the duty area.

- This is an'iron law'. Where there is no supervision, albeit briefly, there *will* be trouble.

- Frustration is a wasted emotion if the problem is systemic.

- The sight of large numbers of well dressed, well mannered, happy young people carrying bags and equipment is the best advertisement a school can have.

- It is better to be proactive and to prevent problems occurring rather than deal with the consequences.

- Our issue, 'bus duty', sounds parochial and immature. In effect it was a key defining feature of our lives.

- Governmental initiatives tend to become increasingly bureaucratised as they move from political soundbite to over regulated delivery.

- It is vital that professionals have the courage of their convictions, are clear in arguing for resources to raise standards and are unambiguous in how that can be achieved. Politicians and local and national government officials need this. Professionals in education, housing, health and welfare have a responsibility to be vigorously proactive.

- Performance Management was, generally, a good initiative continuing on from the NQT framework and being fairly prescriptive over the characteristics of a good teacher and a good member of staff.

- If you are working hard and doing the right thing it will be recognised when it matters and you need to call upon support.

- The governance of new initiatives through partnership Boards leaves tremendous financial control with the DFES, obscures issues of responsibility and accountability at local level and generates a steep learning curve as existing LEA services are simply duplicated.

- New money in schools creates real opportunities.

- A combination of appropriate strategies will have an effect upon discipline in a school.

- Delinquents do not arise before mid-afternoon and stay indoors if it is cold or wet.

START OF EIGHTH YEAR OF HEADSHIP SEPTEMBER 2000

W E HAD ANOTHER PLEASING set of exam results with 25% of students in Year 11 gaining five or more A-C grades at GCSE. To put this in context it helps to realise that we had moved from the bottom of the league table of Liverpool secondary schools to a mid table position. We had appointed eleven new teaching staff and they all looked very promising. We had 170 students report on the first day, which was in line with our expectations, and this grew to 180. We had maintained our low level of exclusions at 10 for the previous year. We were, also, still involved in the building programme for the CLC. A CLC manager had been appointed and was in post.

The building work was significantly disruptive and it is a credit to the staff and students that we managed to improve standards during this time.

We had faced a major setback at the end of August when it became clear that our three new computer suites of leased equipment would not be installed in time for a September start. This was an awful situation for staff expecting to teach the subject right throughout the school but particularly in relation to Year 10 classes – where the new pre-16 GNVQ courses were a significant part of student timetables. Staff were reduced to providing written exercises for weeks on end and this, undoubtedly, detracted from the motivation of the students. **Dealing with national companies who split their operation into discrete business units can be really problematical.** We were to encounter this problem again over the next few years. In the case of the leased computers the company concerned operated separate business units for sales, installation and after sales service. There was antagonism between all three. The installers, in particular, resented the sales team agreeing unfeasibly short delivery times with customers. In the first instance however, where there has been a delay, the only option is to work with the people doing the installation and to develop a relationship in order to get the best out of them. Our ICT department most certainly did this and, before half term, the job was completed. We had lost weeks of teaching time.

Our mistake then was to assume that rapid progress would be made. Nothing of the sort. Staff and students complained that machines were regularly 'crashing' during lessons losing valuable work. In some cases the problem was so severe and so frequent that lessons were becoming a farce. Despite numerous call outs by the after sales staff the problems were unresolved, at which point, the company blamed firstly the students, then the staff, for sabotage. The Deputy and I spent lesson after lesson observing ICT sessions and finally resorted to a device we had used in the past. We asked for all the machines, the server and the wiring to be removed.

Within days we had company directors and representatives from the individual business units on site. They agreed to provide two permanent technicians until the problem was resolved. It was quickly apparent that we had a software problem with the latest version of Windows, which they had supplied. It was uninstalled and we lived happily ever after.

As a school we were now involved in three major projects. The

EAZ was fully operational and, in addition to chairing the Executive meetings, I was also a member of the finance group. We had established a CLC 'implementation group' to steer that project forward and this involved a coordinator from the EIC team, the CLC manager and myself. We were already invoicing the Excellence in Cities team for work undertaken as a direct service to the CLC. This included a proportion of our administration costs. Finally, we were firmly engaged with the PFI process and, early in the academic year, had reached the stage of presentations on the part of those tendering for the contract across the city. It was interesting to note that there was a disproportionate emphasis upon how lavishly appointed a headteacher's new office might be. This was to a great extent misleading as schools had, themselves, to purchase any movable furniture outside of the contract.

At the end of the previous year, as our period of sponsorship with Littlewoods came to a conclusion, we had engaged in an invaluable exercise with Littlewoods managers in developing a future vision for the school. A contingent of around twenty staff had spent an evening at the John Moores Centre brainstorming their ideal for Shorefields. This was then worked up into a set of statements around school development. The top line vision was that we wanted the school to have facilities of a national standard by 2005 and of an international standard by 2010. We wanted our own educational standards to be commensurate with this and wanted the school to have national then international recognition. **It was tremendously important to me, having been in post for seven years, to have this new sense of direction and purpose.** We had also hit upon a vision, which was understandable and easy to communicate.

We were surprisingly successful in attracting staff contrary to the expectations of visiting inspectors and DFE advisers.

There were a number of reasons for this success in recruitment. Firstly, despite being an inner city school, with the attendant problems that implied, we were actually in a very convenient position for the south Liverpool area, which is heavily populated by teachers, and we were also convenient for the Wirral and North Wales.

Secondly, we made extraordinary efforts to attract staff. This included the widest possible advertising, guaranteeing interviews, and repeatedly contacting all those who even enquired. For shortage subjects we headhunted and paid enhanced salaries. If necessary, I would visit applicants in their homes, contact them at work or arrange pre interview meetings. Thirdly, Shorefields was, genuinely, a decent place in which to work. **There was camaraderie amongst the staff, which, in my experience, is rarely found outside of challenging schools.** The senior staff had a reputation for being supportive and supply teachers knew we were very consistent in applying procedures. Finally, the school was, clearly, going places and was improving rapidly. The existing staff conveyed a commitment to, and passion for, what they did and newcomers found this infectious and wanted to be part of it.

We certainly had fewer staff issues to deal with at this point although one classroom teacher was causing concern and two managers were struggling to deal with their roles. The new Deputy was pushing ahead with Performance Management arrangements and was also organising training for all APTC staff. We were trying, with all roles, to link a description of the responsibility with a clear expectation of the performance standard to be attained. It was helpful that objectives for performance management were being set at this time.

One area in which this was crucial was the site responsibility carried by the Bursar and we had to make clear, our expectation, that the postholder would walk the job and be intimately acquainted with any issues. It would not, for example, be easy to engage with our new Health and Safety policy in any other way.

The staff received a tremendous lift in April when Shorefields was allocated a School Achievement Award for raising standards. This was a figure of around £25,000. At that time we had wide discretion over the distribution of this award. In some schools the award was only shared between the teaching staff. We regarded that as reprehensible. I spoke to the staff and proposed that the award at Shorefields was split evenly on a pro rata basis, depending upon whether or not people were full or part time, between everyone working at the school, directly employed or not. The teaching staff agreed unanimously that this should be the case. That was a reflection of their values and of their inherent quality. They were very decent people.

Interestingly, to avoid argument, I had to say that no individual could receive more than 100% of one share. While a part time teacher might, for example, receive 60%, a cleaner, who also worked in the canteen, would receive a maximum of 100%. This was despite the fact that, embarrassingly, her joint hours may go way over a reasonable working week.

The effect of all this was really positive. Some of the canteen staff received around £300, which was a very useful sum at the time. They told me that a local school had shared their Achievement award only amongst the teachers and had bought the canteen staff a bottle of wine – to share between them!

We excluded the Head and Deputies from participating in this bounty. On reflection this was probably unfair and rather sanctimonious. Everyone appreciates a present if they have worked hard.

We had ample time to meet with DFE advisors during the course of the year as they made repeated visits to the CLC. On one occasion I was asked to organise some students to meet a delegation of advisers and MPs. In addition to the usual senior students, as school representatives, we organised the steel band to play in the middle of the building site. We also had a dancing group of Year 8 girls performing a routine to a backing track. The noise was tremendous and we made a great impression. All the students in hard hats performing wildly for the bemused visitors! The message was pretty clear. The politicians were not dealing with a 'command and do' school here. They were dealing with a school determined to take control of every opportunity and use it creatively for the benefit of the students. We distributed laminated sheets to all visitors outlining the benefits we had generated from CLC involvement, even at this point, prior to it being completed.

It is significant that the school log for the period records an intruder on site early in September and that this was a result of the car park gate being left unlocked. As ever this was a strong indication that the life of the school and the security of us all depended upon relentless and rigorous routine. **The stability of a school in our situation is very fragile and the sense of security and well being we had spent so long building up could be eroded very easily.**

It was certainly challenging to have so many workmen coming and going and equipment being moved while the school was fully functional. We also endured one of the wettest winters on record and the log records that the rain persisted for months. This slowed down the building work and generated an atmosphere of sodden misery. In the circumstances it was surprising that we operated as well as we did although, from an overall management perspective, **the issues of supervision, security and support for staff stretched us beyond our reasonable limits.** The simplest example of this was that we could not walk directly from a to b in order to assist staff calling for a pager to back them up. Similarly, at the end of each day, we had the problem of supervising more exits and less satisfactory exits than we had been using previously. We were spread very thinly.

In the circumstances we were extremely lucky to have such high levels of cooperation from most of the students. We did, however, have problems with individuals and it is fair to say that we were struggling to find solutions to the behaviour some young people were presenting.

The level of support from parents when tackling problems was really heartening – although this did not necessarily guarantee progress. In the cases I dealt with personally, which suggests that they were close to the end of our procedures, the parents tended to be desperate for an agreed way forward and for assistance in resolving their problems. There were a number of girls who were, frankly, beyond the control of their families and could be extremely unpleasant. We had a handful of quite serious fights between individual girls and, also, between individual boys. We had two incidents in which generally decent boys had launched 'pre emptive strikes' against others with absolutely no provocation.

While it is certainly true that congestion on the site, the relentlessly poor weather and restricted movement was a source of constant tension, violence could never be tolerated. Finding a way forward with parents, short of expulsion, was often time consuming.

By now our Reintegration Unit was dealing with some seriously difficult young people. It had never been our intention to create a facility to which a student would repeatedly return; yet this had happened. The whole success of the Unit had been around the concepts of removal from mainstream, re-education in a different setting and phased reintegration with ongoing support. We were now struggling with unsatisfactory reintegration on the part of too many students. We were also struggling with the new city wide scheme of 'negotiated transfers' between schools as a means of avoiding exclusions. Shorefields students, and parents, simply did not like the idea of a transfer and were antagonistic to travelling to another part of the city for education. Both white and black students were concerned over encountering local prejudice in another area.

Thus, despite the good level of cooperation on site, we found that, even our, elaborate arrangements for behaviour management were overstretched. Life would have been easier if negotiated transfers had been accepted, if the transfers we did arrange had been successful, if there had been more places in Pupil Referral Units and if there had been more 'wrap around' care for some of our students.

One girl who transferred in to us caused relentless low-level problems. Staff were constantly stopping her and removing jewellery and non-uniform items, punishing her for eating gum, dealing with lateness and objecting to her manner and attitude. It is reflective of the very high standard demonstrated by the overwhelming majority of students that this young woman, new to Shorefields, stood out.

After several months the volume of staff time absorbed by this girl had become exorbitant. We realised, in particular, that staff had confiscated her denim jacket every day for weeks. It was always the same routine. She was wearing the jacket. Staff confiscated it. She made a fuss, challenged and sulked. Other students were amused. Staff were frustrated. Mum came to school to reclaim the jacket.

I rang the girl's mother. I said that this was causing such frustration that I felt like burning the jacket. The mother agreed. She was also fed up. I told her that we had again confiscated the jacket and that I would ceremoniously burn it on the field at breaktime. Mum agreed. She said she was sorry she couldn't be present because it would be entertaining.

And that is what happened. The jacket was on a metal spike when all the students poured out at break time. It was significant that they all recognised the offending article immediately. The jacket was set alight, actually with the help of a Year 8 boy who seemed very adept at this type of thing. The owner appeared and gave a wonderfully aggrieved and histrionic performance. The situation was one of pure slapstick comedy. The jacket burned well. The point had been made.

There is a postscript to the story. I rang Mum immediately. She had already had a conversation with her hysterical daughter by mobile phone and had delighted in telling her that she knew exactly what was happening. I offered to pay for the jacket. She said there was really no need. The point had to be made and she was fully supportive. I pressed the issue and asked how much the jacket had cost. She had no idea. Her daughter did not own the jacket but had merely borrowed it from a friend! I had, unwittingly, burnt clothing belonging to a total stranger.

The second unanticipated outcome of my incautious behaviour was that, for the next week, students were extremely reluctant to cooperate with staff over the confiscation of unsuitable clothing. This was entirely understandable. There was, however, a total absence of denim outerwear from then on.

Months later we received a modest bill for one denim jacket – part worn and recently cremated.

While some of this sounds flippant, there was absolutely nothing whimsical or superficial about our overall approach to discipline and good order. Even the burning jacket was achieved with a certain amount of gravitas on my part. We took issues of standards, welfare and security incredibly seriously and, while every effort was made to support students and their parents, dangerously difficult young people were being expelled.

The consequence of any expulsion was that we would be dragged through appeals procedures as a matter of course. Again, the chair of governors and I attended a series of appeals in relation to two alarmingly destructive young men, both on the fringes of gangsterism in the community, and won through on behalf of the school. We were only successful because we worked so hard at preparing, and then publicly arguing, our case and an essential element in this was the quality of our intervention records.

With 'social inclusion' focussing very much on the rights of the individual, appeals panels were unpersuaded by catalogues of misdemeanours. Everyone knew that there were very difficult young people in schools and that, in the past, they may have been educated selectively due to their emotional and behavioural difficulties. Their poor behaviour was almost a 'given' and we had to demonstrate an appropriate series of escalating responses including – alternative management strategies, individualised education plans and attempts at behaviour modification. A constant refrain of mine was that our records needed to demonstrate, in particular, regular and detailed contact with parents in order to have credibility. Unfortunately, despite perhaps dozens of contacts from the school, a parent, at appeal, was always likely to claim little knowledge of the child's poor behaviour. **Quality record keeping of pastoral business is essential.**

Our main curriculum concerns were around reviewing progress

with our literacy and numeracy policies, involvement in training for the Key Stage 3 strategy and undertaking a greater level of analysis of our CATs and SATs scores by gender, ethnicity and language development. We were also planning the introduction of 'Successmaker', a learning support package, for the CLC. Our department reviews were now very serious affairs culminating in discussion between the team leader and myself, as Head, with the two Deputies present. The benefits of getting it right each time we undertook such a review were considerable.

Our external problems had not really abated since the end of the previous academic year. We had a police presence at the school for the whole of the first half term, which was very helpful indeed, but this had become more sporadic by early November. Predictably, perhaps, the difficulties on the street started to resurface.

A white student was attacked by two white delinquents on the corner of the street. We had the re-emergence of small groups of provocative and disruptive youths and on many occasions we were forced to intervene directly when they began kicking and spitting at passers by. A Somali boy was attacked at one of the public service bus stops and we filed yet another police report.

Amongst the staff there was significant development underway and progress was being made in improving the quality of the Professional Portfolios.

We had a good end to what had been a very difficult year. The CLC finally opened and it really was a spectacular facility. An interesting difference in perspective emerged immediately when it was apparent that neither the architects, the CLC manager nor Council officers had anticipated that we would want students passing through the CLC to access the school. The CLC entrance and the main entrance to the school were one and the same. The CLC and school shared the same reception facilities. The serious suggestion that the students should enter and leave the building by side entrances was unbelievable to me. The whole point of building the Centre where we did was in recognition of the powerful impact it

would have on expectations. **The suggestion that the most deserving people should be kept out of the way in order to keep
the CLC reception clean and tidy for others was outrageous.**
We simply ignored the protests, directed all students in and out of
the beautiful reception area and allowed anyone, who wanted to,
to wander around the new floors of shiny machines. Their humility
was quite shocking. 'Are we allowed to do this?' 'Will we ever be
able to use these rooms?'

Earlier in the year, in February, I had been invited to meet Tony
Blair, Prime Minister, for an Education Seminar at 10 Downing
Street. Along with a number of other colleagues from across the
country, I was there to discuss best practice in secondary education. This really was a great honour and a tribute to the work we
were doing in the school. The Prime Minister led the discussion,
appeared very well informed and was generally concerned to receive feedback on the development of the government's agenda for
education.

During a break, I was able to introduce myself more personally
and the Prime Minister asked me what I felt our greatest challenge
was at this time. Without hesitation I said that it was dealing with
the range of new initiatives and the pace of change. Mr Blair immediately responded that we should apply for Specialist College
status, another new initiative. I found this reply rather perplexing.
He also introduced me to Sir Cyril Taylor, the man responsible
for the Specialist College programme. In our later submission for
Specialist status I made significant capital out of this personal invitation to apply. There was, however, to be no application for the
time being. We were genuinely too busy.

We were very pleased to host a visit by Lord David Putnam, as
head of the new General Teaching Council. He was on a fact-find-
ing mission and we were very proud to have been selected as the
Secondary school he would visit. Lord Putnam was one of an inner
circle of government supporters and advisers and very close to the
centre of educational thinking at the time. His visit was quite de-

manding for us but, nevertheless, was quite entertaining all round.
Estelle Morris was Secretary of State for Education at the time and
Lord Putnam reflected her realism and determination to be properly
engaged with schools.

As agreed, we had organised a familiar timetable of meetings
and observations, tour of the site, lunch in the canteen with students
and the opportunity to meet staff. Lord Putnam, we really called
him David, was very sharp, interested and quick to sift the information relevant to his new role. We had a slight problem in that he was
constantly using his mobile phone, even when observing lessons.
When we learnt of this we simply told him to stop. He was very
good-natured.

Towards the end of the week he insisted on taking the two
Deputies and me out for a meal. We were to meet in an up market
restaurant in Liverpool at 7.30pm. We arrived first. By 7.50pm we
were becoming a little anxious and I looked outside for any sign of
our famous visitor. I could see him standing on the corner of the
street, unsurprisingly, holding a conversation on his mobile phone.
We sent the waiter outside with an ice bucket and a note: 'Place
your phone in the bucket and come inside to eat or we are going
home!' He arrived in good spirits and we had a fine evening.

At the end of the week Lord Putnam was the guest of honour at
the official launch of our EAZ held at the famous Liverpool Institute
of Performing Arts, LIPA. There were teachers and governors from
all the schools in the area, the Mayor of Liverpool and Councillors,
the Director of Education and his senior team, the EAZ team and
invited guests. The place was packed. In his speech Lord Putnam
was complimentary over his visits to Shorefields and Beaufort Park,
one of our feeder schools. I was completely taken aback when he
also told the entire audience that Liverpool, as a city, needed the
same quality of vision as Phil McNulty had for Shorefields. I felt
both gratified and self-conscious over this recognition.

During his visit Lord Putnam had met our Chair of Governors
and was most impressed by his commitment. I explained that we

were applying for national honours for the chair and lord Putnam generously said that we could use him in support.

We made quite a reasonable application with letters from staff, governors, the LEA and other supporters and then awaited the outcome. There was none. Given that it was not possible to trace the progress of applications ours disappeared into a dead zone from which we never received a response. The contribution of our chair to the school, and to a raft of charitable and community causes had been momentous. When we scrutinised the honours lists over the next eighteen months there appeared to be plenty of lollipop ladies and post-mistresses, all very deserving, but what had happened to our application?

After persistent badgering by phone we were eventually told that the process around applications such as ours was relatively arbitrary and that a lot depended upon weight. In other words the actual volume of paper produced in the form of supporting letters. How crass. I have had a relatively jaundiced view of the honours system ever since.

The LEA was again in some upheaval over the loss of a number of senior officers in the Youth and Community management structure. Again, because this was an important part of our business, we felt the impact of the inter-regnum with officers from within the Youth Service jockeying for position and failing to progress any of our long-standing issues.

The completion of the CLC introduced a new range of management meetings as **we attempted to interpret the partially articulated government wisdom around shared use of the CLC facility.** We were already paying, out of the school's budget, to transport local primary children into the centre. This, of course, went way beyond philanthropy and was probably the best money we spent on marketing. We were also, as a school, supplying new computers to all the Youth Centres in the Dingle/Toxteth area. We had a connection on the Brunswick Business Park, where the machines were constructed, and this, again, was a very cheap, educationally sound but superb PR exercise. **One has to speculate to accumulate.**

We were now using 'Navigator' as a vehicle for engaging with the Primary Schools either through the CLC, where children could complete the programme on PCs, or in the schools, where they could prepare hard copy. My relationship with the Primary Heads was at a high point through our EAZ activity, access to the CLC and through social contact. That year we sponsored the wine for the Toxteth Cluster Annual Dinner. This was well received and, again, constituted a sound investment.

In school, with two Deputies, a Bursar and two new, temporary, Assistant Heads I was able to describe a new management structure. This outlined support arrangements for all departments and each pastoral section. We actually had a series of temporary Assistant Heads, drawn from our senior middle managers, but the arrangement was unsatisfactory all around. This was, principally because we were expecting the post holders to carry on with their original, and onerous, departmental management roles.

We were, at the time, starting an involvement with the Liverpool Highsights exercise, a form of self review and target setting which had, rightly, gained national recognition and we were placing a big emphasis upon 'tracking' students in order to monitor performance.

Throughout the year we were bedevilled by problems with the duty system due to inadequate management and, for a school as vulnerable as ours, this was quite unacceptable. In fact we were, in many respects, more physically vulnerable than we had been for years. Not only did we have the chaos of the work on site and monumental problems moving students away safely at the end of the day but we also suffered fire alarms – constantly! Many of these were the result of the building work – electrical breakages, heat and dust – but once young people experience the disruption of alarms there is a tendency for copycat behaviour. We were relentless in pursuing malicious alarms.

The vision, to have a school with national facilities, national standards and national recognition, was published and broadcast widely. This brought us significant benefit. **In a couple of lines we had established a very clear programme of development.**

We were, undoubtedly, seen as an improving school and in late July when we held our major Open Day, New Intake Evening and Governors Report we organised presentations to staff to mark their success. We used the CQEC, Centre for Quality in Education and the Community, brand introduced some years earlier as a vehicle for promoting good practice. The CQEC certificates detailing the performance standard attained by staff in respect of various initiatives and management responsibilities were well received and, later, used in evidence as part of the 'Threshold' application process.

There was a very strong sense amongst staff, governors, parents and students that Shorefields was really going places!

LEARNING POINTS YEAR 8

- Dealing with national companies who split their operation into discreet business units can be really problematical.

- Having been in post for seven years it is tremendously important to a headteacher to have a new sense of direction and purpose.

- Schools should take extraordinary measures to attract staff.

- There is camaraderie amongst staff in challenging schools, which is rarely found elsewhere.

- Value and respect all the staff in the school Treat everyone fairly and justly as important members of a wider team.

- Take control of every opportunity and use it creatively for the benefit of the students.

- The stability of an inner city school is very fragile and a sense of security and well-being can be eroded very easily.

- With building work underway, issues of security, supervision and support for staff may stretch management beyond their reasonable limits.

- Quality record keeping of Pastoral business is essential.

- Serious departmental reviews are an essential tool in raising standards.

- If students are kept away from well-decorated, clean and tidy 'adult' areas of the school you will depress their expectations.

- It is a tremendous challenge dealing with a range of new initiatives and a rapid pace of change.

- An application for national honours should, literally, weigh heavy.

- One must speculate to accumulate. Good PR may require financial investment.

- A clear vision, expressed in a couple of lines, is an incredibly powerful and persuasive instrument.

START OF NINTH YEAR OF
HEADSHIP SEPTEMBER 2001

W E RETURNED TO ANOTHER good exam performance from Year 11, again with 25% gaining 5 or more good GCSEs, and also from our post 16 GNVQ students. Shorefields had, again moved up the 'league table'. We were oversubscribed in Year 7 and had admitted 192 students. Incredibly our record of exclusions showed that we had only excluded 4 students the previous year.

A vacant Head of year position gave us the opportunity to re-consider our Pastoral arrangements and I was strongly in favour of moving towards a more American model of management whereby the Pastoral leaders were all full time with no teaching commit-ment. Having put this proposal to the staff via the Staff Council there was significant opposition and it was withdrawn. This was a pity as the teaching commitment of our Heads of Year prevented them spending the necessary time on the range of monitoring and support activities that were now contemporary. Furthermore, in a school such as ours, significant blocks of time were needed for dealing with parents and following up disciplinary incidents.

We published the new vision for the school, developed the previous year, very widely indeed. Some of our key priorities for the start of this year, other than undertaking the PFI refurbishment, were around a new Performance Management Policy, making our target setting processes more effective and defining a new leadership group for the school. We also needed a new ICT strategy in the light of our increased access to resources and had introduced the ICT based learning programme, 'Succesmaker', which we hoped would raise standards of attainment for the least able.

I was meeting the CLC manager weekly to discuss progress and was involved in pushing the involvement of other agencies, such as Adult Education, in the CLC. The CLC Board meetings, comprising representatives of partner schools and the Excellence in Liverpool Coordinator were, frankly, fractious and stressful affairs with 'partners' attempting to work through the reality of an evolving government policy around CLCs. The hostility towards us as the host school was manifest. I had a number of serious meetings with the Director of Education and Lifelong Learning in an attempt to move away from this frustrating and bitter situation.

We had moved straight from one major new development to another. The CLC had been completed and opened formally as we entered fully into our PFI partnership. After the months of negotiation and tendering during the previous academic year Liverpool had selected Jarvis, a major construction company, to undertake the contract. We would be the first Liverpool Secondary School to be refurbished under the deal and work was scheduled to begin in January '02. Meanwhile Jarvis had taken over facilities management (FM) on all the sites – four secondary and ten primary schools. This involved them taking responsibility for all ongoing repairs and maintenance, heating, lighting, cleaning, security and catering. Our caretaking and cleaning staff were transferred to Jarvis and the catering staff, previously employed by the City Council, transferred to Jarvis's catering sub contractor Castleview.

We were engaged in an ongoing design and development process, room by room, with the LEA, Jarvis and their architects. We were also, separately, dealing week by week with the FM issues generated by the contractor's responsibility for the premises prior to refurbishment. There were very clear standards set out in the contractual Output Specification and, by now, we were paying for them.

A problem for us was the bewildering rate at which Jarvis shed staff. We received assurances over the quality of work from one manager after another, only to find that they had been replaced by the time we were next due to meet. A significant issue appeared to be around the internal tensions in the organisation with Jarvis FM and Jarvis Construction being different companies. Later in the process there were serious disputes between these different parties over where responsibility lay for remedial works. From the viewpoint of the clients – the City Council and ourselves – this was very frustrating.

What was indefensible was the sharp deterioration in the standard of catering provided by Castleview. In the first week it was clear that the canteen was short staffed, that there was no overall management of the whole canteen and dining facility, the conditions were becoming squalid and the quality of food presented had deteriorated sharply. To add insult to injury **the prices had all rocketed, in some cases by more than 100%.** The Cook and her staff were the same people who had worked well in the school for years. What had changed was the expectations Castleview had of the existing personnel, their failure to create a well supported catering management position, their failure to provide additional staffing for even basic jobs, our increased roll, an absence of training and development, and a lack of commitment to providing a nutritious diet for all students. Furthermore, there was, as ever, a dispute between Jarvis and Castleview over who should be cleaning the canteen. The Cook was so short staffed that it was difficult to release assistants from the servery even to wipe spillages. The 'deeper cleans' required daily, weekly and then periodically had not been budgeted for and were unmanaged. The situation was gross and was compounded by the fact that we were serving food in the Canteen at least twice a day, at 10.30am and 12.30pm. Attempting to use the canteen for an impromptu assembly late morning or mid afternoon was out of the question due to its condition. Jarvis and Castleview only sat up and paid attention when we commissioned our own Health and Safety report which embarrassed them and the Local Authority into taking effective action.

We endured months of wrangling over these issues. I challenged the quality of food on a day by day basis, called in Jarvis managers, held meetings with Jarvis and Castleview directors and served them the same food they were serving to students. The sandwiches were inedible and no one could identify the meat purported to be in the nuggets. They were disgusted and humiliated at what their companies were doing and issued instructions to improve the quality of the food being purchased. They blamed the cook, which everyone knew was grossly unfair. Her loyalty to the school and the students was unquestionable. The reality was that her ordering choices were heavily constrained. There were decent meals available but these could only be ordered in tiny quantities. The main emphasis was on a cash cafeteria system, which put a full meal beyond the availability of a child on free dinners. This was totally unacceptable. There were some fancy McDonald's style cheeseburgers available but, like the pizzas, the quantities were relatively small. The bulk of the 'backup food' was chips, nuggets and the notorious turkey twizzlers. Simple vehicles for fat, salt and additives. **The pathetic commitment to providing a 'meal of the day' for those on free dinners was quite offensive.** Boiled fish and boiled potato looks unappetising to anyone and having observed an entire lunchtime session I didn't witness a single student take this option.

Following our protests the quality of the food did improve with more curries, pasta dishes, salads and quality tin baked pies. We also, however, saw an immediate halving of all portion sizes! **We were back to a daily fight with the catering provider and supervised**

the servery each lunchtime, refusing to allow any child to walk away with a meagre portion. The Canteen staff were completely unhappy. They complained of harassment and intimidation by their new employers and, for the first time, there was a deteriorating relationship between them and the students. The ethos behind facilities management in PFI is that it releases heads and senior staff to concentrate on 'educational issues'. In our experience it absorbed vast amounts of time and detracted from curriculum business. **We probably spent a further two years dealing with catering problems and, I suggest, they will always resurface in the absence of the closest monitoring.**

From the perspective of educational management there was a blizzard of innovation at this time. Despite the enormous pressure we were under the Chair of Governors held the view that we should consider Specialist School status. This was a further development putting increased funding into schools and encouraging Secondaries to develop along 'specialist' lines. He was absolutely right. Despite the application being, ostensibly, a rigorous and competitive process the government were also keen to encourage involvement. **There were advantages to any school prepared to seize the moment in applying for specialist school status.**

With our experience of bidding processes and grant regimes we very quickly assembled and submitted a bid to become a Technology College. We were rather cavalier about this and knew that the submission lacked rigour. Many schools spent several years compiling bids and suffered changes to the regulations, changes to the forms and even changes to the political view of their eligibility if they were in challenging circumstances. We knew from experience that it was important to demonstrate interest and commitment, to throw our hat into the ring and to gain attention. Furthermore, the feedback from our bid would assist us in making a better submission in the next round. This is precisely what happened. Our bid was unsuccessful, as predicted, but we had found sponsors, we had invaluable feedback and we had also gained a consultant to steer us through our reapplication.

The publicity we received from merely making the bid was excellent and we went beyond that and changed the title of the school on all brochures and letterheads. We now described ourselves as a 'Technology School', which gave most people the impression that we already had specialist school status.

We also, publicly described ourselves as a 'Multi faith school' and, again, this designation appeared on all letterheads. **This was an example of turning a potential weakness into strength.** There were, clearly, some white parents locally who would not wish to send their children to a racially mixed school. If we had in any way tried to court these people, who were in our catchment area, the school would have failed. We did the opposite. We celebrated the diversity in the school, treated it as a privilege to be in a mixed and complex environment and drew up a policy, which described support arrangements for our different religious groups and attempted to put a recognition of spirituality at the heart of school life.

From a strategic point of view some believed that this was a concession to the significant minority of Muslim students at Shorefields. In fact our strategic target was the local Catholic population. Many of these parents and, indeed, the teachers and some of the clergy were disenchanted with the provision for Catholic boys in particular. There was no school for them in the area and there was a level of dissatisfaction with the wider options available. Some of the local Catholic Primary Headteachers saw us, realistically, as a threat and were highly circumspect in their dealings with me. Others saw us as an opportunity and I was invited to speak to groups of parents, meet members of the clergy and given free reign to promote the vision of a dynamic integrated school, which would transcend traditional divisions.

While there have, historically, been racial divisions within Toxteth itself, the Dingle, the predominantly white area, has also been divided along religious lines between Catholics and Protestants. Traditionally, Dingle has been an Orange Lodge stronghold and there were many years when Shorefields would be near empty on July 12th as students and their families took a day's holiday to join the parades in Southport.

Common sense suggested that, with a declining student population in Liverpool generally, and in our area in particular, it made sense to have more integrated schooling. Interestingly the demographic analysis of school populations, completed the following year, projected Shorefields as the only Secondary school with an increasing roll due to our 'bucking the trend' of school admissions.

Finally, our multi faith designation had some tremendous benefits. By highlighting this as a significant feature of the school and by generating an ethos of tolerance, respect and acceptance we had already won many potential future arguments with parents and students. The truth is that this is the type of environment most people want and will subscribe to. We also found that we were attracting more liberal middle class parents who saw an opportunity for their children to grow up in a multi cultural context.

In the spirit of supporting all groups in the school we hosted a day in the CLC for the Somali community. This was followed by lunch with speeches to parents about the most effective means of supporting their youngsters. We used the opportunity to promote our new after hours lessons in the core subjects aimed at raising attainment amongst Somali students in Key Stage Three.

Once a month we held 'faith assemblies' dealing with specific faith issues. This may have been aimed at older Muslim students, at Catholic students preparing for Confirmation or be a more generalised presentation from various faith leaders to a Year Group.

We also introduced more robust arrangements for lesson observations. We became more prescriptive rather than impressionistic and, for example, expected to see lesson objectives clearly displayed. Our departmental reviews were now generally accepted as a detailed and supportive way of assisting Heads of department and Heads of Year with their management roles. Furthermore the success of these exercises was such that they became the main focus for departmental development planning.

I had attended an HMI Conference for 'Schools Succeeding in challenging Circumstances' and found the recognition of our work heartening and the shared experiences of similar colleagues uplifting. I had a similar experience on the new LPSH (Leadership Programme for Serving Heads), which provided a good insight into leadership styles and gave an opportunity to reflect upon future developments and necessary change back at school.

This emphasis upon reflection was now a popular theme and we were engaged with the Authority on a detailed school self-evaluation exercise. This dovetailed with aspects of our data management arrangements and target setting exercises.

While we continued to work hard within the EAZ to raise standards in the area, and had written very persuasive community submissions for both the CLC and Technology College bids, we were under renewed pressure from the LEA to shed Community staff and scale down our provision. This contradiction was characteristic of the period. **At times it felt like a rearguard action to bid for grant funding in order to replace provision we had taken to be statutory.** This situation merely served to underline my contention that it was impossible to stand still. We needed to be moving forwards, picking up grant funding, considering new initiatives (providing they were congruent with our purposes), gaining experience in partnership building and constructing applications and of course generating income.

As a part of this strategy of moving forward we were involved in wide ranging initiatives. We had overhauled our marketing strategy and now had a professional, glossy and expensive brochure. Our web site was becoming more effective. We had, controversially, introduced a school levy on all families. Some staff opposed this in principle because we were in a deprived area. I argued that this was patronising and an affront to the opportunities we were trying to create. We had a grant funded Raising Attainment Strategy (RAP). We were now receiving significant funds from the EAZ

– for curriculum delivery, classroom assistants and the Unit. The new Neighbourhood Regeneration Company (Include) and the Sports Action Zone (SAZ), were in discussion with us over massive physical changes we proposed to the school by expanding the site. Finally, our most adventurous plan at this time involved the education of large groups of students from mainland China.

Liverpool's Chinatown was in close proximity to Shorefields and a millionaire Chinese businessman contracted with us to educate up to 100 Chinese Sixth Formers annually. We had agreed a curriculum, discussed progression routes, arranged pastoral care and the Chinese community had planned accommodation and domestic support. I met with a large group of businessmen from mainland China who were to sponsor the young people from their province. From our perspective this was a good move financially but, as important, it would immediately raise the academic profile of our Sixth form. We had actually signed a provisional contract when the Learning and Skills Council, the Director of Education and the Chief Executive of Liverpool City Council refused support. This was on a technicality and a poor interpretation of the immigration laws. Frankly, it was a massive lost opportunity for the city.

From a personal point of view this was an exhilarating period of time as a headteacher. The hard work of earlier years had paid off and all the planning for the regeneration of the school was becoming reality. The momentum was incredible. Having started from a position of severe disadvantage we had been forced to address issues of survival well in advance of other Liverpool schools. We had developed real expertise in bid writing and forming the necessary community partnerships to ensure success with grant applications. We had shed staff and were, generally, in a healthier position than many other schools. We had genuinely addressed issues of standards and our approach to behaviour had gained us great respect. Our quiet but relentless approach to marketing using – students, parents, personal contact with Primary Heads, community and faith groups, the newsletter and astute press releases could not easily be replicated. Finally, there was an overwhelming sense of confidence, and trepidation in some quarters, that the involvement of Shorefields as a partner would ensure the success of any given project. **Nothing succeeds like success.** We were now being approached with offers of funding and support, the school was about to be totally refurbished and it looked as though we may actually achieve the vision – a school of national, then international, standards. What an achievement that would be for Liverpool 8.

The Governors annual 'Away Day' at a hotel in the City Centre was quite a triumphal affair. We had an established programme of arriving for coffee in the morning and having four sessions focussed on school development interspersed with coffee breaks, lunch and an evening meal. We then retired to the lounge, often until the early hours. This event involved a great deal of planning and organisation but was a great opportunity to build camaraderie amongst the governors themselves.

By December '01 we were in the first phase of decanting into temporary accommodation prior to building work starting in January and the weight of initiative overload was beginning to tell. Life was now about meetings rather than relationships. The PFI refurbishment itself involved hundreds of meetings around design and development alone. We demanded that all work undertaken at the school contributed to the fulfilment of the vision. The developers and facilities managers were taken aback by the relentlessness and emotional intensity of our arguments. The meetings were invariably hard work, challenging and fractious but this had become an area of expertise for us. It certainly became a way of life.

As we entered the new year, January '02, the extent of the management problems involved in running a school under refurbishment became apparent. We had a temporary 'village' on an area of hard standing behind the school and we had decanted nearly a third of the staff and students into this accommodation. The staff had done a remarkable job of packing up the Science labs and Design Technology rooms and now found themselves seriously disadvantaged in their teaching. The rest of the staff had also undertaken an exercise to rationalise stock and weed out outdated materials in order to make the later decants easier. The attitude of the teaching and ancillary staff was excellent and that of the team leaders was exemplary. We were lucky. Without the Heads of department having a 'can do' attitude we would not have coped. Despite Science and DT being the most difficult subjects to move the really positive leadership in these areas acted as a model for the rest of the school.

The builders had created a compound at the end of the school, which necessitated the closure of part of Dingle Vale, the road outside the school, and the annexation of a large Local Authority playground known as 'Dingle Swings'.

It is interesting to reflect upon the original design of this school and upon the consequences of later development.

Built as Boys and Girls Secondary Modern Schools, on the same site, the original capacity had been around 500 students. The plan was stylish and simple with each school built around a rectangle and sharing a communal hall in the middle. At either end of the building was a playground with adjacent single sex toilets. The schools were bordered on one side by the road, Dingle Vale, and on the other by a playing field – separated from the building by only a narrow path. As the schools amalgamated, and grew, further building took place on the playgrounds – the only space available. The toilets for the new mixed school were no longer arranged rationally at all. Thus by the time of our refurbishment we had inadequate external space and a poor arrangement of facilities inside the building. The original main areas of hard standing were history and, during poor weather, it was difficult to keep students off the field.

Now that the builders compound and the temporary classrooms were occupying any remaining areas of hard standing our management of students outside the building was at crisis point. There was physically nowhere for them to go. The only remaining play area of tarmac could just accommodate the school for marshalling purposes but this necessitated everyone standing still in lines. This was really another unforeseen consequence of attempting to redevelop the school while it remained fully operational.

The builders had no solution to the problems the constricted site now presented. They were also now seriously at odds with the Facilities Management arm of their own business, which was contractually obliged to maintain a high standard of cleanliness in the school. This was impossible given the volume of mud being trampled in each day.

After a short period of acrimonious wrangling, with Construction and FM at each other's throats, and having refuted the ludicrous accusation that students were complicit in the importation of mud, we proposed a solution. This involved the construction of a tarmacced perimeter pathway all around the field. This was one of the few additional items, agreed during the development phase, which required a financial contribution on our part but it was transformational.

While we had achieved a partial solution to our movement problems we, nevertheless, found ourselves on the edge of unmanageability. The rooming changes were very confusing for students and staff and we inevitably lost a proportion of our curriculum time each day with the delays involved in travelling from teaching areas inside the building to the temporary classrooms. In wet and cold weather this was a really unpleasant experience. Senior staff on pager duty also found it much more difficult to support classroom teachers due to the distances involved and to difficulties negotiating a way in and out of the building past the construction work. The forbearance of staff and students was remarkable.

In the later phases of the refurbishment we opted to close the school for longer periods in order to give more time for decanting to 'the village', for moving back into the main building and for establishing teaching bases. A particular frustration was around the failure of the builders to meet agreed deadlines, often due to problems with sub contractors. This meant that students were being kept away from school and staff were waiting by to re-enter areas that were unfinished. On many occasions teachers were moving materials and equipment back into rooms while electricians and plumbers were still working. The unfortunate aspect of all this was that everyone was clearly working very hard indeed. Relations between the school staff and the contractors were good as they were with Jarvis senior managers. In fact, had there not been the highest level of cooperation, creativity and genuine partnership working offered by the school it is hard to see how the project could have been successfully completed.

There are, undoubtedly, significant issues around the disruption to young peoples education and concerns for the welfare of staff arising from such refurbishment programmes.

In addition to our daily supervision and support problems we were spending a huge amount of time in development meetings but, nevertheless, were determined to keep moving the school forward educationally. We maintained our normal monitoring arrangements and, despite some slippage, our pattern of departmental and pastoral reviews. Our curriculum leaders, particularly in Science, Design Technology and Maths were under additional pressure, as we needed a substantial contribution from them towards our Technology college bid. Something had to give and we found, subsequently, that we had been unable to provide sufficient time to developing the emerging Key Stage Three strategy in English, Maths and Science as fully as we would have liked.

In the spirit of genuinely involving the students I took any major issues in the life of the school to the Student Forum. They had considered the plans for the CLC in advance of their finalisation and, similarly, were involved in discussing each stage of the PFI development. This was enormously helpful as they could feedback directly if the building was failing to work as it should or if services were poor. They always had a view on the adequacy of, and access to, toilet facilities, the provision in the canteen, vending machines, queuing, wet weather arrangements, access to the CLC and trips and visits. There were certainly many occasions when the views expressed by the Student Forum transformed the way we ran areas of the school. It was through them that we created access to the CLC pre and post school, during the midday break and during school closure periods. We also created girls only access to ICT and girls only social facilities in response to their concerns.

The Forum was again important when the sports Action zone was established in the area and we held a number of consultation meetings with the new director. Later in the year I submitted a New Opportunities Fund bid for sport and leisure development and this was created as a partnership with the Sports Action Zone, Education Action Zone and the Neighbourhood Regeneration Company (Include).

This bid focussed on the annexation of a large area of Local Authority land, 'Dingle Swings', adjacent to the school site and the leasing of further land from a neighbouring charitable trust. While the other partners produced demographic information and addressed statutory aspects of the bid, I produced the overall rationale, consulted with the local vested interests and, through Jarvis, borrowed and adapted an industrial model to demonstrate the lifecycle costs of the project.

Essentially, this was the fulfilment of an idea I had proposed nearly ten years earlier when we considered the creation of a South Liverpool Educational Campus encompassing ourselves, a neighbouring Primary School, our Community Annexe and the Park Children's Centre, our Youth and Community and Adult Education Centres and a full time day care centre on 'Dingle Swings'. Through 'Include' this now had the working title of the 'L8 Educational Village', which, in some respects, broadened the idea as well as creating a few more conceptual difficulties. It really was incredible how far we had all moved in less than ten years. The regeneration of areas of Dingle was well underway, led by Include, and there was tremendous optimism that a range of structural improvements would bring lasting benefit.

I was certainly conscious of work overload at this time and of being unable to devote sufficient time to the wider radical proposal of 'the L8 village'. What I did was concentrate on the NOF submission. The plan involved taking all the neighbouring Local Authority and Trust land, fencing the sites, resurfacing, providing floodlighting, building community sports and social facilities and placing the whole under our secure management on behalf of the school and the community. I engaged in consultation with local schools, with the Youth and Community and Play Service, with the trustees of the local sheltered home, politicians, Jarvis, Governors and finally held a large public meeting, which was a wonderfully robust and good-natured pantomime.

The result of all this work was that the bid eventually succeeded at Local Council level and with NOF but thereafter stagnated around issues of land transfer and road closure. This was precisely the fate of a similar proposal thirty years earlier. It seems almost criminal really.

We continued to have a great deal of involvement with the Primary schools in our area of Liverpool. This was through involvement in the EAZ and also through a determination to reenergise the Toxteth Cluster, which had been overshadowed by the huge time and effort absorbed by the EAZ and its committees. The Cluster was essentially the power base for Shorefields and the Cluster Primary schools provided our lifeblood. In total there were around twenty five Primary and Nursery schools involved. The relationships here needed ongoing maintenance. On a personal level I had become very friendly with many of the Primary Heads. We attended meetings and residentials together, visited each other's schools and, while a good relationship with them was necessary professionally, it was for my part genuine. We were taken aback when a group of six long-standing heads from the area all retired at this time and they were replaced by new and enthusiastic colleagues with no background of partnership working with Shorefields.

It was quite challenging to establish close relations with this new group of headteachers. Firstly, because they generally saw themselves in competition with other Cluster schools and secondly, as a way of demonstrating high aspirations, they were indicating to parents that more selective Liverpool schools may be more appropriate for their children than the local Community Comprehensive, Shorefields.

There were clear advantages here in being involved in so many initiatives as it created an immediate set of genuine working relationships without the need for artifice. The EAZ, CLC, Technology College bid, and the NOF submission all required the written support of neighbouring schools and, therefore, meetings and discussions. After a couple of Cluster nights out, where we supplied the wine, working relations were as good as they had ever been.

It was during this period that I pushed for the Cluster to reengage with a charitable trust, the Toxteth Educational Trust (TET), an organisation originally established by the Cluster as a fund raising body. We had previous experience of charities exhibiting mission drift and goal displacement and there were real concerns in this area. Our aim was to create a successor body to the EAZ, which was itself time limited.

Relations with neighbouring Secondary schools improved through the same partnership working benefiting our relations with Primaries. We were more or less surrounded by three Diocesan schools and a girls Catholic School. They were all oversubscribed high performing schools and did not see themselves as in competition with us or even, necessarily, with each other. This was a healthy situation to be in. Our main competitors in the County sector were some distance away as were a number of Catholic boys schools drawing from the area. I took the attitude that the provision we offered was complementary to our neighbours and, now that we were oversubscribed, we were treated with increased respect.

I personally visited our neighbours to generate support for the use of the CLC, to gain testimonials for our Technology College submission and to consult with colleagues over the NOF bid. In each case they were being offered something very substantial. In the case of the NOF bid, it was permanent access to playing fields and hard courts, which they had not enjoyed previously. With regard to the CLC we saw groups of students bussed in from neighbouring Secondary schools on a weekly basis. These relations became more formal as we collaborated over plans for use of the new Leadership Incentive Grant (LIG) and later as part of an area based Post 16 collaborative.

There was no doubt that we were under strength manageri-ally to deal with the volume of leadership, management and de-velopment work underway at this time. As the Head I was, to an extent, involved in all activity but was concentrating on the strategic development of the school and the maintenance of relationships and funding streams to give us the wherewithal to do what we wanted. One Deputy was, almost singlehandedly, managing the incredibly complex PFI development along with oversight of Curriculum and Finance, while the other had a similar role in respect of all our Pastoral and Inclusion concerns, Staff Performance and pupil progress. All the key functions of the school were handled between the three of us. We all did pager duty, lunch duty and bus duty every day, dealt with disciplinary problems, met with parents and observed lessons. We met together formally each week and infor-mally each day. I had formal meetings with each deputy once a week. **The volume of business was extraordinary.**

It is possibly surprising that we had not increased senior man-agement capacity given the growth of the school but it must be remembered that our revival had, initially, created large group sizes and this necessitated the employment of more classroom teachers particularly in Science and Design Technology. We had also restruc-tured the school to cope with growth and this had involved address-ing both Curriculum and Pastoral responsibilities. The Governors had agreed to a structure of Head, three Deputies and two Assistant Heads but we had to work towards this. We had appointed a number of our senior curriculum leaders as temporary assistant heads in rotation but this, understandably, created little scope for developing strategic responsibility.

We learned, through a number of poor external appointments, that **there is a significant difference between a good middle manager and a colleague capable of accepting strategic responsibility at a senior level.** It is probably easier to do the job rather than micro manage a person who is not coping. Finally, we became very mistrustful of references.

Despite our setbacks were very pleased to appoint a third deputy for Easter 2002 and we were determined to appoint new Assistant Heads as Key Stage 3 and Key Stage 4/5 Coordinators with wider responsibilities to manage much of the internal working of the school.

Life continued at a furious pace towards the end of the academic year. We continued to have problems with the catering service and the problems of short staffing in the canteen were compounded by the resignation of three of the senior catering staff. In particular the cook and the assistant cook were unwilling to work under the arbitrary tyranny of the new regime and we ensured that they both continued in employment, as highly successful classroom support staff, within the school.

The new canteen and staff room were handed over in June and gave an immediate lift to life in the school. The students were amazed by the quality of the facilities available to them and we had, fortunately, negotiated up the size of the canteen in order to cycle 1000 students through in an hour. The original specification, agreed between the LEA and contractor, would have been under capacity by 30%.

We did have a number of immediate issues. Firstly, the position of the serveries in the canteen, which had been imposed upon us, did not allow for easy management or flow of custom. Secondly, the remote serving points, salad bars, drinks counters and so on, agreed nearly a year earlier did not materialise. We found ourselves in a highly labour intensive situation managing access and egress around the canteen. We were using twice the number of teaching staff to supervise the situation in the canteen alone. Furthermore, the problem of clearing tables and cleaning spillages resurfaced thereby slowing down the rate at which we could move students through the facility. As ever it required a series of difficult meetings to achieve the standards the students deserved. Two things were inescapable. Jarvis were contractually obliged to provide a clean canteen and they were also obliged to provide a facility through which all the students could pass in the lunch hour. The fact that we were encroaching on curriculum time each day, in order to feed everyone, was just unacceptable. Despite these problems, and ongoing wrangling over the quality of food, **the new facilities were a great step forward.** We served hot food during the pre school breakfast club, the mid morning break and during the lunch period.

Similarly the Staff Room facilities were much improved with a huge general meeting space, workroom, toilets and showers. The new staff room opened onto one of our internal quads and offered a very pleasant environment during the summer. It is worth re-emphasising that the quality of these facilities had been achieved through hours of difficult negotiation in design meetings with the contractor, the LEA and architects.

Due to the busyness and complexity of the school, I introduced a termly review of standards. This was a device to enable me to reflect a general view of progress back to staff and was simply done as a 'desktop' exercise. I was concerned to maintain an overview of the school in all its aspects – curriculum, pastoral, community, administration, finance, facilities management, catering, governance etc. **It is only by standing back and evaluating your position that you can properly focus energy.**

Because we always did make a habit of reflection we recognised the need for constant development. We arranged to supply laptop computers to staff. A Governors Pastoral panel was established to help monitor disciplinary cases in the school. We also advertised the availability of personal interviews, for prospective new students, with me as the Head each evening. This was simply a device to imply selection and exclusivity. There was a good take-up.

We engaged consultancy support to develop web based curriculum materials area by area. Finally, shortly after the opening of the new canteen, we arranged a Business in the Community (BITC) event and invited a large group of potential future sponsors into the school to meet students and discuss educational issues.

One area of real success throughout was our bilingual provision – the facilities we provided for students whose first language was other than English. We had the largest number of such students in the city and were fortunate to have a very dedicated teacher in charge of the project supported by a group of highly professional community language colleagues. The methods used and the materials developed became a model within the EAZ and led to a successful publication.

Despite our increased management strength I was still dealing with a significant number of disciplinary cases through until the end of the academic year. These all warranted the Headteacher's involvement and concerned possible expulsions or transfer to other schools. These included the theft of a laptop from a member of staff, an allegation of assault on a visiting teacher, bullying and racial harassment outside the school. We were still outside the school each evening and, sad to say, the problems of getting the students away from the school each night persisted.

On the financial front we had received a grant to install a lift in our Science block, although this needed to be incorporated into our PFI scheme. We had cancelled a planned trip to France due to organisational problems and this was a significant expense for the school. Finally, we received notification of our Technology College status. We had achieved this outside the stated quota of schools supported by the LEA. This involved, as a capital project, the construction of a Computer Aided Design and Manufacturing (CAD/CAM) suite for textiles. We refurbished an abandoned block we had fought to save from demolition under PFI. We would, also, receive substantial revenue funding for the project. The announcement of this latest success, which would have been a cause for celebration in all other schools, was greeted with exhausted indifference by the staff. They just needed a holiday.

LEARNING POINTS YEAR 9

- The teaching commitments of Pastoral staff may, effectively, prevent them spending time on monitoring and support activities.

- The PFI contractor shed staff at a bewildering rate.

- There were serious disputes between the PFI contractors own business units over the completion of remedial works.

- There was, immediately, a sharp deterioration in the standard of catering under PFI.

- Canteen prices rocketed under PFI.

- There were significant gaps in cleaning caused by the dispute between the PFI contractor and the catering sub-contractors.

- It was necessary to commission an independent Health and Safety report to get effective action.

- The pathetic PFI commitment to providing a 'meal of the day' to those on free dinners was quite offensive.

- Maintaining catering standards under PFI was a hugely time consuming daily battle.

- There was harassment and intimidation of the canteen staff by the PFI sub contractor.

- Facilities Management under PFI absorbed vast amounts of management time and detracted from curriculum business.

- Catering problems will always resurface in the absence of the closest monitoring.

- There are advantages to any school being prepared to seize the moment with new initiatives such as the specialist school programme.

- It is important to turn potential weaknesses into strengths. We proudly described ourselves as a multi-faith school.

- Most people will subscribe to an ethos of tolerance, respect and acceptance.

- There are times when grant funds merely replace provision once taken to be statutory.

- In organisational terms it is impossible to stand still. One must always be looking for opportunities to move forwards.

- Once an organisation has momentum, success follows success.

- The PFI design and development process itself involves hundreds of hours of meeting time.

- It is important to recognise when life is about meetings rather than relationships.

- Staff in temporary accommodation during refurbishment are seriously disadvantaged in their teaching.

- Heads of Department require a 'can do' attitude during disruption to the school.

- There is a range of unforeseen consequences to the total refurbishment of a fully operational school.

- Life on the edge of unmanageability is not pleasant.

- Builders fail to meet agreed deadlines.

- Without the highest level of cooperation, creativity and genuine partnership working on the part of a school it is hard to see how a PFI refurbishment can be accomplished.

- There are, undoubtedly, significant issues around the disruption to the education of young people and concerns for the welfare of staff arising out of such programmes.

- A Student Forum provides essential insights during a period of change.

- Even the best schemes, with financial support and government approval, can stagnate over permissions at local council level.

- Involvement in a range of initiatives provides the opportunity for genuine Primary/Secondary working relationships without the need for artifice.

- Once a school is oversubscribed it is treated with increased respect.

- Being under strength managerially impedes progress over development work and general leadership and management issues.

- There is a significant difference between a good middle manager and a colleague capable of accepting strategic responsibility at a senior level.

- Be mistrustful of references.

- There was an arbitrary tyranny towards staff within the PFI regime.

- The new facilities provided under PFI *were* a tremendous and inspiring step forward.

- It is only by standing back and, regularly, evaluating your position that you can properly focus energy.

- If you feel tired, from time to time, think how the staff feels.

START OF TENTH YEAR OF
HEADSHIP SEPTEMBER 2002

IN FACT, SOME STAFF did not get much of a holiday due to their involvement in the running of Summer Schools at Shorefields. The previous year had been disappointing as we found that Summer School programmes run by other agents lacked appropriate supervision and overall control. We could not have this in our school. While some of our teaching staff were involved in the actual teaching of courses, either through our Raising Achievement Programme or through the EAZ, we realised that the premises required overall management when, potentially, hundreds of youngsters could be on site on a given day. The Summer had been divided into three blocks for the three deputies. I was the backup for the whole Summer period and this was an error of judgement. It meant that my mobile phone was switched on permanently and I could be, and was, contactable at any and every point. I did not feel as though I had really been away from work at all and the deputies, and many staff, probably felt much the same.

In considering the examination results, we had done well to

maintain student performance given the remarkable disruption of the last two years and the figure gaining 5 or more good GCSEs was again around 25%. We had only excluded 2 students during the previous year and this was a tribute to the work of the two Units we now had on site, to much earlier involvement of parents, to the limited success of the negotiated transfer scheme between schools, to the involvement of Governors and to one Deputy working flat out on disciplinary issues.

The simple fact of the school being at capacity in most year groups also contributed in a number of ways – as we had predicted. Firstly, it created a greater sense of stability in the school and, secondly, we were no longer obliged to take extraordinarily difficult students from elsewhere.

Our intake was 205 students into Year 7 and parents were appealing against placements in other schools. We had moved away from a straightforward 'negative preference' situation to one in which parents were making very positive choices. I really felt as though we had arrived at a significant place. **The school was now of a size to be taken very seriously indeed. The size of the school was crucial to the realisation of our vision.** If we were to diversify our provision, particularly in Performing Arts and by 'tracking' students through a more vocational curriculum, we would require large numbers in each year group. We had a much wider span of needs than most schools and were very concerned that our teaching should be as appropriate as possible for the individual students.

The refurbishment programme had now reached the Senior Staff and School Administration offices and we moved into the temporary accommodation outside the building. On reflection this was probably a mistake. While, on the one hand, it demonstrated that Senior Management were enduring the same conditions as the staff, on the other it made the possibility of support for those same staff much more challenging. **The capacity for management to manage should be heavily protected for the sake of the staff and the students.** As well as coordinating the routine life of the school I was also overseeing a range of additional initiatives and engaged in negotiations over further developments for Shorefields.

Much of our success to date had been around seizing opportunities and responding quickly and appropriately to challenges. As the Head, I was now marooned in a portacabin on the field behind the school. There were no phone lines to the temporary accommodation and relying upon mobile phones proved useless. I was not in direct contact with our main reception/administration/reprographics/caretaking staff. At the same time, the School Administration officer, who acted as my P.A., was away from work ill. The Bursar was also on long – term sick leave. We were a step closer to unmanageability and, as senior staff, we were literally running around the building in an attempt to cover all the bases.

There were indeed many issues to address at this time.

We had decided to investigate a new information management system, CMIS, to replace the more traditional SIMS. This was part of a deal brokered by some of the Secondary Heads. It involved our new Deputy in extensive liaison with the CMIS team, other schools and our own staff. We had also opted into a new Liverpool initiative and agreed to host a BEST, Behaviour and Education Support Team. This was targeted at those wards with the highest crime and disorder levels and not at undisciplined schools. From our perspective, as a Community Comprehensive trying to push a multi agency and more holistic approach to education this was very attractive as was the involvement of a school based nurse we took on at around this time.

BEST involved the location of a new specialist team at the school. The team was to include an Educational Psychologist, Social Worker, Police Officer, Teacher and Administration staff. It cost hundreds of thousands of pounds to implement.

From the outset we agreed to this scheme providing we had control of deployment and were allowed the overall management role. **We had seen too many bolt-on initiatives squander opportunity through ineffectiveness, lack of drive, or replication.** What was needed was a clear assessment of the work of the school followed by an analysis of how the school and the BEST team could move forward as an entity.

Despite agreements with the LEA, the BEST initiative initially foundered over recruitment problems, the complexity of their strategic and operational thinking, the identification of appropriate casework and the need to demonstrate targets no matter how shallow. The colleagues appointed were excellent but we struggled with systemic problems and real issues of communication and accountability.

The PFI project itself was proceeding well. We had managed to negotiate some significant improvements on the original plans. These included an additional 30% capacity in the canteen, a new Art and Learning Support block, a first floor corridor link into our Science block and a Prayer Room. The latter included a washing area as an ante – room and this was all planned in conjunction with the Liverpool Mosque.

We had recognised that **aspiring to national and international standards suggested commensurate links** and were in contact with a range of schools in the North West who we had identified as successful in raising achievement. We developed a close link with a Catholic School in Strabane, Northern Ireland, and were pursuing links in India, China, the USA and Canada.

A priority for me was still the delivery of an integrated ICT strategy and a feature of this had to be coherence between the facilities of the CLC and the school. We were still struggling with the obscene situation in which our access to the CLC was generating hostility from 'partner' schools in relatively middle class areas. Shorefields was chosen as a 'host' school precisely because of the advantages this would bring to the seriously deprived population we served. Yet, here we were, 2 years later still receiving 'clarification' from the DFES and from the Excellence in Liverpool team around our status. We had done most of the planning work, had suffered all the physical disruption, had relinquished our Annexe to part fund the project, taken significant responsibilities for management and were still contending with redefinitions which obliterated the original concept of 'host' school and, apparently, relegated the host school to mere 'partner' status.

While this reflected the confusion around the country, our situation was more complex due to the design of the CLC. It was in the heart of Shorefields. We shared a front entrance, reception, administration, cleaning and security. My response to this obstructive nonsense, over the status of Shorefields as the host school, was to work harder at generating beneficial activity for the partner schools while not giving an inch in the philosophical and practical arguments over control. My fallback position was always the Governors and I frequently invoked their concerns in meetings and halted discussion in order for them to be consulted.

I managed to amplify and embed an argument over the value of the Annexe we had handed over to the Authority. I did feel a sense of bitterness over the whole business anyway as the Annexe had fallen into disrepair due to failings on the part of the Council not the School. As explained previously, we relinquished control of the building at a point when it was no longer safe to retain it under our management and to facilitate relatively minor works, to the value of around £27,000, in conjunction with the building of the CLC. The Annexe itself could easily have had a market value at the time of £600,000 and would be worth substantially more now. We, the argument ran, had, in effect, covered most of the development costs of the whole CLC. It was essential to keep this argument live as a backstop to our position.

Interestingly, the argument over the Annexe took a new turn when the Authority finally acknowledged that the planned development of the school would be inadequate for the number on roll. This had been another area of contention as our intake continued to rise. It was absurd that we faced a situation in which the school would be refurbished and rebuilt to a high standard only to suffer the teaching of a proportion of students in portacabins. I threatened

to reoccupy the Annexe, now occupied by LEA Advisors and, surprisingly, renovated by the Authority since we left! We received a
grudging acknowledgement that additional permanent accommodation would be provided on our main site.

Attempting to move a school forwards while in contention
with agencies around you creates a very difficult personal position.
Shorefields had deteriorated to a great extent due to a power struggle
around the governing body, due to past failures at Council level and
through tangible opposition from other schools. Most of our initiatives still suffered from bureaucratic incompetence, short staffing, an
inability to form priorities and inertia within the Council. The cabal
controlling the Secondary Heads Group continued to be implacably
hostile to developments at the school. Clearly, we had been afforded a measure of support and confidence by the Education Authority
but to actually realise the opportunities available was taking a great
deal of determination, energy and assertion. It was no surprise that
the announcement of our Technology College status received no
acknowledgement from either the LEA or the Secondary Heads. It
had been a remarkable achievement, against the odds and without
the support of the LEA. This, unfortunately, only served to confirm
a certain maverick reputation within the city.

In these circumstances one must make choices. **A sense of
isolation is manageable if you define your purposes clearly
and know which constituency you are working to.** In my case,
while not rejecting a relationship with other secondary schools, I
focussed on improving Shorefields for the students, making the
Toxteth Primary Heads my main point of reference professionally,
and working closely with any organisations striving to regenerate
Liverpool 8.

Internally, we were still dealing with the fractious issue of the
foreign trip from the end of the previous academic year. This had
become a disciplinary matter involving LEA Advisors, Personnel
Officers, unions and other staff. The issue was instrumental in us
undertaking curriculum reorganisation in the area. I was also strug-

gling with a long-standing problem regarding the competence of a relatively senior member of staff. Not only is this an embarrassment to the organisation as a whole but, due to the level of responsibility, **staff and students are at risk when operational routines are being managed badly.** Unfortunately dealing with problems generated by staff can overwhelm the rest of school business for Headteachers. It is certainly true that 90% of your time spent on personnel issues can involve only 10% of the staff. At least the realisation of this as an issue can help to focus Senior Managers on the need to support, encourage and praise everyone working in the school. **I had a sign opposite my desk which said '10:1' as a reminder to concentrate upon praise rather than criticism in those proportions.**

We had continued with our cluster meetings of parents throughout the refurbishment of the school and, early in the year, we met with Czech parents. There had been a large influx of Czech families into Liverpool and many cited persecution as the reason for their migration to Britain. As ever it was challenging to integrate these students into the school and we faced familiar culture clashes and conflicts. We had excellent language support, which helped enormously when meeting with parents.

We did have a distressing incident when Police and Immigration Officials came to the school to remove a number of students whose families were being deported due to illegal immigration. This was, however, a highly unusual occurrence for us. It served to underscore how unhelpful the media spotlight on illegal immigration was for the vast majority of Eastern European immigrants, who were in Britain quite legitimately.

I was continuing to hold individual interviews with families several evenings a week and this was having a positive effect on the climate of support we were building for the school. While my sole intention was to create an atmosphere of selection and exclusivity and, therefore, at root the exercise was entirely cynical, in practice it was anything but. I had suggested to parents that the extensive period of waiting for Secondary School placements, imposed by the Liverpool system, was unfair educationally and emotionally. There were significant numbers leaving Primary School in the July without having confirmation of their Secondary place for September. In most cases this was because they had rejected the place offered by the LEA. It was certainly disheartening to visit Primary Schools in June and find confusion amongst children over their futures. If nothing else it caused chaos in the natural process of reforming friendship groups prior to moving to the next educational stage. My contention was that **if a child's choice of Secondary School was settled earlier they could sort out their friendship arrangements, be more settled and work better towards the end of Year 6 and look forward with anticipation towards transition.**

The reality for Shorefields was that as the County School for the area we were obliged to take children who had selected us as first choice. There would at some point be a limit on this but we knew at this stage that we wanted to grow and that we would be able to accommodate the numbers applying. This meant that immediately following a personal interview and, having achieved an undertaking that Shorefields would be selected first on Transfer Forms, I was able to offer a place there and then.

The effect of this completely illegitimate action should not be underestimated. Parents and children were delighted that in October of Year 6 they knew where they were going nearly twelve months hence. I was able to meet and form an initial relationship with some great parents who, subsequently, became school governors. The family would leave with a 'completely confidential' signed agreement between us which they promised not to reveal to anyone in case it created too great a demand for places. They *always* showed the agreement to other parents and we were inundated with requests for interviews. This was wonderful and everyone was happy.

By the end of October we were tackling a significant workload. We were involved in intense negotiations over the later phases of the PFI project with plans requiring interrogation room by room.

The NOF bid, over expanding the school site, had stalled at Council level, despite support from the Chief Executive of the Council, and we were applying pressure on officers in Strategic Development and Leisure Services on a weekly basis even to make minimal progress. We were also in correspondence with local Councillors, the Highways Department and Planning over permission for the road closure as a necessary part of the scheme.

The re-engagement of the Toxteth Cluster with TET, the Toxteth Educational Trust, had proved exceptionally difficult, as we had immediately walked into a dispute between the Chair of the Trust and the Manager. The Chair was suspended following a complaint and I became temporary Chair until the dispute was resolved. This involved negotiating with the Charity Commissioners, unions, staff and trustees and steering the organisation through a series of hearings. In the end, unfortunately, despite more than two years of acrimony, frustration at meetings, misdirection and demoralisation we made no progress with TET. The Cluster heads resigned en masse and notified the Charity Commissioners that this was the case.

The EAZ had proved to be of great value to the area but, despite its short life, we were now involved in work to effect its 'transformation'. This was the exit strategy needed to preserve some of the impetus of the initiative at the end of funding and to address contractual responsibilities as the organisation wound down. It has been remarked upon previously that clever ideas and political soundbites take on a new dimension when they move towards implementation. We had another example here of a fine policy becoming turgidly difficult in practice. Having spent significant time building the capacity of the EAZ before it could deliver anything, finding premises, recruiting staff, developing internal policies and wrestling with VAT we now had to take advice on termination of contracts, redundancy payments, disposal of assets, preparation of final accounts and an agreed structure whereby the core of our EAZ would be subsumed under the Excellence in Liverpool programme. More meetings about meetings.

We were continuing to use the resources of the EAZ to improve the School and, with them, had embarked upon a very thorough improvement programme for the Maths Faculty. While much of our observation indicated that the subject was reasonably well taught the examination results were of serious concern. We had support from the LEA, and the EAZ, recruited staff and embarked upon a development programme for existing staff. Clearly, the achievement of comparable results across our core subjects was a non negotiable.

Part of our plan for raising attainment was linked to the use of the CLC. We now had substantial access to Information Technology and had deliberately planned the CLC itself in 'zones' in order to facilitate access. Behind the reception area was a suite of 30 PCs devoted to Modern Foreign Languages and Humanities, in the basement was the 'Cyber Café' for use by the Sixth Form, on the mezzanine we had a Guidance Suite and overlooking the whole there was an English/Maths area of 30 more PCs. In addition there was a CAD/CAM (Computer Aided Manufacturing and Design) block, an Interactive Science Laboratory and an ICT Music Suite. There were more than four hundred computers in the school. While any staff could book any suite, location and proximity to teaching areas was obviously an issue.

Understandably, the physical difficulty of moving around our building had an impact upon CLC use and upon developing curriculum at this time. It is a real credit to staff, particularly in Design and Technology and Modern Languages that their enthusiasm for the new resources was unabated. The Design Technology staff, in particular, were at the centre of the greatest changes. They had embraced the CLC most enthusiastically. In respect of the PFI remodelling and refurbishment programme, they had been engaged in a complex design and procurement process for their own areas of the school, which they now reoccupied, and were undertaking the same process again as part of the Technology College capital project.

The success of the Technology College bid brought its own

pressures, as, ahead of the capital project, we needed to demonstrate progress with the main thrust of the bid, which was about raising attainment through a new perspective on teaching and learning. This involved work with the core subjects, again, and beyond them with the rest of the school.

We were also monitoring and making returns for our Raising Attainment Programme, Leadership Incentive Grant, Social Inclusion funds, Special Needs budget and bilingual allocation. This was all in addition to our main budget, our Community Allocation, the Adult Education provision and the different strands of funding within Excellence in Liverpool, for example for the Learning Mentors and the Gifted and Talented Programme. Thus, we were involved in around fifteen major grant driven or centrally funded regimes and half a dozen minor additional funds. Unsurprisingly, in addition to the Administration officer and the Bursar being on long-term sick leave, our Finance officer was also ill.

In addition to all this financial, project and general curriculum management we also had to run the school and this was a very testing time indeed. I had identified during my last LPSH (Leadership Programme for Serving Heads) day that priorities for me concerned – withdrawing from much operational business, creating blocks of time for strategic work, delegating more assertively and encouraging all other Senior Managers to accept full responsibility for the school. **It is, however, difficult to withdraw from operational business when your Senior Team are genuinely stretched to the limit and all hands are needed at the pumps just to maintain the status quo.**

In truth the refurbishment was having a deleterious effect upon the life of the school and there was little we could do but cope. The site was overcrowded and we had no way of separating out the students. We had new groups of youngsters with language problems who were having difficulty assimilating; our Muslim girls were asserting themselves, since the invasion of Iraq, and we had conflict between them and both black and white indigenous girls; gang conflicts in the area were resurfacing and affecting the life of the school. We had chaos at the end of each day with site work under- way, buses manoeuvring around the builders compound, parents' cars blocking the road, a thousand students leaving the building and the usual gangs loitering with intent. A police presence was now a permanent feature of the end of each day.

In mid November we suffered the sad death of one of our stu- dents. I attended the funeral along with Pastoral Staff and Learning Mentors. Many students had requested leave to attend and we be- lieved that many more would simply absent themselves. The fu- neral was hugely attended by the black community and a colleague Primary Head read the eulogy. It was upsetting to see so many young people confronted by the reality of a friend's death. The service was very dignified. Afterwards I shook hands and exchanged con- dolences with a lot of people known to me personally and with many of our own students. One lady criticised me for not closing the school, but this was said out of grief and I didn't respond.

Returning to Shorefields I arrived in time for the end of school clearance and went straight onto duty with colleagues. I was super- vising buses near the builders compound when I received a phone call to say that intruders were on the site and heading for the mobile classrooms. I knew that at this time there were a number of female staff working alone in these rooms with no means of alerting col- leagues. I made my way through the compound on the quickest route to the mobiles and came face to face with four of the worst delinquents in the area. Upon seeing me they bolted for a security fence and scaled it in seconds. They then turned to argue and hurl abuse. This should have been 'bread and butter' to me but instead of ignoring them and moving on I challenged their behaviour and said we were sick of their repeated intrusions. This brought an incredibly psychotic and violent response. The worst I have ever witnessed. One youth repeatedly threw himself at the fence, screaming, swear- ing, and threatening to kill me. Unable to scale the fence from the outside he started to run around the compound towards the access gates followed by the other three.

The students were leaving the school by now and many were making their way along a narrow footpath between the compound and the Dingle Swings fence. Pushing against them and through them were the four youths still screaming and shouting obscenities and threats. This was not good. I dialled 999 on my mobile with little anticipation of a decent response. Emergency calls from mobiles seemed to be routed to a call centre out of the area and previous emergency operators had never heard of the school or the Dingle, which made a rapid response difficult. My other concern was the students. I felt fatalistic about the oncoming brawl with the four hooligans but couldn't conceive of it taking place in this arena with this audience. All this went through my head. Suddenly the emergency operator answered and I explained that I was under attack. The youths had reached the gates and stopped. Whether it was the fact that I was obviously in contact with the police and talking loudly and assertively into the phone or a concern over their vulnerability once they left the street is immaterial. They stopped issued more threats to return and kill me and then made off.

I continued with my report to the Police and asked for the call to be transferred to the duty desk at the local station. The caretakers arrived at this point and they were dispatched to check on the welfare of staff in the classrooms.

I felt unwell. I had pains in my chest, neck and arm and was exhausted. The angina had been a daily reality for years but had become progressively worse. Following a doctors appointment the following day I was admitted to hospital on suspicion of an imminent heart attack. I had had a heart attack in 1994 and they did not want a repetition. I languished in hospital for two weeks. **At a single stroke I found that I had withdrawn from operational duties, delegated fully and allowed others to take responsibility for the school.** Not a bad result I suppose.

Forced to work from home I concentrated on strategic business and development planning. This included the new School

Development Plan, the Leadership Incentive Grant submissions, Threshold applications, the Governors Annual Report to parents, roles for the new Assistant Heads we hoped to appoint, a review of operational responsibilities within the school and the reorganisation of Governors sub committees.

Moving back into the main building in January, we faced continuing opposition, from the LEA, to the retention of our community staff and were subjected to a farcical review. Our stated aims in deploying our community tutors were to run a Reintegration Unit and to provide a Youth facility, which would occupy huge numbers of young people both during the day and in the evenings. We were very successful on both counts although we had to deploy staff and resources from our main budget in order to support the community tutors. The review allowed for no discussion with senior staff, looked at no evidence and concluded that our Unit was working well catering for around 60 youngsters per year but that our Youth Club, catering for around 650 per week was not. We had already drawn up a Youth Development Plan, which addressed 'curriculum' issues and **we informed the Youth Service that we would not accept their flawed report.** We would accept that we had been involved in a pilot inspection exercise as a learning experience for *their* staff. We refused to support any dissemination or publication of the report, which we regarded as part of a mere cost cutting exercise.

We continued running the Unit successfully and continued with the Youth Club as the biggest informal venue for young people of all racial and ethnic backgrounds in the city.

Having made little progress with TET (The Toxteth Educational Trust) a number of Cluster Heads were keen to build on the experience of the EAZ and move all the schools in the area forward on the back of a recent Government initiative – Network Learning Communities. This involved a genuine commitment to sharing new approaches to learning, perhaps using new technologies (wireless ICT networks were becoming popular) but certainly focussing on an understanding of the most effective learning styles for individual youngsters.

By now I had delegated responsibility for much of our external agenda to our new deputy. This included all EAZ business, the work of the Cluster, liaison over the CLC, Adult and Community provision and driving forward the work around the Technology College.

We had engaged the services of an external consultant to advise over finance and he brought an accountants experience to bear on our finances and our future projections. Liverpool had no assigned finance officers for Secondary Schools and we had been completely self-managing for around 15 years. Some schools had created significant problems for themselves by using additional grant funding to support the core budget. We had never done this. Our core budget supported all our mainstream staff including managers. This was one of the reasons we were relatively slow to rebuild management strength. **Our budget was 'hypothecated' to the extent that we identified clearly the additional purposes of each funding stream.** This provided substantial security against the withdrawal of funding. It also created the atmosphere in which middle managers were much clearer over the outputs expected and understood grant-speak such as 'project activity', 'milestones' and 'beneficiary hours'.

Now that most of the building had been refurbished we had come full circle in terms of addressing the environment. We needed to energise departments to take up display space on corridors and returned to the need for reinvestment in plants. While this had originally been a desperate measure to disguise the decay in the old building, the softening and civilising impact of the plants was now missing. As ever, **the atmosphere in the school required constant maintenance and review and there were a number of new imperatives.** The larger numbers of students necessitated even higher levels of supervision. The internal modifications of the last two years had created a first floor link corridor around the entire building and into the Tower Block making clearance at the end of the morning session difficult. The new Art and Learning Support block

had created a number of blind corners and created an area of external yard space, which was difficult to supervise. The increase in the
sale of packaged food by the Canteen and Youth Club was creating
a colossal litter problem and, finally, fire alarms had become a way
of life, which was hugely disruptive to the school.

**Our response to the supervisory issues was to reorganise du-
ties, be at our posts, create roving duty team leaders and work
harder.**

The fire alarm situation was intriguing. Each time the alarm
sounded we evacuated the entire building. We left the alarm ringing until the source had been traced and only allowed students and
staff back into the building when everyone had been spoken to.
The main causes of the alarms during this period were electrical
problems, oversensitive smoke detectors (for example near solder-
ing work or cooking), accidental breakage and malicious intent. We
took alarms very seriously indeed and evacuating the building was
always difficult given the limitations of the site. It was frustrating
that the alarms were frequently the result of work on site because,
from experience, one alarm often gave rise to copycat behaviour.
We suffered a number of occasions upon which we evacuated the
school twice in a single day. In previous years this would not have
happened as the alarm would have been switched off until we felt
it reasonable to reset it. Again this was not correct behaviour at all
but nor was it right that the lives of so many could be disrupted so
easily. It was a point of principle that we always discovered the
cause of an alarm. This was communicated to the students and staff
with an apology for the disruption, frequently in the freezing cold
and rain. We treated malicious false alarms as 'seriously disturbed
behaviour' – warranting the involvement of Governors, the Police
and Educational Psychologists and consideration of exclusion. The
young people themselves disliked disruption and had no respect
for this type of behaviour. They also knew that we investigated the
whereabouts of every single person in the building each time there
was an alarm. This eradicated false alarms during lessons as the

perpetrators were easy to trace.

The litter problem frustrated Jarvis, the caretaking and cleaning staff, the sports staff and neighbours. I proposed a 'continuous clean' operation which Jarvis initially rejected out of hand. The outside became a mess during the lunchtime and they set about cleaning it from 1.30pm. It was the way things had always been done.

Fortunately, the Output Specification stated clearly that the grounds must be kept clean and free from litter. This, in my view, did not suggest that young people should tolerate unpleasant conditions for an hour each day. Jarvis accepted the principle and grudgingly agreed to test my argument that **a continuous clean would require less staff and less effort.** If it could be done at Disneyland and the Trafford Centre, in Manchester, I was sure we could do it at Shorefields.

Initially, the continuous clean at lunchtime was a total failure. I realised that staff were very reluctant to be seen publicly picking up litter. Because they were embarrassed and half hearted they communicated diffidence to the students and, all in all, the job was no better. On the slightest pretext the 'litter picking' was abandoned in favour of more pleasant duties.

I began monitoring the situation. I rang the caretakers if there was no one on 'outside' duty. I would do the litter picking myself until staff arrived. I organised students to litter pick. Eventually, Jarvis got the message. This was to be done seriously or there would be endless complaints. The difference was remarkable and proved the argument. People do not intentionally drop litter when they see somebody charged with picking it up. On a daily basis we could observe students going out of their way to place litter in the bin bags carried by the 'pickers'. Another result for civilisation and common sense.

Over the coming months I was absent intermittently and also organised more strategic work to complete at home. By July, the refurbishment was complete and was of a high standard. Shorefields was the first Liverpool Secondary School to be refurbished under PFI. Staff, students and the community in the area now had the quality of provision they deserved. **The staff at Shorefields had been outstanding in their forbearance of the difficulties involved in refurbishing a living school while it was fully operational.** It is not an experience I would recommend. Nevertheless, it was pleasing to note that, despite the fifteen months of difficulties over catering, with some remarkably low standards offered, the situation was now excellent. I was proud to be associated with the new catering manageress and her team as the quality of food and the manner of its presentation were first class.

Key to the success of the refurbishment had been our Senior Deputy on behalf of the school, the lead officer for the LEA and the overall contract manager for Jarvis. PFI had helped to create a school to be proud of.

We were nearing completion of the CAD/CAM Textiles block as part of the Technology College development and were well advanced with associated curriculum plans.

In the last two years we had lost ten teaching staff but gained twenty eight. This included the new Community Deputy who was already making an impact. We had interviewed and appointed two Assistant Heads to start the following September, which would bring our management strength to six plus two Senior teachers. This was seriously needed, as Shorefields had become a large complex organisation. For September 2003, for example, we had planned for eight forms of entry with up to 240 Year 7 students and 1100 on roll.

We also had notification of an Ofsted Inspection in September and were busy making preparations. Despite the strongest indication from Ofsted that they no longer required the masses of documentary evidence apparent in previous years we judged it to be in our favour to overwhelm them with detail about the school and its activities.

We had still made little progress with the BEST team although individuals appeared to be working hard and with enthusiasm. An example of this enthusiasm came towards the end of term.

The light evenings had given rise to familiar problems in the neighbourhood and rivalries had surfaced in school. Our assigned Police Officer had alerted his new Inspector to this and the response, at three o'clock one afternoon was alarming. The Inspector arrived at school accompanied by around a dozen Police vehicles. There may well have been sixty officers supported by dogs with further mounted officers as backup. I explained to the new Inspector that, no matter what the scale of the problem, the only response we ever really wanted was a single marked police car. He agreed to keep the officers and, particularly, the dogs in the vehicles and allowed us to handle what turned out to be a normal and peaceful dispersal of students.

This had been a busy and difficult year compounded by my absences. By the year end, we were still engaged in the planning of new initiatives, in particular around Citizenship in the curriculum. We were looking hard at new guidelines on staff workload and were planning another Summer School.

We had obviously made disappointing progress in a number of areas. The New Opportunities Fund bid to expand the site had barely progressed in six months. Our Leadership Incentive Grant collaboration with other schools needed revisiting with a greater degree of harmonisation between partner organisations. Finally, the accommodation problems, our oversubscription had given rise to, meant that we would start our first full year as a 'new' school using temporary additional classrooms.

On a day to day basis fewer problems were coming directly to me as Head. Senior Staff had accepted full responsibility for the running of the school and that my role had to be more strategic. The Ofsted forms clearly showed that there was a need for schools to spend more time considering policy. In order to do this, as Head, I needed to step away from operational roles and, in particular, delegate all responsibility for routine duties. We were looking forward to our new Assistant Heads starting in September and sharing the workload.

LEARNING POINTS YEAR 10

- Summer schools are extremely demanding and may exhaust managers and staff.
- The Head must have time when he/she is out of contact with the school.
- The size of a school is crucial to the realisation of certain curriculum plans.
- The capacity for management to manage should be heavily protected for the sake of the staff and the students.
- Much of our success had been around seizing opportunities and responding quickly and appropriately to challenges.
- Too many bolt-on initiatives squander opportunity through ineffectiveness, lack of drive or replication.
- Aspiring to national and international standards suggested some commensurate links.
- 'Partnership' management of new initiatives may prevent real benefit reaching the most disadvantaged.
- A sense of isolation is manageable if you define your purposes

clearly and know which constituency you are working to.

- Incompetence on the part of senior staff is an embarrassment to an organisation.

- Staff and students are at risk when operational routines are being managed badly.

- Managers everywhere spend 90% of their time dealing with 10% of the staff.

- Senior managers need to focus on supporting, encouraging and praising everyone in the organisation.

- We should praise and criticise in a proportion of 10:1.

- Parental interviews create an atmosphere of selection and ex-clusivity.

- A successful bid brings its own pressures.

- It is difficult to withdraw from operational business when your senior team are genuinely stretched to the limit and all hands are needed at the pumps just to maintain the status quo.

- A major refurbishment will have a deleterious effect upon the life of the school and there may be little one can do but try to cope.

- If you do not believe that a report on the school is fair then it must be challenged or rejected.

- It is important to identify the *additional* purposes of each new funding stream rather than ploughing new funds into core activ-ity.

- The atmosphere in a school requires constant maintenance and review.

- Schools should be cleaned continuously. This requires less staff and less effort and contributes to an atmosphere of common sense and civilisation.

- PFI had helped to create a school to be proud of.

START OF ELEVENTH YEAR OF
HEADSHIP SEPTEMBER 2003

D UE TO THE IMPENDING Inspection, scheduled for the week of September 15th, it was necessary to spend more of the Summer period than usual making preparations for the new academic year. The second Monday of term was booked for the important first visit of the Registered Inspector and he had scheduled a Senior Staff Meeting, Parents Meeting, lunch with Governors and full Staff Meeting for the one day. All of this required preparation.

We were also finalising plans for the Inspection week itself, reviewing progress with the SDP, scrutinising Senior Staff responsibilities and rereading our own self assessment comments on the Ofsted forms. We had brought forward our normal schedule of dates for the completion of exam analysis by departments and the updating of schemes of work. This meant more work for everyone, in August, in order to be best prepared for the Inspection.

We experienced a dip in GCSE performance, unsurprising really given the disruption, and just under 20% gained five or more good grade GCSEs. The Post 16 GNVQ results were very good again and, finally, we had excluded no students during the previous year. This was a remarkable achievement. Our intake in September was 210 Year 7 students and they appeared to be a very promising group of young people indeed. We obviously did not have long to prepare them for the forthcoming inspection.

In order to prepare the Governors, we held a full Governors meeting during the first week in September. **In previous Inspections we had found that Governors struggled with searching questions on school development and strategic planning.** They had been presented with a detailed outline of developments, to read during the Summer, as well as with the summary of key priorities they were familiar with from their termly meetings. We were able to discuss progress since the last inspection in order to build their confidence for meeting inspectors. Most importantly, it was an opportunity for the new Governors and Affiliate Governors to become comfortable with their roles.

As ever **our preparation for the inspection was thorough and was considerate of the inspectors needs.** The room set aside for their use was well equipped. There were tables groaning with catalogued 'evidence' and necessary details about the school. Refreshments were organised, clerical and site staff were briefed and teachers and students had a healthy anticipation of a busy week from the 15th September.

When we arrived at school on Thursday 11th September, two working days before the Inspection, we discovered a break in. The intruders had smashed their way into seven classrooms and, in the process, had damaged doors, door frames and caused real disruption. They had stolen the interactive white board projector from each room and, for those staff who had prepared all their work for the Inspection as a series of 'Power Point' presentations, this was devastating.

The atmosphere in the staff room that morning was one of subdued demoralisation. I singled out a member of the Maths department and told her publicly what a good teacher I considered her to be. I said that I had complete confidence in her ability to teach her subject well in the absence of any resources whatsoever. The staff were told that we would see each colleague affected by the break-in, individually, and attempt to make good any losses before the weekend. Finally, I told staff that the break-in was a good sign. We had been worrying about the Inspection and now, as ever, they were faced with working in difficult circumstances and would just have to get on with it. I genuinely believed this to be the case. **Reality often intrudes to prevent us becoming overly precious about life's events and this can be a good thing.**

The staff thought I was mad, but the general abuse and humour that this generated lifted the tone that morning, distracted from the selfish anxieties about personal performance and reminded everyone that, **in an inner city school, you sink or swim together.**

In the event I was proved correct. The Inspectors were shocked by the break-in and were deeply sympathetic. They were most impressed by the way the staff rallied round and simply got on with the job and this helped to form positive initial judgements. Beyond that there was a further, unanticipated, benefit from the loss of the projectors. While we were able to locate a number of replacements a couple of teachers volunteered to wait for reinstatement until after the inspection. They lacked confidence with the new technology yet had felt under pressure to make use of it that week. The break-in served to reduce their anxiety about their performance, the inspectors, sympathetic over the theft of the equipment had made allowances and everyone was happy.

As in the past, **honesty, good humour and lavishing charm on the inspectors worked well.** I made it absolutely clear to the Registered Inspector that there were staff over whom we had concerns and detailed the actions we were taking. We also made available the Maths Department Improvement Plan, the record of Departmental Reviews and all our monitoring files in order to show our determination to achieve high standards. The Governors, and in particular the Chair, did an outstanding job of representing us and the inspectors were impressed with their loyalty and by their engagement with the school.

Other aspects of the inspection week that went very well included our finance and community management discussions, the inspections of EAL (English as an Additional Language) and most departments, the meetings with parents and a meeting with local Headteachers. The inspectors reported very favourably indeed on the behaviour of students, on progress in the school and on the Sixth form. They also reported very favourably on leadership and management, which was pleasing.

We did have issues, which we tried to resolve through dialogue with inspectors and staff. One, in particular, concerned the use of Individual Education Plans (IEPs) for students on the Special Needs Register. The staff were aware that the Special Needs Inspector, parachuted in towards the end of the week, had been critical of our approach and lacked sympathy for the fact that teachers were contending with entire classes with IEPs. I knew that we had matters to address but felt that staff attempts to modify custom and practice during the inspection would be counter productive. I spoke to the staff during a morning briefing, told them how well the inspection was going and asked them not to change a thing. One of the deputies and I had a barnstorming meeting with the Special Needs Inspector and I then had a robust discussion with the Registered Inspector before we all came to an understanding.

We had a spectacularly good night out at the end of the Inspection and the report itself was very complimentary over the work of the school. Nevertheless, immediately following the inspection, our Senior Management meetings were concerned with pushing the school forward on some of our key issues – Key skills (literacy in particular), Teaching and Learning in the Foundation Subjects (TLFS) and our whole framework for monitoring and support.

Having delegated really extensively I was still concerned over leadership and drive in significant areas of school life. An effective team approach to leadership would, I assume, involve substantial mutual challenge, the modelling of initiatives, the generation of a wider vision and well informed debate. We were certainly moving in the right direction and, collectively, the new team was working reasonably well. It was obviously a challenge to move to my ideal situation in which senior staff would demonstrate individual responsibility, significant professional authority and feel fully accountable not just for the maintenance of systems but also for their future development.

Senior Staff, like all others, need mentoring, support and development and the availability of the NPQH (National Professional Qualification for Headteachers), alongside specialised courses in finance, curriculum and personnel management, is very worthwhile.

Liverpool had organised excellent Middle Management training in recent years but a comprehensive programme for Deputy Heads was no longer available. This was a pity. There is no doubt that managers need to be taken out of their environment from time to time in order to reflect upon what they are doing and where they are going. This is doubly true for those working in highly pressurised and volatile situations.

The day to day operation of the school continued to absorb all of everyone's time, despite there being a good atmosphere and genuine delight over the improved facilities. We were obviously overcrowded and, while the increased numbers would help us to meet our strategic objectives, the lack of proper additional accommodation was a headache and continued to stretch our resources.

A proportion of the students were difficult to manage despite our having many experienced and competent staff and some of the tightest and most consistent procedures in the country. I was still handling a number of individual problems, particularly where parents had become contentious. In these circumstances I saw that my role was to broker an agreement with parents on the way forward. Teachers and, particularly, senior staff need to be sensitive to the importance of treating parents fairly and with respect-even in the most trying situations. The reputation of the school can depend upon it.

More fulfilling were the continuing one to one meetings with parents and prospective students. There was a huge turnout at our Marketing Evening with many parents booking personal interviews on the night.

We were now broadcasting our relationship with the other, highly prestigious, schools in our post 16 collaborative group and made it clear to parents that students attending Shorefields could, if they chose, undertake 'A' level studies in these relatively selective schools. On the other hand we were now widely regarded as a centre of excellence for post 16 GNVQ courses and were being encouraged by our partners to expand provision on the site.

Yet again the adequacy of the site was an issue that could hold back our potential. The BEST team were installed in a Portacabin and they now had a permanent manager. While this was a good development **it is always time consuming supporting someone getting up to speed with their role** and there were still concerns amongst the school staff that they were unclear over the team's objectives. The physical distance from the main building to the Portacabins did not help at all.

We had seen another change of management in the Canteen. While this was only temporary, during the absence of the excellent Cook, it was a big setback as conditions there started to deteriorate immediately. We were back to arguing over standards, complaining about food quality and providing greater levels of supervision as the pace of service slowed. We discovered that the Cook, like her predecessor, could not tolerate the poor standards and bullying culture of the contractor. There was no attempt to contact her or to address the absence.

We sent flowers and rang and discussed levels of support needed to help a return to work. I promised unequivocal backing and within a fortnight we had our Canteen back to an acceptable standard. So much for PFI freeing Headteachers to manage other aspects of the school. **The problem, of course, is that Heads tend to be very experienced managers in comparison to the fly by night super-**

visors of the PFI companies. This, inevitably, pulls us into issues of quality assurance and conflict resolution.

Our new Senior Management Team met regularly, to discuss key issues of educational concern, during October and November. These included – department reviews, target setting, curriculum change, monitoring and staff performance. We were dealing with a number of staff issues relating to performance and capability and it was desperately time consuming. Another exhausting area of business concerned the buses and, again, **one must challenge whether it is right and fair for an inner city school to be so distracted by such basic issues as pupil transport.**

Our arrangements for safely dispersing the students at the end of the day were a constant source of concern. Obviously, the three buses we now had relieved the pressure but they were always vulnerable and were often seriously overcrowded. Frequent requests for additional buses had been rejected and we were now informed that one of our existing contracts was being cancelled and that no replacement could be found. This was with immediate effect and we were left with students both morning and evening with no transport. There were, immediately, a number of serious attacks on students making their way home at night.

In desperation we arranged a private company to cover the gaps and informed Merseytravel that we expected them to issue a contract to provide services.

This really was intolerable. We were a demonstrably successful school with an increasing roll. We had a series of good Ofsted reports. We had Specialist College status with wide ranging additional funds and had recently been refurbished. We were providing a massive service to local communities and to Liverpool as a whole yet, despite our best efforts, our entire agenda, all of our time and the welfare of students and staff was jeopardised on a nightly basis by delinquency in the area and by the non-arrival of buses. Ridiculous!

A measure of the seriousness with which we viewed this business was that Senior Managers formally discussed it on at least five occasions in six weeks, Governors met with councillors in December and Governors also devoted part of their Away Day to the issue. **As ever, exerting massive pressure brought recognition of the problem and a solution for the rest of the academic year.**

This, at least in the short term was pleasing, as this year, my final year of headship, saw the school arrive at a significant point. The refurbishment and rebuilding was to a high standard and the resources available to students and staff were outstanding. The Ofsted Report found that students had good attitudes to learning, their behaviour was very good and the quality of teaching and learning were both good. They found the leadership and overall effectiveness of the Sixth Form to be very good. In terms of leadership and management generally they said:

'The headteacher's leadership is extremely effective. His commitment to the school, clear sense of purpose and high aspirations are significant factors in promoting the school's ethos of hard work, achievement, respectability and personal fulfilment. He leads and gives direction to a newly strengthened senior management team, whose members are equally dedicated in promoting the aims and values of the school.'

This was obviously very pleasing. The original aim, of course, had been to give people what they wanted and to survive. In doing this and in fighting to retain County Secondary School facilities in Liverpool 8 we had, by 2004, probably exceeded our own expectations and even had a wider impact.

In July 2004 the last event I attended in connection with Shorefields was a joint training day, organised by the EAZ, with all the Toxteth schools. This was held in the Conference Centre at Aintree Racecourse and was a presentation by Alistair Smith, the guru of 'accelerated learning'. There were hundreds and hundreds of teachers and ancillary staff in attendance for this riveting, motivational, performance. **What a distance we had travelled in**

a decade! From isolated, under resourced, devalued professionals working in appalling conditions in an area of profound social and economic disadvantage to this unapologetic, assertive, strongly collegial and visionary group who knew that attention was on them to play their part in the tide of regeneration sweeping the area.

I am very pleased to have been part of the story.

LEARNING POINTS YEAR 11

- Governors need to be well prepared for their role in Ofsted inspections.
- The school, as a whole, should be thoroughly prepared for an inspection including giving consideration to the needs of the inspectors.
- Reality often intrudes to prevent us becoming overly precious about life's events and this can be a good thing.
- In an inner city school you sink or swim together.
- Honesty, good humour and lavishing charm on inspectors works well.
- Senior staff need to be very protective over the reputation of the school.
- It is always time consuming supporting someone getting up to speed with their role.
- PFI does not necessarily free up Headteachers time to run other aspects of the school.
- Heads tend to be very experienced managers in comparison to

the fly by night middle managers of the PFI companies.

- Under PFI, Heads must still be concerned with quality assurance and conflict resolution.

- One must challenge whether it is right and fair for an inner city school to be so distracted by such basic issues as student transport.

- Solutions to basic problems often require massive pressure to be exerted.

- Huge, area wide, educational improvements had been achieved in a decade.

CONCLUSION

Iᴛ ɪs ʀᴇʟᴀᴛɪᴠᴇʟʏ ᴇᴀsʏ to understand that schools require focus, staff need to be motivated and made accountable, students need to learn (be engaged, take ownership and responsibility and behave), that we need a partnership with parents, that there must be sound re-source management and responsiveness to innovation and change. But *how* in reality can these things be achieved? How does a school move out of a deficit situation? At what point is it appropriate to suggest that a school has 'turned around'?

Do we give sufficient weight to the challenging circumstances in which many of our teachers work? Do we provide sufficient re-sources for the fragile situation in which success/ failure for an in-dividual student, a group or the school is perpetually in the balance? Are schools themselves sufficiently accountable and to whom? Do we have appropriate arrangements to ensure that challenge and sup-port from outside and inside schools guarantees an improvement in standards?

As a society we have a responsibility to create the highest stand-ard of education and the greatest opportunity for our most disad-vantaged citizens and to provide whatever structured multi agency support schools need in order to manage and deliver this.

The societal benefits we enjoy in 'getting it right' educationally are immense in a rapidly changing social, economic and technological world. Our reality is that, despite significant progress, many of our teachers and schools struggle to 'hold the line' educationally.

Hopefully, this book will add value in an environment where developments around the quality of educational leadership, the preparation for leadership and management, multi agency working, a real upward investment in deprived areas, issues of accountability and a sensible debate over teachers conditions are genuinely contributing to change in Britain.

GLOSSARY

APTC	Ancillary, Professional, Technical, Clerical
BEST	Behaviour and Education Support Team
BME	Black and Minority Ethnic
CCTV	closed circuit television
DFE	Department for Education (used also for DFES)
DGT	Dingle, Granby, Toxteth
EAZ	Education Action Zone
EIC	Excellence in Cities (later EIL-Excellence in Liverpool)
ELLS	Education and Lifelong Learning Service (mainly referred to as LEA)
ESF	European Social Fund
ERA	Education Reform Act
EAL	English as an Additional Language
FM	Facilities Management

FSM	Free School Meals
GEST	Grant for Education Support and Training
GNVQ	General National Vocational Qualification
GCSE	General Certificate of Secondary Education
HMI	Her Majesty's Inspectorate
ICT	Information and Communication Technology
IEP	Individual Education Plan
JNC	Joint Negotiating Committee
LEA	Local Education Authority (later to become ELLS)
LFM	Local Financial Management
LIG	Leadership Incentive Grant
LPSH	Leadership Programme for Serving Heads
MESH	Merseyside Education Super Highway – also used for 'Project United' and 'MEON'
NGFL	National Grid for Learning
NUT	National Union of Teachers
NAS/UWT	National Association of Schoolmasters/Union of women Teachers
NC	National Curriculum
NF	National Front and BNP British National Party (right wing groups)
OMR	Optical Mark Reader
PC	Personal Computer
PSE	Personal and Social Education
PFI	Private Finance Initiative
SMT	Senior Management Team

SIMS   Schools Information Management System
SEN   Special Educational Needs
SRB   Single Regeneration Budget
TES   Times Educational Supplement
TVEI   Technical and Vocational Educational Initiative

ISBN 1-4120-5586-5

9 781412 055864